BEER, BACON AND BULLETS

CULTURE IN COALITION WARFARE FROM GALLIPOLI TO IRAQ

GAL LUFT

CONTENTS

PREFACE

Reflecting on my decade-and-a-half of service in the ranks of the Israel Defense Forces (IDF), it occurred to me one day that I had spent almost as much of that time working *with* Arabs as I did fighting *against* them. For nearly five years, I was deployed in combat assignments in South Lebanon, a magnificent yet forbidding territory where the ground is soaked with so much shrapnel that a compass needle gets confused. There, I lived and worked with Maronite Christian, Druze, Sunni and Shiite soldiers of the South Lebanon Army (SLA), all of them Arabs who defended their villages in the south while we defended Israel's north from infiltrations and rocket attacks. I had never worked with Arabs before, nor did I speak their language, and collaboration with people whom I had previously seen mainly through my binoculars involved some non-trivial adaptations. Later, in 1994, Palestinian leader Yasser Arafat arrived to take charge of the Gaza Strip, giving rise to what was known as the Palestinian Authority. In the months that followed, my soldiers and I gained more cross-cultural experience, working closely with the Palestinian Security Forces, a nascent army under the guise of a police force. As part of the Oslo Agreements, we found ourselves patrolling, guarding checkpoints and participating in other joint general security missions with Jordanians, Yemenite-, Lebanese-, Syrian-, Iraqi-, and Egyptian-Palestinians. Only those who know the Middle East cauldron of turmoil understand how uncharacteristic the spectacle was of Jews and Arabs working together. This experiment ended in colossal disaster with the outbreak of the Second Intifada in September 2000 and disintegration of the peace process. Our erstwhile partners turned their guns against us, and the radical group Hamas eventually took over power in Gaza, condemning the Palestinians there to years of poverty and isolation. In my military career, I had other opportunities to work with Arabs. As a young officer I was assigned to the IDF's only non-Jewish battalion comprised mainly of Druze and Cherkes (immigrants from what is now Chechnya). The only Jewish officer in the battalion, I was fortunate to witness their culture up close and personal. Though at times I felt I was on a different planet, the glimpse into Druze culture was transformational. Years later, as battalion commander, the person I spent most of my time with was an Israeli-Arab. It was my Bedouin tracker with whom I spent days and nights in a Jeep, patrolling the security fence along Israel's borders. When the electric fence alerted of a possible infiltration, the two of us had to rush to the spot and search for infiltrators' footprints. In those hours, first in the line of fire and joined in fate, this Arab was my closest ally. All of these experiences solidified my belief in the importance of culture in military cooperation. I learned that culture could stand between effective collaboration and a military blunder. Watching from afar the U.S. military interventions in the Persian Gulf, Somalia, the Balkans and Afghanistan, I also learned that no two cultures are alike and that different cultures pose different challenges. It was only natural that I decided to research the topic in depth as part of my doctoral work at the Paul H. Nitze School of Advanced International Studies (SAIS) at Johns Hopkins University. This book is a product of that research.

Writing about culture is like walking in a minefield - difficult to do without hurting someone. The biggest danger in dealing with culture is the tendency to commit generalizations or present the characteristics of one's own group or race as superior to those of other groups or races. Ethnocentrism, parochialism, stereotypes and cultural prejudices are difficult to avoid. Making sweeping generalizations is often unavoidable when describing any cultural and social phenomena. To understand cross-cultural tension among cooperating militaries, I had to examine various cultural groups and their perceptions of each other, to what degree those perceptions percolated into the military and how these perceptions affected cooperation in the field. The findings were often ugly and may be hurtful to some readers. This is certainly not my intention and I regret in advance any offense this book may cause. But it is important to remind ourselves that political correctness and cultural sensitivity are relatively new phenomena and that most of the historical data in this book come from times when Westerners and non-Westerners alike were unapologetic about their cultural prejudice. Admittedly, most of the sources used in this book are Western. This is mainly due to the dearth of documentation and personal testimonies among non-Western militaries. As such, this book is much more reflective of the attitudes of Western militaries toward their Asian or Muslim partners than the other way around. I did not try to question the validity or fairness of those perceptions or to pass value judgments on one cultural group or another. All I tried to do was to portray the unvarnished feelings and perceptions of the time, biased as they may have been.

To this end I used numerous primary sources, letters, notes, battlefield reports, telegrams and personal memoirs that I found in the Public Record Office in London, the National Archives in College Park Maryland, the Library of the Greenwich Maritime Museum, the Library of Congress, the Military Museum in Istanbul and the Moshe Dayan Center for Middle Eastern and African Studies in Tel Aviv. I thank the helpful staffs of all of those institutions for dealing with my frequent interruptions and odd requests. I also thank the librarians of the SAIS, Georgetown and Haifa University libraries, whose great efforts provided me with some of the most obscure books and journals. Additionally, I thank those who in many ways enriched me intellectually and helped me improve the manuscript. A great debt I owe to my mentor, Professor Eliot Cohen, a wonderful teacher with a sharp pen and a golden heart, who inspired, guided and exemplified to me the highest standards of scholarship. Professors Stephen P. Rosen, Francis Fukuyama, Thomas Keaney, Kenneth Pollack and Ambassador Shirin Tahir-Kheli as well as Jonathan Korin and Rob Satloff and the staff of the Washington Institute for Near East Policy have all been generous with their time and advice. A special thanks to all the veterans interviewed for this book who responded to my interrogations with patience and politeness. I also harbor deep gratitude to my dear friend and co-director at the Institute for the Analysis of Global Security (IAGS) Anne Korin whose integrity, morality and wisdom have been my compass. A special thanks to two remarkable teachers who sadly passed away before this book was published. Professor Alvin Bernstein's tales on the role of culture in ancient history made me understand that technology, the intricacies of political alliances and national interests may change, but human nature doesn't. Professor Frederick Holborn, a treasure trove of anecdotes and insights on American foreign policy in the 20th century, was incredibly generous with his time, always happy to share his wisdom and to be a first responder to my hypotheses. Finally, I would like to thank my family, which, spread across five continents, has given me the inspiration to delve into the world of culture, demonstrating that people's culture may not be similar but their cause can certainly be.

INTRODUCTION

*Madness would be near the man who sees things through the veils at once
of two customs, two educations, two environments*
T.E. Lawrence, Seven Pillars of Wisdom

In the summer of 1967, the commander of U.S. forces in
Vietnam, General William Westmoreland, discovered that the first
contingent of the Royal Thai Volunteer Regiment, known as the
"Queen's Cobras," arrived in Vietnam with a baggage train containing hundreds of wooden coffins, one for each member of the regiment. Westmoreland also noticed that the higher the rank of the
soldier, the more decorated the coffin.[1] He soon discovered that the
source of this puzzling conduct was rooted in Thai tradition to pay
respect to the deceased with a proper burial ceremony and frequent
visits of family members to the place the beloved is laid to rest.
The Thai military, mainly for morale purposes, wanted to reassure
its soldiers that in case they die their bodies would be returned
home and buried next to their ancestors rather than abandoned in
a foreign land.

In contrast, on March 21, 1991, during the Gulf War, a Saudi
C-130 transport plane carrying a party of Senegalese soldiers on
a return flight from Mecca, where they had gone to perform the
Muslim pilgrimage rite - or *Hajj* - crashed on landing. Ninety-
one Senegalese, one fifth of their contingent, were killed. As the
Saudis prepared for the repatriation of the bodies, the families of
the dead said that they preferred them to be buried in Saudi Arabia.
Their wish was fulfilled.[2] Unlike Thai tradition, Islam prohibits
any delay in burial of the dead. Shipping the bodies of the Muslim
soldiers back to Senegal was, therefore, perceived by the families as
improper. They much preferred to have their sons buried in proximity to Islam's holiest places.

These two anecdotes demonstrate some of the peculiarities
involved in the conduct of multinational operations in which

nationals of different cultures join together to fight, and sometimes die, for a common cause. In both cases, the coalition members' national culture had a direct effect on troops' mindset regarding their possible death in battle. In both cases, their habits and attitudes differed from those of their counterparts. In both cases, unique needs and sensitivities were met with genuine sympathy by coalition commanders. But this is not always the case.

This book is not about how soldiers of dissimilar cultures die at war, but rather how they live and work together in a combat environment and how they overcome their cultural dissimilarities. Military cooperation between nations often brings together forces of diverse cultural backgrounds. This phenomenon goes back to antiquity, as early as the first battles to have been recorded in any detail. In 853 BC, a league of twelve kings including those of Hamath, Aram, Damascus, Phoenicia and Israel, stood up against the attempt of Assyrian emperor Shalmaneser III to expand the boundaries of his empire. Each of the militaries had its own unique cultural characteristics. Each spoke a different dialect, prayed to a different god, ate different food, and adhered to a different set of rules and social norms. How they got along we will probably never know since ancient historians have left us very few answers. But since then, history has supplied us with many better documented cases in which war made strange bedfellows.

Muslim Syrians and Christian Crusaders fought together, and lost, the 1244 battle of Gaza; Russia and Turkey, two long lasting enemies, collaborated to defeat Napoleon in the 1798 battle of Corfu; French, Dutch and Javan troops fought in 1810 against the British; Europeans joined forces with Japanese soldiers to crush the 1899 Boxer rebellion in China; Britain and France joined the Ottomans during the Crimean War against Russia; in World War I it was the Germans who collaborated with the Ottomans; American troops supported China in World War II, a prelude to decades of military cooperation between the U.S. and other members of the Sinic civilization in Korea, Thailand and Vietnam; on numerous occasions, Western powers fought combined with Islamic militaries in Trans-Jordan, Turkey, the Persian Gulf, the Arabian Peninsula and as far as Central Asia; during the Cold War, Cuban soldiers fought alongside Africans in Angola against the then exclusively white South African army.

Nowadays, coalition warfare has become the norm. Whether as part of a humanitarian intervention, peacekeeping mission or combined combat operation like the Gulf War and the Global War on Terrorism, nations join forces to act against an emerging challenge. This is done not only to divide the ever increasing cost of war among several member states but also to facilitate solidarity and commonality of mission among nations. Unlike pre-existing alliances, such as NATO, that usually have enough time before the war to integrate their forces, train together, and establish working relations, coalitions are usually established hastily without allowing member states the time to familiarize themselves with each other. As a result, problems and tensions that could have been resolved over time are more likely to hamper the performance of the coalition.

Advisory missions are another type of military cooperation. Militaries of technologically and economically established nations often send military missions to underdeveloped countries in order to provide them with advanced training methods, introduce new doctrines and technologies, and assist in the implementation of reforms and reorganization. There are many examples of such collaboration. French, British and German advisors trained the Japanese army after the Meiji Restoration and the Ottoman Empire prior to World War I; German and Russian advisors worked in China in the 1920s and 1930s; the Americans took over in 1941-45, and after World War II they sent advisors to other countries such as South Korea, Vietnam and Saudi Arabia; in Jordan, in the 1940s, British officers under John Glubb made the Arab Legion into the most effective Arab military in modern time; and Soviet advisors operated in Egypt in the 1960s and early 1970s. U.S. soldiers are currently training the Iraqi and Afghan security forces. Military advisors are usually deployed in foreign lands on relatively long missions. Their main challenge is to familiarize themselves with the host country, its people and its culture, and lead the host military through difficult reforms. Their success depends on the development of good, open relations with their clients. But in some cases such missions fail due to constant friction with the hosts. One example is the Soviet mission in Egypt in the 1960s until the early 1970s, which exhibited paternalistic behavior and cultural insensitivity toward the Egyptians. The 20,000 Soviet advisors treated their hosts with such rudeness, indifference and insensitivity that officers of the Egyptian army began resenting them no less than they did its Israeli enemy. Often under the influence of heavy drinking, prohibited by Islam, Soviet officers, failing to understand the cultural importance of honor and self-respect to the Arabs, made insulting dinner remarks that the Egyptians to demand their removal.[3] At one point, Egyptian officers began urging the military to start a *jihad* against the Soviets.[4] The antipathy toward the Soviets resulted in the July 1972 decision of Egyptian President Anwar Sadat to expel them from the country.

This example of the severe impact culture can have on the relationships of collaborating militaries is not isolated. In this book, I examine how cultural factors such as language barriers, religion, customs, philosophy, values, stereotypes, heritage, gender roles, education, mentality, ethnic background, economic and social outlook affect the way militaries collaborate. The book grapples with the question "does culture matter?" and if so, in what ways? In which potential fields could it hamper cooperation and when could it achieve the exact opposite? Has social, doctrinal and technological progress changed the way culture affects military cooperation? How do military organizations address the problem of cultural dissimilarity, and which techniques are used to mitigate cultural tension? How do general trends and perceptions about other racial and cultural groups in society as a whole affect cultural attitudes in the military? And finally, how important is military leadership and the role played by individual coalition commanders to accomplishing effective cross-cultural cooperation? The following chapters will show that culturally related issues *could* affect the operational relations among military forces of dissimilar cultures and in some cases even impact the outcome of campaigns, if not the entire war. But we shall also see that cross-cultural tension can be managed and mitigated if enough attention is given to the partner's cultural sensitivities. This in itself can facilitate more stable, better relations and, hence, increase the probability of success.

Why culture?

For most of the second half of the 20th century, the field of social sciences treated cultural-driven explanations of international phenomena with a great deal of suspicion, skepticism, sometimes disdain. "Culture, in the sense of the inner values and attitudes that guide a population, frightens scholars," wrote David Landes. "It has a sulfuric odor of race and inheritance, an air of immutability."[5] Researchers who dare address the topic often do so by treating culture as a residual variable that explains behaviors of societies when all other plausible explanations fail; the result, in many cases, is effusive, unsatisfying and unconvincing. The concept of culture also poses a difficult challenge to the researcher due to its intangibility and its dependency on generalizations counterintuitive to methodological and empirical patterns of scholarly thought. Yet, since the 1980s, more and more scholars have examined phenomena on the international stage -such as economic development, political development, and human rights - through cultural prisms. Many of these works have demonstrated how values shape human progress and nations' fates, thus concluding that culture *does* matter.[6] This conclusion also applies to military affairs. In fact, when it comes to our military activities in the age of globalization, culture is as important an element as ever before. With the increase in combined military operations, mainly for peacekeeping purposes by international and regional organizations such as the UN and NATO, the number and diversity of countries contributing forces to such missions has been on the rise. In 1950, 19 countries took part in the UN multinational force in Korea. Forty years later, the number of countries taking part in the Gulf War stood at 28. Four years later, the NATO-led coalition in Bosnia- Herzegovina brought together troops from 37 states, and following September 11, the coalition against terror combined military and intelligence services of more than 70 countries. This trend is likely to continue. Whether in Africa, Asia, or the Middle East, the ongoing war against terrorism as well as emerging humanitarian crises around the world will surely create more and more opportunities for Western militaries to join forces and cooperate with counterparts from nations of dissimilar cultures. The tasks facing these coalitions are likely to be monumental, and their enemies are likely to be formidable. For this reason alone, they must employ their scarce resources exclusively against their opponents, not against each other. Furthermore, in the post-September 11 world, the U.S. found itself embarking on a long chain of military interventions in Afghanistan, Iraq and other parts of the Islamic world. At the same time, tension between the West and the Muslims has been mounting. This raises the specter of what the late Samuel P. Huntington described in his 1996 book as a Clash of Civilizations.

Huntington postulated that international conflict in the post-Cold War era would evolve along cultural or civilizational rather than ideological or political fault lines. He divided the world into nine distinct civilizations and underlined the social, economic and cultural differences among them, suggesting that these differences would likely carry the seeds of future conflict.[7] What Huntington missed in his analysis was that the cross-cultural conflict he described could also be the catalyst for cross-cultural cooperation. Inter-civilizational fault lines such as the Middle East, Central Asia, Central Africa and East Europe, are also the areas where such cooperation is most likely to occur. In fact, Huntington's world order fosters no less cooperation than conflict. There are several examples from past conflicts when intra-civilizational feuds brought about intervention by members of foreign cultures. The war in the Pacific during World War II was a result of a conflict between two Asian nations, China and Japan, that broke out in 1937. The U.S. interventions in both Korea and Vietnam were the result of a war between two culturally compatible, rather than dissimilar, peoples. So was the intervention in the first Gulf War in which the U.S. and its allies sided with one Arab country that was assaulted by another. September 11 and its aftermath led to an abundance of opportunities for cross-cultural military cooperation. The U.S.-led coalition against terrorism has brought the U.S. military to collaborate with a large number of Muslim and Asian countries. American troops and personnel are currently present in Afghanistan, Iraq, Pakistan, Oman, Bahrain, Qatar, the United Arab Emirates, Kuwait, Saudi Arabia, Turkey, the Balkans, Uzbekistan (until 2005) and Kyrgyzstan (until 2009.) Multinational forces are now deployed in South Lebanon in the aftermath of Israel's war against Hizballah in 2006, and there are growing calls to deploy an international force in Sudan in an effort to stop the genocide in Darfur. Joint exercises are conducted with the Egyptian and Jordanian militaries. In some places, the U.S. deployed its forces merely to increase its presence in the region; in others, American troops assumed the role of instructors and advisors modernizing the local militaries. In Afghanistan, Americans train the Tajik, Pashtun, Uzbek and Hazara soldiers who formed the new Afghan army, air force and border police force. In the Philippines, U.S. forces helped train the local army against the local terrorist group Abu Sayyaf. Perhaps the most challenging cross cultural experience is currently taking place in Iraq. What started with a small deployment in southern and northern Iraq on a mission to train Iraqi opposition groups for a future uprising against Saddam Hussein ended with a full scale deployment of close to 150,000 troops from 34 countries predominantly from the U.S. and Britain. Whether they came from Birmingham, Alabama or Birmingham, England, Western soldiers found themselves amidst people whose culture was foreign and mysterious to them at almost every level. Once Saddam Hussein's Ba'ath regime fell in 2003, their job was to train Iraqi soldiers to take over security tasks in the war torn country. This proved to be a daunting task. The mother of a newly deployed U.S. soldier in Iraq asked her son over the phone how he deals with the 11 hour time difference between the U.S. and Baghdad. His answer was: "it is not the 11 hours difference that makes it so difficult, it's the 800 years difference."

Important as culture may be, it is not the only dividing force between coalition partners. There are factors that can handicap relations which are just as important if not more. Divergent war aims and strategic interests, disagreements on the allocation of forces, technological and doctrinal incompatibility, poor logistic and intelligence coordination, and contentious relations between commanders appear in one way or another in most cases of military cooperation. Sovereign states rarely share similar strategic goals, and even if they do, their accord is usually either short-lived or they end up disagreeing on the ways and means of achieving their goals. Coalition partners are often strict about preserving their operational independence, their sovereignty and the identity of their forces. In some past coalitions, an amalgamation of forces was unachievable due to considerations of pride. In other cases, constitutional restrictions prevailed over operational imperatives. The U.S. Expeditionary Force in 1917 and the French contingent in the Gulf War were two military forces that refused to submit to the command of other nations and also refused, at least at the beginning, to amalgamate their forces into other partners' forces. No coalition relations are viable without a common understanding among all powers that each will have to cede at least some of its sovereignty for the common benefit of the collective. Failure to accept this fact can cause deep tension. Gaps in technology and doctrine can cause irresolvable conflict between counterparts. The engagement between militaries with different levels of social, economic and technological development can cause disproportion in strength and firepower. The amount of military power coalition partners bring to the theater determines their influence on the management of operations.

Doctrinal incompatibility may also be a source of friction. Some militaries are better prepared to perform specific missions or maneuvers. This gives them an edge over other coalition partners not capable of performing similar missions. Coalition commanders take into consideration the level of technology and equipment in the hands of member states, which can determine the allocation of assignments and division of labor among members. In modern coalitions, technological incompatibility is specifically problematic since it directly affects the ability of the members to communicate, exchange intelligence, coordinate their forces and control the moves and positions of their units. Differences in logistics doctrine, stock levels, and dependencies on the supply of certain items may also be a source of disagreement. Coalition partners often quarrel over the control over sea and airports, highways, and rail lines in an attempt to give priority to the supply of their forces. Intelligence collection is also a challenge. Coalition partners maintain their own separate intelligence systems and in many cases, mainly for reasons of secrecy, are very reluctant to share their full intelligence capabilities with their allies. Finally, personal relations between coalition commanders are perhaps the most important factor affecting fruitful cooperation. "I am tired of dealing with a lot of prima donnas," erupted General Dwight D. Eisenhower exasperated by the inflated egos of fellow American and British generals during the preparations for D-Day. "By God, you tell that bunch that if they can't get together and stop quarreling like children, I will tell the Prime Minister [Churchill] to get someone else to run this damn war. I'll quit."[8] This was not the only tantrum in the history of coalition warfare. Nor was it the first time coalition commanders felt that strained personal relations with their colleagues impeded their work. And indeed, lack of trust, understanding, teamwork and even a basic antipathy between commanding officers can exact a high price from many coalition undertakings. A main source of weakness of the German-Austrian relations in World War I was the clashes between Austria's Chief of Staff Conrad von Hötzendorf and his German counterpart Erich von Falkenhayn. U.S. cooperation with China during World War II, as will be described in Chapter 4, was severely impaired by the thorny relations between the U.S. commander General Joseph Stilwell and his Chinese counterpart Chiang Kai-shek. Coalitions with more compatible commanders, demonstrating mutual understanding and goodwill, operated in a more positive spirit which contributed to their overall effectiveness.

The book begins with the delineation of the boundaries of the term 'culture' and reviews the integration of cultural studies and military affairs. It offers three plausible explanations to the origins and catalysts of cultural tension in coalition operations. First, that the level of exposure of military organizations to other cultures in the pre-coalition stage determines their ability to minimize cross-cultural tension with fellow coalition partners. Such prior exposure provides individuals and the organization with a better understanding of potential partners' sensitivities and minimizes the risk of culture shock when dealing with unfamiliar cultures. Second, the disparity of power between the partners can cause the senior partner to show less cultural sensitivity toward the junior partner. In other words, coalition members contributing the majority of the force may feel less obligated to treat the smaller players with equality and respect. Rarely does one come across a coalition of equal partners or a case in which all partners are senior partners. Since the burden of participating in a coalition is never equally shared, senior partners are often perceived as those who bring the greatest contribution of military power to the partnership. But disparity of military contribution does not necessarily indicate disparity in power. Other forms of contribution such as political capital, geographical assets or logistic support could be more meaningful than pure military hardware. Coalition counterparts unequal in their military power, as a result, could find themselves equally dependent on each other. As the leader of the Arab world, Egypt, for example, brought to the 1991 Gulf War coalition political capital worth a great deal more than the two divisions it contributed. Turkey contributed no military forces and, yet, provided a crucial element for victory: airbases from which coalition planes launched air attacks on Iraq. Saudi Arabia supplied the host territory as well as logistical support for all the coalition forces. Its importance to the war effort was not less than that of the U.S., the main force contributor. The third proposition is perhaps the most problematic. It asserts that the general attitudes of the home society toward the culture of the coalition partner could percolate into the collective consciousness of military personnel and hence affect their ability to tolerate the cultural differences of their allies when called to work together. Societies infected with cultural chauvinism, ethnocentrism, biases against minority groups and racial segregation cannot excise such feelings from their militaries, assuming that the military is a genuine representative of society's general attitudes. Military personnel of such countries tend to view other cultures through the subconscious prism of their own cultural conditioning and, therefore, may look down at those from cultures they perceive to be inferior. To make matters worse, many military organizations are characterized by disproportional representation of the more traditional sectors of their society. When such militaries work together with forces from cultures that are perceived as inferior, there are likely to be negative implications on the mutual ability of the sides to collaborate. Cultural biases could also generate fear of cross-cultural transmission. In other words, there is the fear that in the course of the military relations certain values and habits would pass from one group to another and hence 'contaminate' one's culture. Such fear among coalition counterparts, as the U.S. experience with Saudi Arabia in the Gulf War showed, can develop when coalition members perceive the interaction with contingents from other cultures as a threat to the existence of their social-political fabric. Their main concern is the introduction of new norms and ideas that could potentially penetrate and destroy their fragile social order. As a result, they may prevent their contingents from engaging members of other cultures, thus putting great strains on the coalition's work.

To examine these issues, this book will present five cases of military cooperation between countries of distinctively different cultural backgrounds and civilizational affiliations. All five cases bring together Western militaries and a non-Western counterpart. The fact that many good cases of military cooperation between countries of similar cultures, such as Europeans and Americans, have been excluded from this book does not indicate that cultural differences cannot affect working relations even among people who share a similar language or religion. They can, and they have. But the influence of culture on cooperation among culturally compatible forces has been considerably reduced. During the 20th century, Western militaries had so many opportunities to work together, especially members of NATO, that they have managed to overcome most cultural barriers. Since future coalitions are likely to emerge in those areas of the world dominated by Asian and Muslim populations, the book focuses on cases that brought Western forces to work with those cultures. Doing so, it will examine whether some cultures are more compatible with each other and, if so, why.

The cases selected offer a sufficient degree of interaction between the cooperating militaries. Some coalitions - such as Germany and Japan and the U.S. and Soviet Union during World War II - were characterized by strategic coordination but very little contact between operational units. These cases are unsatisfactory in terms of demonstrating the cultural dimension. The cases selected here present coalition relations at the theater level and in which soldiers of all levels of command had a chance to work and interact with members of other cultural groups.

The first case study, in Chapter 2, describes the relations between the Ottoman Empire and Germany during the First World War. Many Western historians described the alliance in the context of the Gallipoli campaign - the greatest victory for the Turks and their German allies that gave an impression of an effective alliance. But the battle of the Dardanelles was only one of many campaigns and is not reflective of the true nature of Turkish-German relations which were, as we shall see, heavily burdened by mutual antipathy and cultural incompatibilities. Thousands of miles away from Constantinople, two empires colluded against Germany in an attempt to end its presence in East Asia.

Chapter 3 describes the cooperation between Great Britain and Japan in the same war focusing on their combined operation against a small German colony in China called Tsingtau in the autumn of 1914. The battle of Tsingtau is one of the most obscure episodes of World War I, but it offers a glimpse into a positive example of cross-cultural cooperation between people who were culturally remote from each other. The experience of the British Army is particularly interesting since Britain, as part of its colonial endeavors, was the nation with the longest tradition of cross-cultural cooperation. As such, it could implement many of the lessons learned the hard way during decades of cooperation with Indian, African and Asian counterparts.

Chapter 4 presents another coalition between Western and Asian armed forces: the U.S. military mission in China during the Second World War. Unlike the British, the Americans had little experience fighting alongside non-Western allies. The China-Burma-India (CBI) Theater was perhaps the least visible front of the war but it offers a remarkable story of military collaboration among people who were as remote from each other as one could expect. America at that time was a racially segregated society where Asian people were greatly discriminated against. But the Chinese, a proud nation with an ancient heritage, were also consumed with the idea of racial hierarchy. In their view, Chinese culture was superior to all others. Could two such peoples cooperate on an equal basis? The answer is evidently negative. Despite the eventual victory over the Japanese, the Sino-American coalition was burdened by both cultural and non-cultural pressures that threatened its existence throughout the war.

From the jungles of Burma, we go to the Arabian Desert. Chapter 5 presents a second U.S.-led coalition but this time with a Muslim country, Saudi Arabia, during the 1990-91 Gulf War. This coalition ended in one of the quickest, most decisive military victories in modern military history. So sweet was the victory - "By God, we've kicked the Vietnam Syndrome once and for all!" exclaimed President George H. W. Bush - that in its aftermath, very few soldiers or statesmen had the desire to spoil America's moment by delving into the sources of tension that eclipsed U.S.-Saudi relations. We told ourselves a story of how well things went during the war. But as time goes by and particularly in the wake of September 11 and the deterioration in relations with Saudi Arabia, it becomes apparent that the popular narrative of the Gulf War differs from the reality that actually took place in the desert.

Finally, Chapter 6 introduces the unique patron-proxy relations between the Israeli Defense Force (IDF) and the South Lebanon Army (SLA) from 1985 until Israel's unilateral withdrawal from Lebanon in May 2000. This was not a coalition in the traditional sense of the word as one of the sides, the SLA, was not operating on behalf of a state but on behalf of an ethnic group within one. But the Israeli experience in Lebanon is useful for our purposes, since collaboration with non-state actors - in recent years the U.S. military worked together with several non-state actors such as the Kosovo Liberation Army, the Northern Alliance in Afghanistan and Iraqi opposition groups - is emerging as the most prominent form of military cooperation and should be studied with care.

Chapter 7 will assemble and review the lessons learned from a century of military cooperation in multiple theaters. Several doctrinal, technological and organizational approaches to facilitate cohesion building and improvement of cross-cultural dialogue can be offered. Cultural preparation could include joint training, language studies, cultural acclimatization programs, do's and don'ts manuals, and the appointment of specialized liaison officers. Doctrinal manuals, briefing books on cultural issues and the existence of military affiliated institutions that include cultural familiarization training are all indicators of high organizational awareness to the potential hazards of cross-cultural cooperation. But perhaps more than any other factor, it is the level of exposure of the individuals appointed coalition commanders and that of officers commanding coalition contingents that determines the spirit and the climate of the coalition. We shall also discover how critical the personality factor is. Coalition command requires a certain personality and character conducive to cross-cultural interaction. Audacity and tactical genius are not sufficient qualities for the commander of a multinational force. We will run across several coalition leaders: Liman von Sanders, Enver Pasha, Nathaniel Bernardiston, Kamio Mitsuomi, Joseph Stilwell, Chiang Kai-shek, Norman Schwartzkopf and Khaled bin Sultan. They are just part of a long list of epic supreme commanders stretching from the Duke of Marlborough, the Duke of Wellington, Marshal Foch, Dwight Eisenhower, Douglas MacArthur, Matthew Ridgway, William Westmoreland, Wesley Clark, Tommy Franks and to our present-day's George Casey and David Petraeus. Some of these military leaders leaned toward parochialism, lust for glory and national biases. Others were known for their interpersonal, diplomatic, motivational and integrative skills. The latter group did not always win over their enemies, but they certainly won the hearts of their counterparts.

1
CULTURE AND WAR

⌘ ⌘ ⌘

Culture - what a word!
Jacques Barzun, From Dawn to Decadence

Culture is a prime determinant of the nature of warfare
John Keegan, A History of Warfare

What is culture?

Not many words in the English language have as many definitions and interpretations as the term 'culture.' Though most people would agree that culture and its associated traits pervade every aspect of our lives and behavior, anthropologists, sociologists, artists, linguists, and other social scientists are still grappling to nail down one comprehensive definition that captures the full scope of its components.[1] When it comes to definitions of culture - and there are many - there are two schools of thought. The first sees culture as merely a collection of a group's basic traits such as language, religion, customs, habits, laws, values, philosophy and symbols.[2] A second, more popular view adheres to a much broader definition of culture encompassing more than just a basket of traits. It sees culture as a collective programming of the mind, or as Francis Fukuyama defined it, "an inherited ethical habit," that distinguishes the members of one human group from another.[3] Culture, according to this school of thought, is much more than the sum of its traits. It consists of the shared values, understandings, assumptions, experiences, perceptions, myths and goals that are learned from earlier generations, imposed by present members of a society, and passed to succeeding generations. It is a shared outlook that results in common attitudes, codes of conduct, and expectations that guide and control certain norms of behavior and bring about a common, often unarticulated, worldview.[4] This approach also assesses cultures in terms of group traits such as individualism, achievement, relation to authority, conception of self, concepts of masculinity and femininity, control of aggression, etc.

Such broad definitions of culture may cause confusion with a different characterization that has become known as national character. Unlike culture, the term national character has not been widely accepted. Some people even believe that it does not exist. Samuel Taylor Coleridge viewed national character as "the invisible spirit that breathes through a whole people," and Alex Inkeles defined it as "a particular way of looking at the coherence of culturally defined values or behavior patterns."[5] Most of the students of the national character school grappled with the bilateral relations between individual behavior and that of the group as a whole, trying to find causal connections between the cultural matrix and the group personality structure. The underlying assumption was that there *are* enduring personality characteristics common to most adult members of any given society and that society's behaviors and reactions are likely to follow distinctive trends that therefore can be predicted.[6]

Another challenge facing culture scholars is posed by the complicated interactive relations between culture and social structure. While culture deals mainly with symbols and meanings, social structure involves tangible social organizations of various sizes from the family to the entire nation. But social structure is a product of culture. The way people view their place and role in the universe, their respect for authority and hierarchy, and their religious beliefs are all cultural components that shape social structures. I subscribe to an inclusive definition of culture, treating it as a set of nonhereditary explicit and implicit behaviors and patterns of thought common to most members of a national group. I focus both on the affect on military cooperation of basic, tangible traits of culture and those aspects of mentality derived from those traits.

Three reservations should be stated regarding the study of national cultures in the context of military affairs. First, the cultural disposition of different countries is not uniform. Some countries, irrespective of size or population, are multicultural with little in common among the various cultural groups. Others are multicultural but with distinctive cultural patterns shared by most members of the different groups. Large, densely populated countries such as Indonesia and India, for example, have 69 and 50 different cultures respectively each with distinct cultural traits. A tiny country like New Guinea has 26 cultures and even tinier, Micronesia, has 19. Other countries such as Austria, South Korea and Saudi Arabia are almost culturally uniform. The U.S. - despite the proliferation of ethnic and racial groups and small minorities of Indian cultures, Amish, etc._- is also treated by anthropologists as culturally homogenous.[7] In order to distinguish a national group as culturally homogenous, it is not necessary for all its members to share similar cultural traits, but it *is* necessary for the majority of the population to accept, respect and adhere to cultural traits of the collective while preserving the culture of the minority group as secondary.

The second caveat is related to the treatment of culture in the context of military matters. The assumption that every military, as an institution residing within a host society, always being a reflection of the host's cultural scene is misplaced. Military organizations are sometimes dominated by members of a distinct confessional or sub-cultural group and do not necessarily carry the cultural traits of the community that they are bound to defend. This could be said about the condottieri employed by the Italian city-states, the Japanese samurai class, the Jannisaries of the Ottoman Empire, the Punjabis in Pakistan and the Sikhs in India. These groups were the agents that carried the nation's culture to the field where engagement with alien cultures of coalition counterparts took place.

Third, culture is a multidimensional term with dozens of different manifestations in society. Art, music and literature are among the first things that come to mind when discussing culture, but in the context of the military their impact is negligible. This is not to say that art and music do not play a part in the lives of soldiers in the field. Alexander the Great took on his expedition to the East several prominent cultural figures. So did Napoleon Bonaparte in his 1798 expedition to Egypt: he took writers, philosophers, a poet and even one musicologist. Ancient Indians and African tribes combined singing and dancing in their pre-battle morale boosting process; many royalties and dignitaries in the 17th and 18th centuries hired painters to capture in colors battle scenes from their military campaigns; Australian soldiers en route to the Dardanelles front in World War I received their inspiration by reading literary classics such as Homer's description of the battle of Troy. And so on. But in order to establish how culture affects military performance and cooperation, we have to focus on those cultural traits that have a meaningful impact on military life and operational effectiveness. Operationally relevant traits can be language, religion, ethics, sexual practices, and etiquette. These traits influence the way people communicate with each other and behave toward each other. This is not to say that a specific trait could not become a hinge factor that by chance could change the results of a battle. Some traits have had greater operational relevancy in past periods than in modern times simply because the outcome of a single battle often determined the outcome of an entire war. For example: disparate annual calendars and time measurement systems posed a serious obstruction to military cooperation, especially when it came to coordinating forces in different locations. Until as late as World War I, allied forces such as the Germans and the Ottomans operated under different calendars and time systems, a factor that often caused confusion and miscommunication. Food taboos also had impact on military effectiveness and cooperation. Western soldiers were known to consume alcohol when socializing and trying to alleviate pre-battle stress. Often, excessive consumption of alcohol prior to a battle impeded soldiers' performances in the field as well as their commander's capacity for effective decision making. Militaries belonging to cultures where drinking alcohol is prohibited enjoyed a culturally driven operational advantage over militaries allowing free alcohol consumption. Norms of cleanliness and hygiene also carried operational implications. Prior to World War II, in most theaters of operation, more soldiers became dysfunctional due to disease and poor hygienic conditions than due to enemy action. Militaries from cultures with high standards of orderliness and cleanliness have been able to maintain a higher degree of public health in their units in comparison to militaries in which these norms were not heeded.

Is culture destiny?

The notion that certain national groups share specific cultural characteristics affecting their military, economic and political performance has its origins in antiquity. Some of the military classics emphasized select aspects of a group's way of life, ethos and behavior as an explanatory variable and a predictor of the nation's military behavior. The Greek historian Thucydides who gave us the ultimate portrayal of the Peloponnesian Wars was one of the first to suggest that certain peoples have distinct group characteristics that distinguish them from other groups, and that the nation's military behavior is a reflection of these characteristics. One can find several allusions to these ideas in his description of the various city-states involved in the Peloponnesian War. In the famous debate at Sparta, for example, the Corinthians, pleading for Peloponnesian support, pointed at the differences in culture and mentality separating the Spartans and the Athenians. The Spartans were portrayed as narrow-minded, insecure, conservative and indecisive. The Athenians, on the other hand, were seen as innovators, open to changes, decisive and imaginative. These traits, according to Thucydides, shaped the strategic culture and military behavior of those two city-states.[8]

Many of the leading military writers of the 19th and early 20th centuries saw culture as predictor of a nation's military effectiveness and strategic behavior. Simplistic characterizations about the calmness of the English, the dash of the French, the tenacity of the Russians, the fearlessness of the Chinese, the Tartars and the Mongols are scattered in many fictional and non-fictional accounts. German military writers of the 19th century excelled at proliferating such ideas. Carl von Clausewitz, for example, despite his later conviction in the rationality and instrumentality of war, treated strategy as a reflection of society and its culture. He noted stark contrasts between French and German cultures and national characters and their respective military performances. According to

Clausewitz, "the French have limited, but within these limits, very nimble intelligence," "They lack originality of mind and deep sensibility." They "rarely think deeply of the essence of things," and because they focus on external appearances, they lack the ability to grasp a wide circle of ideas and to "delve into the realm of abstractions." Regarding the Germans, "we find that their spirit, their character, and their customs are almost completely the opposite." The German intellect, claimed Clausewitz, is deeper, their emotions are calmer, and they are "much less vain than the French." "I cannot conceal from myself how far the German national character has contributed to our present condition, and how fully it explains it," he concluded after the German defeat by the French in Jena, 1806.[9] Impressed by Clausewitz's gospel, Prussia's Chief of General Staff Helmut von Moltke saw German *kultur* and superior character - "physical fitness, mental alertness, order and punctuality, loyalty and obedience, love of our country and manliness," - as the principal tool that enabled Germany to bring her opponents into submission during the wars of unification.[10] His followers at the German high command led by one of the fathers of German militarism General Friedrich von Bernhardi held even more parochial views influenced by the writings of modern German philosophers such as Treitschke, Schlegel, Kant and Hagel. Bernhardi saw Germans as "the greatest civilized people known to history" and preached for synergetic relations between the people and their armed forces. In order for German moral, cultural and intellectual superiority to express itself, Germany should project its power outward by using military force. The army, claimed Bernhardi, was not only a vehicle for cultural transmission but also an instrument for social change, a "grand school for the whole nation" to shape German *kultur*.[11]

French writers were no less ethnocentric. Though not a pure military thinker, Alexis de Tocqueville offered his own unique observations about French social behavior and its implications on the country's doctrinal preferences and military performance:

> The Frenchman can turn his head to anything, but he excels in war alone and he prefers fighting against odds, preferring dazzling feats of arms and spectacular successes

to achievements of the more solid kind. He is more prone to heroism than to humdrum virtue, apter for genius than for good sense, more inclined to think up grandiose schemes than to carry through great enterprise. Thus the French are at once the most brilliant and the most dangerous of all European nations, and the best qualified to become, in the eyes of other peoples, an object of admiration, of hatred, of compassion, or alarm - never of indifference.[12]

Later military writers such as the French Colonel Ardent du Picq believed that combat behavior may be manifested in various ways according to "the character and the temperament of the race." His book *Battle Studies* is scattered with culture-driven observations of national combat behavior, in most cases supported by very thin evidence.[13] But it seems these views were also prevalent in the Anglo-Saxon world. Winston Churchill, in his work *History of the English Speaking People*, offered cultural explanations for a nations' military competence. The Vikings' ability to generate military power, for example, was attributed to dominant characteristics of their culture such as self-discipline and teamwork, necessary to the operation of the long boat. These values were transmitted, according to Churchill, into other spheres of civil and military life. The Saxon race, he asserted, with its pluck and doggedness, shaped the character and temperament of British military officers.[14] Churchill's American contemporary, Alfred Thayer Mahan, a geo-strategist who explored the sources of maritime power, linked the notion of a nation's culture to its propensity to become, or not to become, a naval power. He suggested that the tendency to trade, derived from society's esteem for the trading profession, and the necessity to produce something to trade with, is the cultural trait most important to the development of sea power.[15] Distinguished as the above writers were, their assessments of societies' military performances in relation to their culture were circumstantial and tainted with parochialism and cultural chauvinism. Conclusions were based on anecdotes and impressions rather than on serious empirical study. This outlook characterized a period ending only after World War II in which colonialism, imperial rivalry, racial discrimination, and

Western ethnocentrism dominated the international system and popular thought.

The treatment of national culture and character resumed after World War II but through new, much subtler approaches. The idea that a nations' strategic behavior is shaped by its culture and national character was revived and popularized by three intellectuals: Ruth Benedict, Hans Morgenthau and Raymond Aron. Commissioned by the Pentagon during World War II, Ruth Benedict's *The Chrysanthemum and the Sword* was a source of great controversy among anthropologists and Orient scholars. Despite the book's limitations, stemming mainly from its reductionism and lack of historical perspective, it clearly depicted certain features of Japanese national culture - such as its submissiveness, respect for hierarchy, emphasis on honor and most important its "shame culture" as opposed to the West's "guilt culture" - and its unusual military performance during the war.[16] Morgenthau was the first post-World War II writer to recognize the existence and impact of national character as a key element influencing national power, placing it at a similar level of importance with power sources such as quality of government, geography, natural resources, industrial capacity and strength of the armed forces.[17] His contemporary, Raymond Aron, grappled with the degree diplomatic-strategic conduct is affected by the possible influence of culture and national character. He concluded that along with other factors, the psychocultural heritage of a group might determine the strategic behavior of a political unit and predict its foreign policy style.[18] During the Cold War, there was keen interest in the link between culture and nations' strategic behavior. Rudolph Rummel in *Understanding Conflict and War* alleged that people organize their cognition and perception of reality in terms of cultural meanings and values. He was one of the first modern writers to present a compelling case that human perceptual interpretation, expectations, motivation and behavioral norms in the context of military affairs are affected by society and culture.[19] His work paved the way for the development of the strategic culture school of thought, a term first coined by Jack Snyder in 1977 in the context of the Cold War. Snyder pointed to different U.S. and Soviet attitudes toward the use of nuclear weapons. He explained the differences in that the two superpowers were influenced by different strategic cultures.[20] The term was later defined as "a nation's traditions, values, attitudes, patterns of behavior, habits, symbols, achievements and particular ways of adapting to the environment and solving problems with respect to the threat or use of force."[21] Strategic culture is usually deeply rooted in the "early" or "formative" military experiences of the state or its predecessor and affects mostly state elites rather than the general population.[22] The concept of strategic culture became useful to understanding the rationale behind nations' choices on matters of national security. Nation's strategic behaviors could be viewed through a cultural prism. Colin Gray, in *Nuclear Strategy and National Style,* maintained that distinctive U.S. and Soviet national styles came into play in each power's nuclear strategic planning. He also asserted that it was the lack of American understanding of its rival's national style that led to poor U.S. policy.[23] China's strategic culture sparked a debate between those who identified the pacifist bias in Chinese tradition as a predictor of its strategic behavior and others who observed a transformation of modern Chinese strategic culture into a more aggressive, nationalistic style.[24] In the case of Israel, strategic culture influenced the military's resorting to what one Israeli scholar called the "cult of offensive."[25] The Israeli defense and political establishment since the 1950s cultivated the doctrine of preemptive offense as the only viable way to defend a small country besieged by hostile Arab neighbors. But whereas many focused on the geo-strategic imperative that brought about the cult of offensive, other Israeli writers presented an array of associations between Israeli culture in the pre-state period and its impact on the formation of the strategic thinking of the country's founding fathers.[26] Stephen P. Rosen added a new perspective to the study of strategic culture by analyzing the affect social structure has on the ability of societies to generate military power. In his study, he examined the influence of India's unique caste system on its military power. He concluded that certain societies have consistently produced more effective militaries mainly due to variations in the divisiveness of the dominant social structures of these societies.[27] But as argued earlier, social structure is, more than anything, a product of culture. The way people view their place and role in the universe, their respect for authority and hierarchy, their religious beliefs, are all cultural components that shape social structures. If so, we can derive that there is a direct link between culture and societies' ability to generate military power.

Typical culturally driven problems

Complicated as military collaboration is, cultural dissimilarity can make it even more difficult since it increases the potential for misunderstandings and antagonism. In other words, the fact that people come from different cultural backgrounds creates more opportunities for them to disagree on what and how things should or shouldn't be done. Culture has been a source of tension in every form of multinational cooperation, not only the military. Perhaps the most widely studied field of cooperation is the business world where people of different cultures collaborate for the purpose of gaining wealth. Studies on business organizations have shown that the multinational firm is the most problematic and challenging business environment. They found, for example, that poor intercultural communication skills are the most daunting management problem to the extent that approximately 40 percent of expatriate managers who left their assignments early were forced to quit because of poor adjustment to the local cultural environment. Cross-cultural differences are also the cause of failed negotiations resulting in losses to U.S. firms of billions of dollars per year.[28] A pioneering work on the cultural dimension of the working environment by Geert Hofstede, an influential Dutch expert, on the interactions between national cultures and organizational cultures, compared 40 cultures and showed striking cultural differences among employees of a single multinational corporation. The study concluded that national culture explained 50 percent of the differences in employees' attitudes and behaviors, more than professional role, age, gender or race.[29]

Intercultural military coalitions are subjected to similar perils. Culturally driven problems may appear as a result of communication gaps as well as perceptual, attitudinal and ethical differences.

Communication problems are ranked among the primary causes for tension, confusion and inefficiency in multinational forces. Two forms of communication should be addressed: verbal and non-verbal. Verbal communication is the interaction through written or spoken language or as T.S. Eliot wrote: "speaking the same language means thinking, and feeling, and having emotions, rather differently from people who use different language."[30] Whether spoken or written, language is the principle device of communication between humans and the bond between members of a group. While it is a vehicle to convey ideas, desires, and feelings, it is also the main source of miscommunication.[31] No one could expect to be able to communicate with all 6,000 linguistic groups in the world. Most languages, in fact, are used by miniscule groups or tribes that due to geographical isolation developed their own form of communication. This is why a sparsely populated country like New Guinea has almost 1,000 languages, while a huge country like India has only 14. There are two mechanisms to overcome language barriers: language study and translation. Since language study is a tedious and lengthy process, translation is the preferred remedy. But translation has many shortcomings.[32] It does not always evoke the intended meaning of the original, and often distorts the meaning of ideas. In addition, different cultures employ unique vocabularies to describe the environment in which their people live. Vocabulary is a cultural matter. A cultural group that is technologically advanced, possesses knowledge of a larger array of facts, and makes finer discriminations in thought must inevitably have more words. When modern militaries cooperate with less developed militaries there exists a potential for vocabulary gaps with operational implications. U.S. military forces fighting alongside their Korean counterparts during the Korean War were surprised to find no Korean equivalents for basic military terms such as "sector," "zone," "regiment," or "squad." A military language had to be improvised, and the result was cumbersome and, at times, unintelligible. A machine gun, for example, became "a-gun-that-shoots-very-fast," and a vehicle headlight was "a-candle-in-a-shiny-bowl." "Such translations," wrote one military historian, "made radio communications a nightmare."[33]

Vocabulary reflects the culture, the social structure and the political climate of the people who speak it. In certain non-democratic political systems, words like "compromise," "debate," or "privacy" do not exist. Another problem: a single word can have multiple meanings and thus depends on the context in which it is used for clarity. Additionally, words or expressions often have different connotations in a foreign language. A senior Soviet military advisor in Egypt learned it the hard way. Wanting to convey to his Egyptian colleagues the fact that they were on the horns of dilemma, he said: "you are like a man with two wives and do not know which one to choose." This seemingly innocent expression was received very badly by the Egyptian generals who viewed it as an attack on Egyptian manhood and family values. The advisor was immediately expelled.[34] Language is in many cases a transmitter of implicit social messages and behavioral norms in a specific society. In the army of imperial Austria, for example, all officers in the same regiment addressed each other in the German informal "Du" form regardless of rank or social status. Failure to use the familiar form was perceived to be offensive and equivalent to a challenge to a duel.[35]

One strategic decision every combined force should make early on is what its official working language will be. The decision should be based on considerations such as location of the coalition's headquarters and preference of the majority of its members. In most cases, the coalition's senior member enforces its own preferred language. In cases of two or more dominant powers, more than one official language could be used. With approximately one billion people worldwide speaking English in various degrees of fluency, it has become the favored language for conducting international relations, and most multinational organizations conduct their business in it. As a result, leaders and military officers from English speaking nations do not feel a need to study other languages. American political and economical dominance has led many Americans to believe that they can conduct business anywhere in the world strictly from an American perspective and exclusively in English. But the dominance of English has not changed the fact that many junior partners continue to use their domestic tongue simply because their troops and commanders are not equipped with foreign language skills.

These forces are, therefore, required to invest in adequate translation services. Translation of battle orders issued by general headquarters and other military documents requires time and accuracy. Errors in the process of translations could result in loss of costly resources. Can language barriers have implications for the outcome of military operations or are they mere irritants? In some historical cases, language was a principal reason behind miscommunication and battlefield chaos. The best example of the linguistic effects on military performance is the Austro-Hungarian army, which was composed of various ethnic groups: Germans, Hungarians, Czechs, Slovaks, Poles, Serbs, Croats, Romanians, Italians and others. Linguistically speaking, there was little common ground. No fewer than ten different regimental languages were used. Most units used two, three and even four different official languages. Officers could hardly converse with their troops; troops in some units could hardly converse with each other. The language gap between Austrian officers and their multi-ethnic units contributed greatly to the 1788 defeat of the Austrian Emperor Joseph II by the Turks in the Battle of Karánsebes and had a strong impact on the performance of the army in many other cases during World War I.[36] Other militaries also suffered the destructive effect of language gaps. Dutch, French and Indonesians fighting together in the East Indies in 1810-1811 faced language difficulties that resulted in chaos in the transmission of orders. Meetings between French and British World War I generals with a poor understanding of each others' languages resembled a dialogue of the mute and the deaf. Particularly telling is the testimony by General Matthew Ridgway, commander of the U.S forces in Korea, about his failure to stop ROK soldiers fleeing the Chinese offensive of December 1950 due to his unfamiliarity with the Korean language:

> I jumped from my jeep and stood in the middle of the road, waving them to a halt. I might as well have tried to stop the flow of the Han. I spoke no Korean, and had no interpreter with me. I could find no [Korean] officer who spoke English. The only solution was to let them run and set roadblocks far enough back where they could be stopped.[37]

Apart from the spoken word, different cultures convey their ideas and thoughts using different tones of voice. Some societies, such as those in Asia, have a much more monotonous, self-controlled style than Latin or Anglo-Saxon societies. Some organizational psychologists discovered that raising the tone of voice is considered, in certain Eastern cultures, inappropriate for people holding positions of power. The higher the position, the lower and flatter the voice of the manager would be. Western commanders feel no compunction raising their voice in front of their subordinates, but doing so in front of people from other cultures could hurt their prestige and credibility.[38] Problems caused by non-verbal miscommunication also strain working relations. Non-verbal communication, "the silent language" as referred to by anthropologist Edward Hall, is a much less tangible form of communication but no less influential on the conduct and the success of multinational operations. In fact, studies show that approximately 75 percent of all communication is non-verbal.[39] What people do is frequently more important than what they say. Human beings constantly communicate by means of implicit, coded, transmitted forms of information exchange and via messages delivered by non-linguistic devices such as body language, facial expressions, customs, biases and other behaviors. These patterns of behavior prescribe our handling of time and space, our attitude toward work, change, learning and gender.[40]

Methods of communicating feelings and ideas differ from culture to culture. Some cultures are more expressive, while others are more restrained. Interaction between members of emotional opposites can cause misconceptions about the way people really feel about each other's ideas and personalities. Cultures also differ in the way they value personal space, the physical boundary that separates individuals from their external environment. The distance kept when interacting and the degree of physical contact are two of the main parameters to determine cultural appreciation of space. Arabs, Latin Americans and Asians, for example, are known as high contact cultures. They stand close to each other and touch each other a great deal during casual conversation. North American and North Europeans on the other hand are low contact cultures and have a much more distant style of body language.[41] Many people from cultures in which physical contact has offensive or sexual connotations become offended when touched by a member of the same sex, while others interpret physical contact with members of the opposite sex as a sexual advance. This problem was especially noticeable in the relations between American soldiers and their Korean and Vietnamese partners. Many American veterans reported that in Vietnamese culture there was nothing embarrassing in the display of affection between men. American soldiers were offended and aghast when touched by their Vietnamese partners.[42]

Servicemen deployed overseas tend to isolate themselves in golden ghettoes and interact with each other rather than with the people of the country. As a result, they may fail to understand the sensitivities of the host society and when encountering what they perceive as culturally bizarre behaviors. What passes as acceptable behavior in one culture - such as bribery, violence in the family, promiscuity or gender inequality - may be interpreted unfavorably by others and vice versa.[43] Perceptual problems are not only the result of disrespect for others cultures, they also originate from differences in outlooks on fundamental issues such as the perception of time and the environment surrounding us. To be late to an appointment with an associate may be considered extremely rude in one culture and totally acceptable in another. What to one's culture seems like the long-run may be perceived as short-run in other cultures. The fact that cultures' sense of time beats to different rhythms often creates difficulties in long versus short term planning and decision-making.[44]

Edward Hall distinguished between two types of cultural perceptions of time and their relations to the business environment. The first, a monochronic culture, stresses scheduling, concentration on one thing at a time, and an elaborate code of behavior built around promptness in meeting obligations and appointments. Schedules in this culture are sacred, and time commitments are taken very seriously. A polychronic culture is just the opposite. It emphasizes human relationships and interactions rather then arbitrary schedules and appointments. In polychronic cultures, many things may occur at once, interruptions are frequent and there are few formalities. While the monochronic worker concentrates on doing one assignment at a time, religiously following plans and regulations, and emphasizing promptness, the polychronic worker tends to do many things at once, is highly distractible, is subject to interruptions, and is open to changes of plans.[45]

A second distinction offered by Hall has to do with the way workers process information and how they act on the information they have acquired. He distinguished between cultures of high context communication in which most of the information is collected through a wide network of information, including interactions with broad groups of family and associates, and cultures of low context communication in which people need detailed background information in order to perform their jobs. Arabs and Japanese who have extensive information networks among family, friends, colleagues, and clients are considered high context. Examples of low context peoples are Americans and North Europeans who, by and large, compartmentalize their relationships, separating the work from personal. Consequently, every time they interact with a new group they need detailed background information. Hall also observed that these context processing differences could cause great tension. High context people tend to become impatient and irritated when low context people insist on giving them detailed information they perceive to be unnecessary. Too much information often leads people to feel that they are being talked down to. Low context people become confused and feel left out when high context people do not provide them with enough information and detailed instructions.[46]

Cultures differ in the way they value other issues such as success, responsibility, individuality, authority, family, social structure and patterns of decision-making. There are considerably different ways to perceive individual life and our capacity to influence the future. These views mainly originate from the implicit and explicit messages conveyed by religion. Perhaps the most important fundamental of religion has to do with its attitude toward the meaning of life and the role and purpose of a human being in the world. All religions offer their believers comfort and mechanisms to deal with their biggest concern, that is, their own demise. Most of them subscribe, in one way or another, to the notion that our present life is temporary and is a corridor to an eternal afterlife. The value each society places on human life can have a profound effect on its civilian and military behavior. That is to say, society's religiosity determines to a large extent its ability to stomach casualties, because that determines how highly it values the afterlife. Militaries from societies that value martyrdom and self-sacrifice usually enjoy greater freedom of operation than those from societies where individual life is sacred. Militaries from societies with a high sensitivity to casualties are likely to reflect their sensitivity by relying on firepower and air power, a reluctance to engage in high risk operations, conservative training programs and an adherence to often exaggerated safety standards in the daily life of the troops. Different attitudes toward life among foreign militaries working together can cause tension regarding certain ethical and moral issues applicable to military life such as rules of engagement, treatment of civilian populations in enemy territory, environmental issues, the use of certain types of weapons, torture, abuse, and the treatment of prisoners of war. Culture may also determine the different attitudes toward the idea of surrendering a battle. Japanese military culture during World War II abhorred the idea of Japanese troops taken alive. Surrender in battle was perceived as unethical, a betrayal of emperor and country. Consequently, the Japanese military provided no instruction to its soldiers as to how they should behave in captivity. As a result, most prisoners of war freely responded to interrogations and cooperated with their captors to a degree that most Europeans would consider traitorous.[46] Compare this to American prisoners in Japan, Korea and Vietnam who were held to a strict code of honor. They were trained to believe that they would be treated very badly by their captors and were thrown off balance whenever they were treated softly. American culture treated U.S. soldiers who surrendered and became prisoners of war with understanding and empathy. In recent years, it has even become customary to reward returning U.S. prisoners of war with honors and decorations.

Attitudes toward the future can determine the pattern of long-term planning in military organizations. When people believe that they have the power to shape their future, they are willing to invest in planning. Others are more fatalistic, believing that everything is predetermined by God, and, therefore, there is no gain in investing much in planning. Even though most Americans believe in God, they belong to the first type of free will culture. The great majority believe that it is a person's own efforts that account for success or failure in life and that one's destiny is in one's own hands.[48]

Cultures have different levels of tolerance of uncertainty. Attitude toward uncertainty determines the willingness to take risky decisions and to institute major changes in the organization. Avoidance of uncertainty is closely related to religion. Countries with religions that stress absolute certainties such as Catholicism and Islam showed the highest level of uncertainty avoidance. Protestant and Buddhist countries, less concerned with the absolute, showed a much higher level of tolerance toward uncertainty.[49]

Societies may also demonstrate dissimilar views toward authority in their political, social, tribal and family institutions. Attitudes toward authority influence people's willingness to challenge and disagree with their superiors, to express their true opinions and to propose and promote change. In countries where authority is stressed, employees fear to disagree with their bosses, close supervision is valued by subordinates, managers make decisions paternalistically and authoritatively, and power holders are entitled to privileges. By and large, this is the case in Asian and Middle Eastern countries.[50] Attitude toward authority determines the hierarchy of the organization, the working relations between supervisors and subordinates, and the acceptable ways to express disagreement without insult. Social observers often note that in certain cultures, challenging authority is a social taboo. As a result, people there have difficulties expressing frankness negativity or dissent even during the simplest daily interactions. In some cultures, especially those with a long history of authoritarianism or a stratified social structure, it is difficult to use the word no, especially during an interaction with someone in a higher social status. For example, U.S. troops in China, Korea and Vietnam noted that many of the local people had difficulty saying "no" to their superiors. Koreans would sometimes use the word "yes" to convey "no" in answer to an American's question, but the American would understand the answer as "yes." For example: An American question: didn't you fire back at the enemy? A typical Korean answer would be "yes," meaning, "I didn't fire back."[51] Especially illuminating was a comparative experiment in Iran and Great Britain: in Iran, 20 percent of people on the street gave a foreigner directions to a place even though that place did not exist; in Great Britain this never happened.[52]

Why the individual's motivation to succeed is stronger in one culture than another is a question addressed by few scholars.[53] Different cultures assign different values to tangible and intangible rewards for hard work and professional achievements. Hofstede examined the relations between the individual and the collective in different societies. He constructed an individualism index that predicts the level of improvisation tolerated by the organization, the preference to work in small or large groups and the degree of autonomy given by managers to their subordinates. The index clearly showed that the U.S. and Western European countries have high scores whereas Asian and Muslim countries are at the bottom of the list. This means that Western cultures focus on the individual, in contrast with non-Western cultures where the focus is on the group.[54]

Views on gender equality, marriage, promiscuity and sexual practices can differ quite starkly between societies. Most cases of host-guest relations are characterized by the influx of male soldiers of an alien culture into a foreign land, laying the groundwork for cross-cultural sexual relations that have the potential to create severe tension with the indigenous population. In his book *Rich Relations*, historian David Reynolds described the sexual implications of the 'occupation' by almost three million "oversexed, overpaid, overfed and over here" U.S. troops who passed through Great Britain in the months preceding D-Day. Though the U.S. and Great Britain are probably as close culturally as two nations could ever get, many British citizens felt resentful of the way American servicemen treated and, in their opinion, exploited British females.[55] A more negative sentiment is likely to arise when the two groups are not culturally or racially homogeneous. Potential sources of tension between hosts and guests could emerge when members of the guest military perceive the indigenous population to be more relaxed about sexual matters than their own culture. Soldiers can often view their overseas deployment as a sexual haven, a place where they can escape the confines of wives and girlfriends left behind, where they can fulfill their sexual needs through liaisons with members of foreign cultures. But in doing so they often misbehave and treat local women, including married women of high social status, as lesser beings. This can be interpreted by the host society as sexual imperialism and create a general resentment against the guest military. At the same time, phenomena such as interracial relations, mixed marriages, and religious conversions of brides are examples of cultural transmission between a host society and its guest. For example, the Allied abandonment of official brothels during World War II led not only to the reduction in the number of soldiers who contracted sexually transmitted diseases but also enhanced intercultural relations due to increased cases of promiscuity and an acceptance of marriages between host and guest populations. One popular demonstration of such cultural transmission was the *querida* system, a semi-official arrangement that occurred during the U.S. occupation of the Philippines, where a man and a woman could live together as long as they wished and then separate without commitment, even if there were children. Many American servicemen, including senior commanders such as Generals John Pershing and Douglas MacArthur, maintained *queridas*.[56]

Promiscuity could have negative operational implications when soldiers using the services of local prostitutes become infected with sexually transmitted diseases. Between one eighth and one third of the British garrison in India during the 19th century was infected with syphilis, and between five and fifteen percent of the allied soldiers fighting in the Mediterranean, Burma and Europe during World War II suffered from sexually transmitted diseases. Such high numbers of sufferers added an additional strain on the already over-burdened medical staff, clearly degrading the operational preparedness of the units.[57] Today's raging AIDS epidemic exposes soldiers deployed in East Asia and Africa to similar risks.

Finally, culture dictates attitudes toward gender and especially the role and status of women in society. This point is becoming increasingly important as more women in Western countries join combat units of their militaries, deploy overseas and often climb to high ranks. Participating in coalition with militaries from countries where gender discrimination still exists, these servicewomen could face a serious disadvantage. Their counterparts may not take advice or orders from them and in extreme cases may not even be willing to communicate with them. The U.S.-Saudi Gulf War partnership, described in Chapter 5, demonstrated some of the problems arising when Western female soldiers found themselves working in an environment where women are treated as second class citizens.

But let's begin with the men.

2
PASHAS AND PRUSSIANS: OTTOMAN TURKEY AND GERMANY DURING WORLD WAR I

⌘ ⌘ ⌘

Ben bir türk'üm, dinim, jinsim ulundur
(I am a Turk. My religion and my race are noble)
Mehmet Emin Bey, Turkish poet.

Deutschland über Allah
Punch Magazine

By 1914, the Ottoman army was the prime casualty of the illness that had struck the "sick man of Europe." Unless fighting alongside coalition partners, as in the case of the Crimean War, the Ottoman army at the turn of the 20th century was too weak to win a war on its own. The 1875 Bosnian revolt, the defeat to Russia in 1878, the loss of Egypt in 1882, and the debacles of the Italo-Turkish War and the Balkan Wars all left Turkey and its military defeated, fragmented and humiliated. Realizing the urgent need for outside military assistance, Ottoman sultans constantly courted the great European powers asking them to send military missions to Constantinople in order to upgrade and reorganize their decaying military.[1] Hence, the British were invited to train the Turkish navy, while the French and the Italians trained the police and gendarmerie. But the weakest component of all, the ground forces, required a series of radical reforms in order to rise to European standards. It was only natural that the declining empire sought the help of the emerging military power of the time - Germany.[2]

German-Turkish military relations officially began 78 years prior to World War I with a four-man German military mission to

Constantinople headed by the young captain, Helmuth von Moltke, who later became the Prussian Chief of Staff during the Wars of German Unification. The Ottoman army made a poor impression on Moltke. He found an army of diseased and malnourished soldiers, dominated by corrupt and lethargic officers. Moltke cynically called it "a European army," deriding not its spirit or doctrine, but its external appearance. It was an army with "Russian uniforms and French standards, equipped with Belgian guns, wearing Turkish hats, riding on Hungarian saddles, using English swords, and trained by instructors from all nations."[3] This portrayal reflected the magnitude of the challenge Moltke and his team faced. Though the German mission that ended after only three years failed to transform the Sultan's army into a European one, it set the stage for future military relations between the two powers. Then came defeat in the war against Russia. Struck by disaster, the Sultan, Abdul Hamid II, appealed to Germany to send a second, larger mission to which he was willing to grant extended powers. This mission to Turkey, named for the officer who headed it, Colonel Otto Kaehler, began in 1882, but, again, had limited results. Kaehler's untimely death in 1885 left a void soon filled by Colmar von der Goltz - one of Germany's foremost military thinkers - who became the most influential and highly regarded German officer in the Ottoman court. In his twelve years of service in Turkey, Goltz reorganized the military education system, revised its curriculum, and wrote more than 4,000 pages of doctrine and field manuals. He also instituted field maneuvers with live fire, a rarity until then. But like his predecessors, his work was hampered by the corruption, apathy and low standards of achievement that were so deeply rooted in the Ottoman government system.[4] The attempt to instill German military professionalism and norms in the Turkish army also included the training of Turkish officers in Germany. In 1883, a group of 10 Turkish officers went to study and train in Germany. Some of these officers, and others who followed, were later promoted to high positions in the Ottoman army and filled important roles during World War I and the subsequent Turkish War of Independence.[5] The Ottoman Empire's moral and political decline created much domestic turmoil which eventually brought to a bloodless coup orchestrated by the Committee of Union and Progress (CUP) in 1908, followed by a failed counter-revolution in which the Sultan was deposed and exiled. The Young Turks of the CUP, led by a triumvirate, took command of the empire. But even these political changes failed to improve Turkey's strategic posture. On the contrary, defeats in Tripoli and the Balkans ensued.

By 1913, the year a new military mission headed by the German general Liman von Sanders was established, Turkey was in many respects a changed place. The Empire shrank after losing all of its holdings in southeast Europe in the Balkan Wars; its military prowess was severely degraded; and the Sultanate was considerably weakened. A wave of nationalism loomed, inspired by pan-Turkish ideologists such as Ziya Gökalp and Ismail Gaspirali who preached for Turkey to face east and unite with its Turk brothers in Russia, Persia and Central Asia. To Enver Pasha, Turkey's new minister of war and de facto strongman, a man who had been Turkey's military attaché in Berlin, Germany was a natural ally not only because of its military promise but also due to the extensive civil support it granted Turkey.[6] Germany, more than any other European power, helped Turkey in its social and economic reforms. German advisors were assigned to various Turkish ministries, rising to senior positions, even undersecretaries of state; German professors held key positions in Turkish academia; affluent Germans financed influential newspapers published in Turkey, shaping Turkish public opinion. Most importantly, Germany financed the Anatolian and Baghdad Railway Companies that connected the Asian part of Turkey with Europe and promoted Germany's strategic goal to create a land route to the Indian Ocean.

With the winds of war blowing in Europe and the realization that a war with France would essentially involve a clash with Russia, Turkey's stock in the eyes of the Germans mounted even further. An alliance with Turkey, it was thought, would serve several strategic purposes. Turkey's strong anti-Russian sentiments could be exploited to open a front in the east, weakening Russia's forces and preventing them from assisting the French. To weaken Russia even further, Turkey could block the passage of Russian ships through the straits leading to the Black Sea, thus denying Russia three-quarters of its strategic imports. Turkey could also assist Austria in its war against the Serbs and, finally, Germany could exploit the fact that Turkey was the center of Islam to inspire religiously-motivated domestic unrest in Muslim dominated French, British and Russian colonies in North Africa, the Middle East, India and Central Asia.

It was less clear what Turkey had to gain from allying itself with Germany. Most Turks felt it would be unwise for Turkey to abandon its neutrality. But the idea of restoring Turkish national pride by settling the score with a weakened Russia and the promise of territorial gains in Transcaucasia was appealing to some of Turkey's young leaders. Enver's dream was to regain substantial territory in Macedonia, Thrace, eastern Anatolia, Egypt and Cyprus. He also planned to liberate the ethnic Turkish population in the Caucasus and central Asia from Russian and Armenian oppression. This was only possible with outside help.

Turkey's fall into Germany's embrace was also a result of its growing aversion to the other European powers, mainly France and Britain. One cannot precisely determine the impact Ottoman disenchantment with British policy toward Turkey had on its decision to join the Germans. It is clear, however, that Winston Churchill's August 1914 seizure of the two battleships, *Reshadieh* and *Sultan Osman I,* the purchase of which was made possible through a patriotic popular donation collection throughout the Empire, deeply hurt the Turks' feelings, causing an unbridgeable rift between London and Constantinople.[7] Turkey, therefore, drifted away from its European friends as it struggled to restore its lost pride and fulfill its aspirations of uniting the Muslims of the world. To achieve all that, it needed the support of a militarily strong ally. The French and British clearly showed that they were in no position to provide such service. Germany, thus, became an ally by default.

The strategic landscape

The defensive alliance between Turkey and Germany was signed on August 2, 1914. Only three members of the Turkish cabinet were informed of the step.[8] The Turko-German treaty stated, among other provisions, that: "In case of war, the German

Military Mission will remain at the disposal of Turkey. As agreed upon directly between the head of the Military Mission and His Excellency the Minister of War, Turkey will grant to the German Military Mission an active influence and authority in the general management of the army."[9] The aforementioned German Military Mission under Otto Liman von Sanders - a Pomeranian nobleman considered one of the most experienced division commanders in the German army – had begun its work in Turkey in the winter of 1913. When the Great War began, the mission already numbered 70 officers and advisors. The contract between Liman von Sanders and the Ottoman Navy Minister Mahmet Pasha granted the German general unprecedented powers. In addition to his role as head of the mission, Liman was a member of the Ottoman Supreme War Council with a vote on a broad set of issues related to training, doctrine, organization, appointments and discipline. He was also allowed to conduct visits and inspection tours in all military installations, enjoying the authority to remove and punish subordinate Turkish officers.[10] The Turks also agreed to entrust the First Army in Constantinople under Liman's command, a decision that immediately sparked a diplomatic crisis with Russia. For the Russians, Liman's appointment essentially meant that if they were ever to land in the Bosporus area, they would come up against a German corps. The crisis was finally resolved with the repeal of the appointment. But by then, Germany was already deeply involved in Turkey's domestic and military affairs, and Liman's far-reaching authority was a well-known fact among the European powers.[11]

The general view among Germans about the state of the Turkish army prior to the beginning of the war was that it was worse than worthless. Most of the units were not in operational shape; there was a shortage of food, medicines and essential equipment; and many of the units had suffered losses due to plagues and malnutrition. The Chief of the German General Staff, Helmut von Moltke the Younger, referred to it as "a total zero. [...] An army without weapons, ammunition, and uniforms. [...] The wives of the officers beg in the streets." A letter by the German Kaiser, Wilhelm II, summed up the situation of the Turkish army in one word, "horrific."[12] Despite the weakness of the Ottomans, Liman and his friends had faith in their potential. They invested great

Ismail Enver Pasha

efforts in improving the training and supplies of the Turkish army. Germany soon became Turkey's main arms supplier transferring battleships, hundreds of planes, artillery, tools, trucks, uniforms, food and ammunition.[13] By the fall of 1914, German military personnel deployed in the Ottoman Empire climbed to about 2,000. Their main goal was to ease the Ottomans' fear about the poor status of the Dardanelles defenses. This was promptly taken care of by a large contingent of German experts in shore artillery and engineering sent to fortify the gateway to the Bosporus. So visible were the German advisors on the Dardanelles front that the U.S. Ambassador in Constantinople, Henry Morgenthau, commented upon his visit to the region that he had the impression that he was in Germany.[14]

In the three months between the outbreak of World War I and the Turkish October 29 surprise attack on the Russian Black Sea coast that marked Turkey's joining the war, Germany's political and military leaders expressed their desire for immediate Turkish fulfillment of their alliance obligations. But the Turks procrastinated. Their reluctance to fight was rooted in a strong sense of insecurity, lack of preparedness, and failure to secure an effective alliance with Bulgaria and Romania.[15] Before the movement of the two German warships *Goeben* and *Breslau* into the Black Sea, the Turks were at Russia's mercy on the sea and, until they were rendered stronger, it was impossible for them to furnish the diversions against Russia and England needed to relieve the pressure on Germany in the other theaters of war. Their hesitance dismayed the Germans and caused the first bits of tension between the allies. The quarrel was a harbinger of things to come. Once Turkey joined the war, it did not take long before it was embroiled in three challenging campaigns. All three campaigns generated more tension with the Germans. The first was Enver's suicidal campaign against Russia in which he, ignoring Liman's vigorous opposition to a winter offensive, led 100,000 soldiers through the forbidding Caucasus mountain range in January 1915. Enver's ambitions verged on recklessness. He envisaged a Turkish advance into Afghanistan and from there to India completely ignoring geographic, logistic and weather considerations. To his distress, Liman was proved right. Frost, hunger, disease and enemy action annihilated 86 percent of his Third Army.[16] Disaster of such magnitude demanded repercussions, and Liman demanded the resignation of Enver's German chief-of-staff, General Bronsart von Schellendorff who, against Liman's orders, had agreed to go along with Enver's plan. But Enver, undeterred by the brewing crisis with the German head of mission, stood behind his chief-of-staff and refused to dismiss him.[17] Simultaneously, Djemal Pasha took command over the Ottoman Fourth Army and led it into a hopeless surprise attack across the Suez Canal.[18] Here too, Liman clearly disagreed with the operational plan. In his meeting with Enver and Djemal, he pointed out the small possibility of success, but his advice was, again, ignored. His predictions were proved right again. The Suez operation was terminated once it was discovered that the pontoons brought especially from Germany by German engineers could not be used since the Turkish commanders failed to provide appropriate training for their troops. Naturally, the incident, which led to a humiliating withdrawal, was a source of additional distrust and allegations between the Germans and the Turks.[19] The Turks blamed the Germans for the defeat, and a wave of anti-German feeling culminated in three German officers being shot by their Turkish comrades.[20]

The campaign to defend the Gallipoli peninsula from the March 1915 allied naval attack and the subsequent landing was the only military success the German-Turkish alliance scored in the first two years of the war. Though the battle was Turkey's most important military victory in the war, it could surely have ended differently if not for the German role in fortifying the straits, planning for the defense and supplying the Turks with sufficient war materiel. Another important factor that contributed to the success was Liman's able command over the Ottoman Fifth Army during the entire campaign. But the joint success in the Dardanelles did not mitigate the tension between the partners; on the contrary, it only deepened the rift. The Turks viewed their victory as an exclusive achievement and took great pride in being able to win the campaign without the Germans. They felt that they owed nothing to the Germans for this victory, even though the Germans taught them all about modern warfare. Furthermore, it was perceived as a victory over the white race and a sign of Turkish resurrection, which only increased their jingoism and anti-German feelings.[20] In a meeting with Morgenthau, Enver conveyed his feelings toward his coalition counterpart:

Why should we feel any obligation to the Germans? What have they done for us which compares to what we have done for them? We have defeated the British fleet - something which neither the Germans nor any other nation could do. We have stationed armies on the Caucasian front, and so have kept large bodies of Russian troops that would have been based in the Russian front. Similarly we have compelled England to keep large armies in Egypt, in Mesopotamia, and in that way we have weakened the Allied armies in France. No, the Germans could never have achieved their military successes without us.[22]

As the war progressed, the size and involvement of the German force deployed in the Ottoman Empire rapidly grew. By the summer of 1916, some 10,000 German troops fought alongside the Turks. This number swelled to 25,000 by 1918. There is no dispute among historians that the sizable German presence had a crucial role in the transformation of the Turkish army into an effective fighting organization, improving its performance over time.[23] Besides the tactical disagreements and personal quarrels, there were also happier moments in the alliance, when German and Ottoman soldiers reached a reasonable level of operational cooperation. Twice in 1917, the allies cooperated effectively to defeat the British at the gates of Gaza. That same year, they also agreed to establish a German-Turkish army group of 14 divisions to repel the British army in Mesopotamia. The Jilderim Army or Army Group F included 6,000 German soldiers and 62 German officers commanded by the deposed Chief of the General Staff General Erich von Falkenhayn. It was an ambitious military conglomerate, though due to the war circumstances its power was never materialized in battle. In addition, Turkey agreed to assist Germany on the Western front when the situation there became dire. Approximately 100,000 Turkish soldiers organized in seven divisions ended up fighting on European fronts in Galicia, Romania and Macedonia.[24]

But it was the Russian withdrawal from the war, as part of the March 1918 Brest-Litovsk peace agreement, which brought the Turks and the Germans closer than ever to breaking their alliance.

During treaty negotiations, the Turks pressured Germany to force a Russian withdrawal from occupied Ottoman territories. Aware of Turkish ambitions in Central Asia, the Germans were reluctant to do so. They wanted to secure the peace with Russia and refused to allow further complications to the already shaky relations. Dismayed by Germany's lack of sympathy, Enver organized a military expedition to advance toward the Caspian Sea. The Germans responded by deploying infantry and artillery battalions in Georgia to keep Enver at bay. The Turks resented this move, and a wave of Germanophobia rose among Ottoman officers. The regional headquarters instructed Turkish soldiers to disarm the Germans and treat them as prisoners of war. Turkish maps found after the war identified the German positions in Georgia as "enemy" positions.[25] The crisis escalated even further when on August 4, the German Generalquartiermeister Erich Ludendorff sent a stern message to Enver warning: "Unless the Turkish advance on Baku is halted at once and the troops are withdrawn to their original positions, I shall have to propose to His Majesty the recall of the German officers in the Turkish High Command."[26] Despite the warning, in mid-September the Ottoman forces launched an attack on Baku and quickly occupied the city only to evacuate it weeks later due to heavy military and diplomatic pressure.

In sum, the German-Turkish alliance was a frustrating affair, best characterized as merely a marriage of convenience. Germany and Turkey were at odds over many strategic issues. The Germans wanted the Turks to be strong for the sake of Germany's own military purposes; the Turks cared very little for Germany's hegemonic aspirations in Europe. Both the military and political leadership in Germany regarded the Turkish alliance as crucial to the German war effort, especially regarding the Russian front and the Western front. When it appeared that the Western front was more challenging than predicted, Germany hoped that by opening a new front in the east, the British, French and Russians would be forced to move forces out of Europe and thus alleviate the pressure.[27] The Germans were also wary of Turkey's independent agenda, especially its ambitions in the Balkans and the Transcaucasia. They made efforts to contain Turkey and prevent a likely confrontation with Bulgaria. Popular World War I literature describes Turkey as subservient to

Germany, attributing its behavior to Germany's relative strength and its use of manipulative and coercive policies in the years prior to the war.[28] This view was refuted by historian Ulrich Trumpener who forcefully argued that though Germany was more powerful than Turkey, the Ottoman army never turned into an instrument of German foreign policy. On the contrary, the proud Ottomans understood well the German calculus and refused to become Germany's pawns. The influence of the German military mission on strategic decision-making was much less significant than portrayed in other accounts. Even though Enver had a large number of high ranking German officers in his staff, they were subordinate to his orders, and he retained complete control over all important issues. Liman's role, according to this view, was exaggerated. His actual role was that of an advisor rather than a policy-maker. Many of his recommendations on strategic issues were ignored or rejected by Enver.[29] The disputes between the two force commanders were not only over operational issues; they were driven no less by mutual personal antipathy. Without delving into the specifics of each of their many squabbles, one could attribute the tension primarily to their incompatible, presumptuous and capricious personalities.[30] Liman, a 59-year old German aristocrat, was regarded by his compatriots as "arrogant, hot-tempered, crusty, suspicious and sensitive." He had never before served outside of Europe and was unfamiliar with the culture and sensitivities of his Oriental partners.[31] His failure to adjust to his unique environment caused periodic fights with Enver and other Turkish officials, severely straining the alliance relationship. Enver was more exposed to German culture than Liman was to the Ottoman. His service in Berlin opened a window to the Western way of life and provided him the opportunity to study the language. Many observers misinterpreted his fluency in German and his style of moustache as evidence of Germanophilia. Morgenthau even said that Enver was barely more Turkish than German.[32] But they were wrong. Enver was not fond of the Europeans. He was interested in their culture but resented it at the same time. "Your civilization is a poison, but a poison that awakens people," he wrote once to a German friend.[33] Enver's actions starting with his rise to power were born out of a warm sentiment to the Arabs and resentment of the Europeans, including the Germans.[34] Both Liman and Enver were hardly ideal coalition commanders. They held ethnocentric views and had little affinity for each other's cultures. Consequently, they failed to establish mutual trust and understanding and constantly tried to undermine each other's authority. Despite the fact that their offices were in the same building, at times they were not on speaking terms for weeks on end. Enver at one point appealed directly to the Kaiser to remove Liman from his position. According to some sources, there was also a plot by conservative Turkish officers inspired by Enver's resentment to assassinate von Sanders.[35]

Otto Liman von Sanders

How did the Turks view the Germans?

As a bridge between east and west, the Ottoman Empire had to always reconcile its tendency to aspire toward the economically promising Christian West with its demanding role as the undisputed center of Islam and guardian of its holy places. Sultan Abdul-Hamid II, who until 1909 also served as the caliph, the highest religious authority and spiritual leader of all Muslims, was clearly biased toward the latter. Fearing the growing influence of the European powers, the Sultan turned his back on the West and called for Muslims of the world to unite in fighting every sign of intervention by the infidels. But the official policy of separation from the West was never fully implemented. In the military sphere, for example, Turkey simply could not afford to relinquish assistance from European powers and thus remained completely engaged with the West. In other fields such as culture and commerce, despite the Sultan's xenophobic attitude, Constantinople remained host to intensive Western cultural activity. It was a place that imported many features from the West, adapting them to Turkey's specific needs. The agents of Turkey's Westernization were primarily those members of the governing class who left home, spent years in Europe and in many cases received a Western education. They also were the European scholars, diplomats, soldiers, artists and businessmen who lived in the various districts of the Ottoman Empire.[36]

Of all European cultures, it was the French, at least until the turn of the century, that most deeply penetrated Turkey's life. A large majority of the educated class studied French as a second language; several French newspapers were published in Turkey; French Catholic missionaries were active; and French scholars dominated the higher education system.[37] However, France's alliance with Russia marked the beginning of a shift in the dominant foreign culture from French to German. If until 1909, almost everything to do with German culture was loathed in Turkey, the Young Turk revolution changed the situation. Germany, for its part, saw great importance in spreading its culture in Turkey at the expense of the French and the British. The Germans made efforts to prove to the Turks that they were their real friends and that their culture was superior to the other European powers. Before and throughout the war German efforts continued to infuse German culture into Turkish society including German exhibitions and other educational organizations.[38] The Germans tried to increase the teaching of the German language and establish it as the dominant European language in use in Turkey instead of French. Germany encouraged Turkish students to study in Germany, granting them stipends and accommodation. As the political affinity between Germany and the Ottomans grew, so did the role German culture played in Turkish high society. Germany's cultural penetration was meant to serve more than just an educational purpose. Its logic was explained by German officials such as Paul Rohrbach, a German specialist on Near East affairs, who stated a month before the war the essence of Germany's *kulturpolitik*:

> We have set before ourselves the necessary and legitimate aim of spreading and enrooting German influence in Turkey, not only by military missions and the construction of railways, but also by the establishment of intellectual relations, by the work of German Kultur - in a word, by moral conquests; and we are determined, by specific means, to reach an amicable understanding with the Turks and the other nations in the Turkish Empire. Our ulterior object in this is to strengthen the Turkish Empire internally with the aid of German science, education, and training.[39]

Certain aspects of Germany's *kulturpolitik* were successful, but it was not well received overall by the Ottomans. The attempt to proliferate a Christian culture in a Muslim domain was perceived as offensive. A belief spread in Turkey that the Germans wanted their culture to dominate the entire world by virtue of their military and economic force and that Turkey was one of their prime targets.[40] Naturally, such sentiment fueled suspicion and hostility toward the emerging cultural threat straining relations between the two strategic partners.

Despite the pitfalls of the 19th century, the Ottomans remained a proud nation with high self-esteem and a strong sense of cultural superiority. They took great pride in their history and contribution to humanity. Most of all, they emphasized their practice of granting defeated nations cultural autonomy as opposed to other subjugating nations that oppressed their vassals. This made them believe in the superiority of their morals. "Every great nation has demonstrated superiority in some particular field of civilization," wrote Ziya Gökalp, "The Turks have excelled in morals. Turkish history from its beginning is an exhibition of moral virtues."[41] But this perception of moral superiority led to utter contempt for all other races. American Ambassador Morgenthau noticed that "the common term applied by the Turk to the Christian is 'dog,' and in his estimation this is no mere rhetorical figure; he actually looks upon his European neighbors as far less worthy of consideration than his own domestic animals."[42] The Ottomans' belief in their cultural superiority debilitated their ability to live on an equal basis with non-Muslims even in their own home. Until a short time before the outbreak of the war, neither Christian nor Jewish residents of the empire were allowed to bear arms and fight in the armies of the Sultan. When the discriminatory law was finally repealed, and non-Muslims began to join the military, they faced serious obstacles on their way to command posts due to their religious background. The Turks' view of their European colleagues was shaped by their religion, which held other belief systems in low regard, treating non-Muslims as infidels. So deeply rooted was the notion of religious hierarchy that Muslim soldiers could not tolerate the idea of submitting to the authority of non-Muslims.[43] German, French and British military and civilian missions that operated among the Ottomans often complained about the tendency of Muslims to refuse to take orders from non-believers. In 1905, when the Sublime Porte, the court of the Ottoman Empire, decided to send to Germany Turkish NCOs to receive training on a new design of an artillery piece, the Germans declined to receive the group on the grounds of prior experience in which Ottoman soldiers refused to be ordered around by non-Muslims.[44] The problem of insubordination to 'infidels' was not only religiously driven but also a result of the strong sense of pride of the Turkish officer. German officers complained that the Turk disliked to be called on by a foreigner even if that foreigner was senior in rank. By and large, Turkish officers did not disobey the orders of superior officers, but, instead, they used excuses and delaying tactics to avoid being perceived by their soldiers or colleagues as losing face.[45] To their agony, proud Turkish officers witnessed how German officers gradually assumed remarkably senior positions in the Ottoman army. Toward the end of the war, German officers commanded three out of seven Turkish armies and one of two army groups. Fourteen German officers served as chiefs-of-staff in Ottoman army groups and army commands, and an additional seventeen became corps and divisional commanders. Staff assignments at the Ottoman General Headquarters were held mostly by Germans. General Erich von Falkenhayn, after his removal as Chief of the German Army General Staff, became advisor and then commander of Ottoman army in Palestine; Lt. Gen von Seeckt served as Chief of General Staff. The heads of the departments of operations, railroads, quartermaster, weapons and munitions, traffic, coal, engineering and fortresses were also German.[46]

The Turks did not trust the German officers who positioned themselves in the army's highest ranks. They resented the fact that the defense of their nation was entrusted to foreigners. Mustafa Kemal, later to become Ataturk, was one of those who held such views. In a letter to Enver he urged "not to rely on the mental ability of the Germans, headed by von Sanders, whose hearts and souls are not engaged, as ours are in the defense of our country."[47] If the Germans lost, it was thought, Turkey would be used as a tool to satisfy the appetite of the victors and be put out of existence. If they won, Turkey was to become a German colony.[48] Ambassador Morgenthau recalled Enver's view of the Turko-German alliance: "The Turks and the Germans care nothing for each other. We are with them because it is our interest to be with them; they are with us because that is their interest. Germany will back Turkey just as long as that helps Germany; Turkey will back Germany just as long as that helps Turkey."[49]

German attitude toward the Turks

To understand the popular view of the Turk in Europe, specifically in Germany in the period prior to the war, one has only to look at the writings of some of the shapers of public opinion and of those Europeans who visited Turkey and spent time among the Ottomans. The letters of Moltke the Elder depict Turkey as "a land consumed with laziness" and "a nation constantly in slippers."[50] Thomas Carlyle depicted the Turk at the outbreak of the Crimean war as "a lazy, ugly, sensual dark fanatic."[51] Heinrich von Treitschke, one of the most influential German pundits at the end of the 19th

Century, observed in the Turks "indescribable intellectual laziness" and "profound slumber of the soul." "The Osmans are decaying, body and soul," he concluded, "Their generative strength is being extinguished in the sodomy and voluptuousness of the harem."[52] "The Musulman," summarized Andre Servier in his controversial book *Islam and the Psychology of the Musulman,* "bound by his religion, cannot accept Western progress. The two civilizations are too different, too much opposed, ever to admit mutual interpenetration."[53] One need not continue enumerating the prejudices and stereotypes used to characterize the Turks and their culture in order to realize the popular feeling of antipathy and disdain toward the Orientals. Many of the commentators on life in the Ottoman Empire were military advisors who served in Turkey and acquired first-hand experience with the country and its people. These officers sent home periodic reports with vivid descriptions of what they perceived as Turkish barbarism. The sentiments conveyed by a handful of officers pervaded the German military and when German troops were massively deployed in Turkey, most of them were already infected with a strong cultural bias. One secret document circulated in 1909 among German officers selected to become military instructors in Turkey provides a good reflection of the general attitude in the German military toward Turkish culture. The paper shed an unfavorable light on Turkish culture and mentality as viewed by the German General Staff. It suggested that the Turks are a passive and phlegmatic people, who tend to trust their good fortune, rather than plan ahead and pay attention to details. Additionally, it said they lack initiative and independent thought, are unable to make decisions and refuse to assume responsibility for their mistakes. "The Oriental grasps quickly new ideas, but meticulousness in mundane issues quickly evokes in him a sense of boredom, especially in light of the fact that he is incapable of understanding the link between him as an individual and the general efficiency of the army," it said. The document also described the deep-rooted corruption and the tendency to prefer the satisfaction of private, rather than collective, interests.[54]

Liman was also known for his prejudice against the Ottomans. In his memoirs he described the slow wittedness of the Anatolian

soldier and his difficulties in comprehending sophisticated training methods.[55] He found the Turkish officers incapable of making judgments and decisions on important military issues, and he
considered them inferior in every aspect to the European officer.[56]
Other German officers also looked down at the Ottomans and often
quarreled with them. Most German officers failed to accommodate
themselves to the peculiarities of the country and the Turkish administration, and thought it necessary to apply German standards, ethics and methods to Turkish conditions. One senior German officer
Kress von Kressenstein ridiculed Liman's approach of forcing the
weak Turkish soldier to march in a Prussian fashion "as if they were
Pomeranian grenadiers." He also proposed to adjust German field
manuals to the education level of an average Ottoman officer only
to be rudely rejected by his head of mission.[57] The Germans' feelings of disdain toward the Ottomans stemmed from a chauvinistic,
perhaps racial bias. German soldiers treated the Turks with a great
deal of paternalism, referring to them as "primitives," *Banausen* in
German jargon, and "Barbarians." Most offensive to the Muslims
was the Germans' habit of describing the Turkish behavior with the
objectionable term "piggish."[58]

Germany's officer corps was of remarkable social homogeneity
and had very little contact or experience with members of other
cultural groups. German officers prior to World War I were noble-
men dedicated to the preservation of their aristocratic institution
and tightly confined by a strict set of traditional values and social
policies. The German officer corps was religiously orthodox; nine
out of ten officers belonged to the Evangelical church and were
encouraged by the military establishment to take their religious
obligations seriously.[59] The German officer was also older in years
in comparison with the Turkish since the German army required
waiting many years before an officer was promoted to a higher rank.
A major would be in his forties while lieutenant colonels would
usually be in their fifties. In contrast, Ottoman officers were unusu-
ally young and inexperienced. Enver was 33 years old in 1914.
Most of his fellow generals were in their early 30's. As a result,
many German officers felt uncomfortable working under people
who were sometimes young enough to be their sons. They did not

trust the young Turkish officers and perceived them as amateurs. The Turks, on the other hand, often felt overshadowed by the age and experience of their German colleagues.

Tongue-tied allies

Mark Twain's famous essay "The Awful German Language" portrayed the tough challenges facing students of the German language. Vigorously complaining about the difficult grammatical structure, long sentences and confusing number of parts of speech, Twain advised his readers to spare themselves the agony of learning this forbidding tongue.[60] In Turkey with its high degree of illiteracy, it took little persuasion to keep people from studying German. Familiarity with any foreign language for that matter was too much to expect from soldiers who in many cases could not even print their own names. Command of foreign language was so rare in the Ottoman army that it merited a special distinction worn on the uniforms. Officers with linguistic capabilities wore above their stripes a ribbon indicating knowledge of a foreign language. Each language was distinguished by a different color.[61] Only a small group of Turkish officers could speak German and even fewer were fluent. Even those who had spent years living in Germany did not develop German proficiency. One of the few German-speakers was Enver, but even in his case communication in German was difficult. Trumpener claimed that many of the misunderstandings between Enver and Liman were due to the fact that Enver was not in perfect command in the German language.[62] Many more, however, spoke French, the most commonly used foreign tongue in Turkey. The Ottomans had a long tradition of close relations with French-speaking peoples, and French was the commonly accepted second language. As a result, a large majority of the educated classes spoke French. European travelers could find their way through the country's main arteries of transportation if they had basic knowledge of French.

On the German side, one could not find German officers posted in Turkey with knowledge of the local language. Those who had already been posted in Turkey made hardly any effort to familiarize themselves with the vernacular.[63] Why is it that after so many years of military cooperation with Turkey, the German army had not produced a cadre of Turkish speaking officers? One reason was that in Germany, perhaps due to cultural biases, the study of non-European tongues was not a popular practice. A second reason was the lack of awareness of the importance of cultural acclimatization for those who were about to serve in foreign countries. Most of the officers sent to Turkey were informed about their post only a short time before their departure, leaving them very little time for linguistic and cultural preparation.

Unable to communicate in each other's tongue, the two allies were forced to adopt a neutral language, which ironically happened to be their enemy's. There is no indication that the decision to use French as the official coalition language was ever made consciously. It was perhaps a result of years of joint cooperation in French prior to the war in which both sides became comfortable with this common language. Despite the animosity between France and Germany, French was still a widely used language among Germans. Command of the French language became one of the main criteria to be sent as a military advisor in Turkey.

How did communication work? Senior commanders' communication was usually conducted in French assuming that most officers involved spoke the language. But at the lower levels of command where there were fewer bilingual officers, the troops had to rely on the services of translators. When a German army or corps commander drafted an order in German or French, this order would have to be translated to Turkish so that everyone along the chain of command could understand it. Similarly, when units forwarded their reports written in Turkish to higher headquarters, they would have to be translated into French so the German officers could read them. This system was cumbersome and required constant reliance on translators. Since very few Germans had knowledge of Turkish, most translation was done by Turkish translators, and there was almost no possibility to verify its quality or accuracy. From time to time, German officers would ask their translators to do a 'reverse translation,' in other words, translate a translated document back to the original language so its content could be compared with the original. Altogether, the language barrier was more than just an irritant; at times it affected operational performance. Language difficulties caused delays and complications in the preparation of plans and orders.[64] Turkish translators harboring anti-German sentiments deliberately misinterpreted German orders in order to stir more confusion and friction.[65] The language barrier was so problematic that it was raised and discussed at the October 1917 German-Ottoman Military Convention. There was a common acknowledgment of the problem and a mutual feeling that both sides needed to do more to improve their language skills. The resolution stated: "both Germany and the Ottoman Empire shall promote the study of each other's languages in their respective armies."[66] But it was too little too late. The language problem affected not only what was said but how it was said. The Ottomans often complained that the sharp, short, abrupt and decisive tone of command used by the Germans sounded like 'whipping' and was perceived as part of an overall German attempt to place the Turks in a position of inferiority. The way German soldiers addressed their Turkish counterparts was a constant irritant and a source of antagonism and tension.[67]

Beyond the practical implication of language as a form of communication, this aspect of culture also had a political dimension. By the end of 1915, Turkey was undergoing a semi-cultural revolution that included a language purification campaign. It was a result of the growing calls for enhanced Turkish identity and the rise of Turkish nationalism. The reform was designed to 'clean' the Turkish language of some of its Arabic and Persian elements. One of its side effects, however, was a wave of anti-European sentiment mostly directed against France and Britain. The Turks removed road signs, inscriptions and shop signs in English and French. The Germans were thrilled by the downfall in Turkey of their enemies' languages. But the nationalists wanted a total purification from *all* Latin-European influence. A few weeks later, Talaat Bey, the Ottoman Minister of Interior, issued a decree to also remove signs in German. This immediately became a source of tension between Germany and the Ottomans. The Germans felt they should not be treated the same as the Entente. They felt that the move would be interpreted by the Entente as a sign of weakness and non-confidence which could invite more allied attacks on the

Turkish front.[68] But the Turks did not cave. Their intransigence was a clear signal to the Germans that cultural sovereignty would take precedence over alliance considerations.

At what time is noon today?

Apart from the language barrier, German and Turkish officers did not communicate well with each other due to too many mentality gaps. The German military culture has always emphasized virtues like precision, discipline, orderliness, detailed planning, efficiency, cleanliness and effective time management. These qualities were not strongly emphasized in the Ottoman army. All haste is from the devil, says the Arabic proverb, and indeed the Ottomans resented the Germans' haste and adherence to strict timetables, and often self-imposed deadlines. In many cases, they could not understand why something that could be delayed to a later date had to be done immediately.[69] This attitude reflected a general view toward time. Whereas the Germans viewed time as a scarce resource to be fully utilized, the Turks lived on a different rhythm. To make things worse, Turks and Germans worked under different time systems. The fixed element was not noon but sunset, which had to be estimated. The hours of the five daily prayers were fixed according to the Turkish system. Turkish time devices therefore had two rows of figures, one marking the Turkish time system and the other the European. European time often conflicted with daily habits causing confusion and resentment. One anthropologist of the period ridiculed the situation citing a common question on the Turkish street: "at what time is noon today?"[70]

It wasn't just watches. By the time World War I started, there were three calendars in use in Turkey. First was the widely used Lunar Calendar. The religious authorities determined the new lunar month with two witnesses. But this was not a suitable system for military and government purposes, because in bad weather one could not determine the date. Therefore, the lunar month at times began on different days in different places causing confusion. During the war, the religious establishment made a special concession allowing the use of telegraph to spread the news of the new month.[71] The second calendar in use was the Julian or Roman calendar taken from the Greeks in the second half of the nineteenth century, but without using the Christian dates. Another difference was that the New Year began in March. The third calendar, used by the Germans, was the Gregorian calendar, which was finally officially adopted by the Turks.

If for the Ottomans haste was from the devil, for the Germans the devil was in the details. Too many Germans could not get used to Turkey's peculiarities and tried to apply German methods and standards to the conditions in the Ottoman Empire. Germans were accustomed to pay a great deal of attention to small details both in the process of planning and in the execution of military operations. The German officer saw himself responsible for treating with care every small detail to ensure smooth execution of the plan even if this required meddling with minutia. German inspections were strict and lengthy. The Turks had a diametrically opposed attitude. They believed in a hands-off approach and thought it improper for officers to deal with small details and intervene in the daily life of their subordinates.[72]

German officers were also known to be neat, obedient and methodical. They placed high priority in their training on discipline, order, control, process and personal hygiene. German officers serving in Turkey were shocked by the absence of sanitary arrangements and of sufficient medical help. This resulted in terrible medical conditions that decimated the ranks of the Turkish soldiers in a manner unthinkable by German standards. Throughout the war, some 401,000 Turkish soldiers died of malaria, typhus, dysentery and other illnesses, many of them attributed to a lack of personal hygiene. Alarming conditions also existed in Turkish army hospitals. Turkish officers had very little awareness of public health issues, and as a result soldiers were deprived of proper medical treatment. Temperatures were taken only of sick officers, while the ordinary soldier was not considered worth treating. Many died daily. Liman von Sanders described how he found several locked rooms in every Turkish hospital he inspected. The Turkish medical staff assured him the keys were lost. When he insisted on opening the rooms, he was shocked to discover the rooms full of dying patients hidden away from him.[73] The Turks were not interested in the introduction of German order and control. They were concerned mainly with their financial benefits. During inspections of military installations, German and Turkish officers differed on the level of responsibility commanding officers should have on their troops' living and hygienic conditions. The Germans saw this as a purely operational issue with direct implications on the preparedness of the units. Turks thought otherwise.[74]

One of the biggest mentality gaps the Germans encountered was the Turks' attitudes toward the future and uncertainty. As mentioned earlier, some deeply religious societies tend to belittle the importance of planning, since they believe that everything has already been determined by divine powers. The Turks exhibited such an attitude. Liman mentioned that they had a negative attitude toward planning, since they believed that despite the best planning, things often turn out differently from what one wants.[75] This was in contrast to the methodical, analytical pattern of thought that characterized the German officers who were taught from an early stage of their careers that success of military operations is dependent on careful planning based on sound intelligence and up to date information. German officers in Turkey sensed their allies' disregard for planning and tried to assume as many staff positions as possible in Turkish armies and corps. The Turks quickly learned to utilize the Germans' planning skills and agreed to post as many German officers as chiefs-of-staff and heads of departments in the Ottoman General staff.[76]

Hajj Wilhelm's gambit

The Ottoman Empire was comprised of territory containing the greatest imaginable racial and cultural differences. The 30 million people living in the Empire in 1914 were divided up as follows: 16 million Turks, 9 million Arabs, 1.5 million Greeks, 1.5 million Armenians, 500,000 Jews and groups of smaller minorities. This means that eight of ten people were Muslims. Indeed, the Empire was above everything the hub of Islam. The Sultan, who was also the caliph, the highest religious authority in the Muslim world, had the power to make religious rulings and appoint clergy. The holiest cities of Islam – Mecca and Medina – were in the hands of the Ottomans. Islam pervaded every part of life: law, education, commerce, and family. The empire took pride in its religious tolerance and respect for non-believers. Non-Muslim cultural groups enjoyed considerable religious and cultural freedom. They were also fairly represented in the Ottoman parliament. But these cross-cultural relations were not as harmonious as they seemed. The Ottoman social system depended on the unequivocal acceptance by non-believers of the sovereignty and dominance of Islam over the Empire's legal, political and educational state institutions. This social contract between the Empire and its non-Muslim residents was key to the relatively high degree of peaceful coexistence over many generations.

Conversely, the first decade of the 20th century brought with it a wave of Turkish nationalism accompanied by efforts to create a pan-Turkish identity. These efforts, in turn, created a great deal of tension vis-à-vis non-Turkish groups, especially the Armenians, Greeks, Kurds and Arabs. A competing nationalist movement, the Pan-Islamic movement, was based on religious commonality under the banner of Islam. Pan-Islamic missionaries tried to inspire the Empire's millions of Muslims by emphasizing the differences between them and the 'infidels.' Whether pan-Turkism or pan-Islamism was to prevail, non-believers of the Empire held the short end of the stick. The rise of pan-Islamism was greatly encouraged by Sultan Abdul Hamid II, who throughout his reign showed a propensity to use Islam as a tool of foreign policy. In a period of imperial decline, religion was a popular means to cement the fragmented Turkish population as well as a catalyst for further territorial expansion in the east. The Ottomans' exploitation of Islam for political and strategic purposes was not a policy pursued by the Sublime Porte alone. In many respects it was an outcome of skillful German manipulation in the years prior to the war and was designed to draw the Ottoman Empire away from the other European Powers into Berlin's embrace. Islam was a key force shaping the nature of the German-Turkish coalition both in the battlefield as well as in the diplomatic arena.[77]

Germany's joining the colonial race late proved to be a blessing in disguise, since it prevented the Kaiser's acquisition of colonies occupied by Muslim majorities. By 1914, Germany had colonies in New Guinea, China, East and South West Africa, but none had substantial Muslim populations. Britain, France, Italy, Austria-Hungary and Russia, on the other hand, all ruled over large Muslim populations in Central Asia, India, North Africa and the Balkans. The fact that Germany was the only Christian power not in control over Muslims put it, in the eyes of the Ottomans, on higher moral ground than the rest of the Europeans. The Germans knew how to take full advantage of their unique position, seeing great potential in the exploitation of pan-Islamic sentiments.[78] Abdul-Hamid II made up his mind to engage openly in the pan-Islamic stir only after receiving encouragement from the German Kaiser Wilhelm II in his 1898 visit to Constantinople. The Kaiser did all he could to express his friendship and support of Islam. In a unique gesture, he delivered a pro-Islamic speech at the tomb of Saladin proclaiming that "three hundred million Muhammedans that are scattered through the world may rest assured that the German Emperor will eternally be their friend."[79]

A pamphlet widely distributed throughout the Muslim world following the Kaiser's speech in Constantinople in 1898 proclaims Kaiser Wilhelm to be the protector of all Muslims.

The Kaiser's suggestive rhetoric was soon complemented by an industry of rumors circulated in the Empire's bazaars that the German Emperor had been secretly converted to Islam and made a secret pilgrimage to Mecca.[80] Throughout the Ottoman Empire, Friday prayers were concluded with an invocation for the welfare of both the sultan and *"Hajj* Wilhelm," implying that he had indeed made the sacred pilgrimage.[81] German consuls traveled in their districts in a propaganda campaign designed to persuade the Turks that the Hohenzollerns were not real Christians but, in fact, the descendents of the Prophet Mohammed. They selected from the Koran passages insinuating that the Kaiser was the Savior of Islam.[82] To live up to his reputation as a benefactor of the Muslims, the Kaiser arranged a conference to promote and proliferate new ideas regarding pan-Islam. In 1911-12 the Germans established a special pan-Islamist center, with Enver as one of its leaders . The German pan-Islamist center issued publications and organized a vast net of agents in Turkey, Iran and the Muslim areas of Russia. German publications supported the Pan-Islamic idea, favoring the liberation of the Caucasus from Russian domination.[83] In Germany itself, pamphlets were published describing the suffering of millions of Muslims under the tyrannical rule of the colonial powers. One pamphlet *Deutschland, die Turkei and der Islam* by Hugo Grothe was especially visible and circulated Pan-Islamic ideas among German intelligentsia.[84]

Some observers claimed that Germany had signed the 1914 secret treaty with the Ottomans mainly because they were counting on the damaging effect of pan-Islamism and pan-Turkism on the Allies' war effort. Evidence for such thinking could be found in Morgenthau's meeting with the German Ambassador in Constantinople, Hans von Wangenheim, in which the latter remarked "Turkey itself is not the really important matter. Her army is a small one and we do not expect it to do very much. But the big thing is the Muslim world. If we can stir the Mohammedans up against the English and the Russians, we can force them to make peace."[85] It was also Wangenheim who, on August 6, guaranteed the Grand Vizier that one of Germany's war aims, in exchange for Turkey's participation in the fighting, would be to amend Turkey's border with Russia in order to annex Muslim communities.[86] In the period between the start of World War I and Turkey's entry to the war, Germany made an independent appeal to the Muslim world calling on Muslims to rebel against the European occupiers. On September 9, 1914, the Kaiser issued a statement that Germany did not consider Muslims residing in enemy states as belligerents and that Muslim prisoners of war captured by the Germans would be sent to the caliph in Turkey rather than held in German prison camps.[87] In addition, Germany began sending money, agents and propaganda material to African and Asian colonies of the Allies. The prime target of the German subversive efforts was India and the Caucasus.[88] German agents distributed leaflets in India accusing the British of crimes against Islam.[89] Germany also launched a propaganda campaign within the borders of the Ottoman Empire through Turkish newspapers owned by Germans, such as an editorial in *Ikdam* calling on "all Mohammedans, young and old, men, women and children, to fulfill their duty" and fight the infidel.[90] Despite these efforts, it was clear that the only way to mobilize the Muslim world against the Entente would be by a proclamation of Holy War, *jihad*, by the leaders of the Islamic establishment in Constantinople. On several occasions prior to Turkey's intervention in the war, Germany's political and military leaders secured Ottoman promises to declare such a Holy War. As Turkey was getting ready to go to war, it too became eager for this proclamation.

Finally, German pressure brought the Young Turks and the caliph to declare a *jihad* against the French, Russians and British. The war proclamation of November 13, 1914 was a masterful piece of religious incitement. Signed by the most prominent religious dignitaries as well as the Sultan, the 10,000-word document was full of quotations from the Koran as well as numerous appeals to racial and religious hatred. It called for an all-out war against the infidels, described plans for the assassination and extermination of Christians and promised eternal punishment for all those Muslims who did not take part in the struggle:

> All Mohammedans living in the territories exposed to the persecutions of the above named oppressive powers, such as the Crimea, Kazan, Turkistan, Bukhara, Khiva, India, China, Afghanistan, Persia, Africa and other countries,

must consider it, in concert with Ottomans, as their most supreme religious duty to participate in the Holy War, with their bodies and goods, keeping in mind the inspirations of the Koran [...] Muhammedan warriors! With the aid of God and the intercession of the Prophet, you will defeat and crush the enemies of religion, and you will fill all Muhammedan hearts with eternal joy in accordance with the divine promise.[91]

The declaration of Holy War by the Sublime Porte is still considered to be one of the most controversial episodes of the war. By playing the religious card, the Turks hoped not only to reap strategic benefits but also to instill in their troops a deep belief in the cause and morality of the war and, hence, improve their combat performance. But the *jihad* proclamation harbored serious strategic and operational problems. First, how to exclude the Germans, who were also Christians, and yet preserve the genuine nature of the divine call to arms? Morgenthau claimed that a "German hand has exercised an editorial supervision" presenting the *jihad* as a war only against infidels who rule over Muslims. Since Germany had none, it was excluded. [92] But this type of logic created a problem vis-à-vis Germany's main ally Austria-Hungary. The Germans overlooked the fact that Austria-Hungary had a large Muslim minority in Bosnia and Herzegovina. The *jihad* proclamation became a bone of contention between Germany and Austria-Hungary in October 1914 when Enver presented his war plan to his coalition partners. The Austrian Foreign Minister Count Leopold von Berchtold reacted negatively, fully realizing the potential for regional instability due to the use of the religious weapon.[93] A compromise was reached. The Ottomans would add a reservation to the text which stated as follows: "Know ye that the blood of infidels in the Islamic lands may be shed with impunity *except* those to whom the Muslim power has promised security and who are allied with it."[94] This policy was a double-edged sword. While it excluded the Christians who were allied with Turkey from the peril of *jihad*, it caused a great deal of irritation among those neutral countries that also ruled over big Muslim communities. In the case of Italy, a proclamation of Holy War would mean unrest in Italian possessions in

Northern Africa, thus increasing the likelihood of Italy joining the war on the side of the Entente. Berlin had to reassure the Italians that their assets in Africa would not be harmed. This guarantee was far from satisfactory, and the fear of losing Italy's neutrality continued for six more months until Italy finally joined the side of the Entente.[95] A similar problem occurred with Bulgaria, which had a large Muslim population in the Bulgarian Thrace. A *jihad* could cause a great deal of tension between Turkey and Bulgaria and, again, another exception had to be issued. The exclusion of so many Muslim communities from the Holy War injured the credibility and authority of the proclamation. This fact contributed to the failure of the German-Ottoman attempt to give the war a religious character. The idea of *jihad* scared the allied forces, especially the British whose army relied on the 57 million Muslims in India as a main source of recruits. It was former First Sea Lord John Fisher who as early as 1911 warned that "the world has yet to learn what the Mohammedans can do if once their holy fervour seizes them."[96] And indeed, a few units, like the British 130th Baluchis and the 5th Native Light Infantry responded to the call from Constantinople and refused to fight.[97] Indian Army soldiers from the Singapore garrison incited by the Turko-German propaganda murdered 40 of their officers before their mutiny was crushed by the British.[98] But these were isolated incidents. As a whole, Germany's idea to invoke the religious element to achieve a strategic gain turned out to be a sham. By and large, the Arabs and the other Muslim communities did not buy into the *jihad*. German missions attempting to convince the Emir of Afghanistan and the Shah of Persia to join the Holy War were met with polite but non-committal responses. Many of the Muslim communities were consumed with hatred toward the corrupt regime of the Porte; others traded their religious sentiments for pledges of independence willfully granted by the advancing armies of the Entente.

Pan-Islamism proved to be a myth, a creation of German and Ottoman wishful thinking. Enver, who believed in effective Muslim and Turkish solidarity under Ottoman leadership, was surprised to discover how weak this leadership was. For the Ottomans, the *jihad* policy was a disaster. It exposed the divisions between the various factions and tribes of the Islamic world and raised doubts about the merits and authority of the caliphate, abolished soon after the war as part of Ataturk's reforms. Furthermore, the failure of the attempt to exploit Islam created a rift between the Turks and the Arabs. The deep-seated opposition of the Arabs to the Porte existed before the war, but the cynical use of religion to promote the Porte's self-interest only increased those sentiments. From a strict military point of view, the *jihad* strategy was not needed to encourage Ottoman soldiers to fight harder. The typical, deeply religious Turk was brave and dedicated enough to fight to the end without it. In addition, the strategy was never really workable. Many of the Entente forces had Muslim soldiers incorporated in their units, like the Muslim Indians in the service of the British army or Muslims in the French army. The loyalty of those soldiers to the crown and to their non-Muslim comrades superceded their sentiments toward their co-believers. It was German naiveté to believe that in the heat of battle soldiers could distinguish between Muslim and non-Muslim enemy troops and spare their co-believers from fire. German military officers seriously deliberated how to differentiate believers from infidels in the battlefield to prevent Muslim soldiers in the Entente armies shooting at them. The German military attaché in Constantinople Maj. Laffert even suggested that German troops display green flags to protect themselves from Islamic bullets.[99] The *jihad* was also made operational by the Germans with regards to the treatment of Muslim prisoners of war. The Germans used to separate Muslim POWs from non-Muslims in order to pressure them to join the *jihad* against their rulers. In exchange for a shift in their allegiance, Muslim POWs were promised many incentives. They were told they would have the great honor of being presented before the caliph in Constantinople and were promised resettlement in Turkey without further military service. This proved to be a false promise. Many of those who fell for it were sent to Turkey only to be used in the service of the Turkish army.[100]

Domestic tremors

The immediate result of the declaration of *jihad* was a wave of popular demonstrations in Constantinople as well as a series of violent clashes and acts of vandalism against non-Muslim establishments in the city. The wave of religious fervor led to a purge in the Ottoman Army of all Jewish and Christian soldiers serving in combat units, reassigning them to what was called 'the working corps.' Alexander Aaronsohn, a Jew from Palestine who had served in the Ottoman Army, described the purge:

> We were disarmed; our uniforms were taken away, and we became hard-driven "gangsters." I shall never forget the humiliation of that day when we, who, after all, were the best-disciplined troops of the lot, were first herded to our work of pushing wheelbarrows and handling spades, by grinning Arabs, rifle on shoulder.[101]

The *jihad* affair would have probably been viewed as just another of the many grotesque episodes of the war if not for its horrific by-product, the persecution of the Christian population in Syria and the Armenians, which remains in the minds of many the darkest chapter in Turkey's modern history. I have no intention to describe here the events that did or did not take place in Van and other places. Historians will probably continue to debate the events of 1915 for many years to come with no assurance of ever revealing the truth about the responsibility of one side or the other for the atrocities that took place.[102] I would rather focus on the German angle, namely, how did Turkey's broad interpretation of the German backed declaration of *jihad* affect coalition relations between the two countries. Germany's share of responsibility for the Armenian misery is fiercely debated by historians. One school of thought claims that the Armenian persecutions were not only welcomed by the Germans but also instigated by them.[103] British historian Arnold Toynbee even alluded to a secret deal in which in exchange for Turkey's involvement in the war, Germany gave the Young Turks free hand to exterminate the Armenians.[104] The alternative view is that Germany, through poor judgment and a considerable amount of moral callousness, sowed the seeds of hatred that brought about the massacres of the Armenians. Once news about persecutions of Armenians reached Berlin, the Wilhelmstrasse showed apathy and an excessive concern with political expediency. As a result, the Germans did very little to exert influence on the Porte to end the violence and the deportations. Ambassador Morgenthau was one of the harshest critics of Germany's policy on the matter. Throughout the crisis, he repeatedly met with his German colleagues in an attempt to urge the Germans to take active measures to save the Armenians. Wangenheim conceded that although Germany did not support the Ottoman policy it valued strategic expediencies more than moral or religious ones. "Our one aim is to win this war" was the official German response.[105]

Despite the many unknowns in the story, there is almost a consensus among modern historians on the following issues: First, the persecutions were not welcomed by the Germans. On the contrary, on several occasions Germany expressed its aversion to the Ottoman policy, even when the survival of the coalition was needed more than ever. Hence, on August 9, 1915, the German Ambassador in Turkey submitted a formal protest against the deportations, and on January 11, 1916, the German Reichstag debated the issue.[106] Second, contrary to Morgenthau's claim that Germany had the power to stop the massacre but did not do so, the facts show that direct protection of the Armenians was completely beyond Germany's capacity. Most of the German officers positioned on the eastern front had no command functions. The most they could have done was to express disagreement or alternatively quit their jobs. There is, however, no evidence that this is what they did. Not one German officer in Turkey broke silence in the face of Armenian suffering. Third, the Armenian saga *did* have a detrimental affect on coalition relations. Many Germans, especially members of Christian conservative groups, saw the folly of Germany's *jihad* policy. The side that legitimized and popularized the religious weapon became a victim of the same weapon. For those who viewed world politics as a power struggle between Muslims and Christians, a policy that resulted in the massacre of Christian Armenians was self-defeating. German intellectuals called for a reevaluation of Germany's *kulturpolitik* and for cultural disengagement from what was then perceived as Turkish religious fanaticism. Especially illustrative was a call from one of Germany's leading intellectuals:

If we persist in treating the massacres of Christians as an internal affair of Turkey, which is only important to us because it ensures us the Turks' friendship, then we must change the orientation of our German Kulturpolitik. We must stop sending German teachers to Turkey, and we teachers must give up telling our pupils in Turkey about German poets and philosophers, German culture and German ideals, to say nothing of German Christianity.[107]

Kaiser Wilhelm's promotion of the idea of *jihad* was a strategic blunder which gave the war a religious dimension that ultimately began to work against German interests. Germany was humiliated by the unresponsiveness of the Muslim world and was deplored by the international community for its passive stance in face of its ally's mistreatment of the Armenians. Furthermore, once the *jihad* genie was out of the bottle, religion became a destabilizing element in the relations. In the summer of 1915, German politicians in Berlin demanded that the Kaiser ask the Sultan to hand over to Germany the Church of the Holy Sepulcher in Jerusalem so it could be given as a gift to the Pope. Others advocated purchasing buildings surrounding King David's Tomb in the Old City. Such discussions increased the Turks' suspicion that Germany was conspiring to take over the third holiest city in Islam.[108] Later, when von Falkenhayn, under the pressure of General Allenby's advancing army, was forced to evacuate Jerusalem, he was blamed for plotting to deliberately hand the city to Christian hands.[109] In 1918, Turkey and Germany disputed the future of Russian possessions in the Caucasus. Enver, feeling that the German armistice with Russia disregarded Turkish interests and betrayed the Muslim world, launched a campaign to the Christian Georgia and Armenia popularizing it as a "Pan Islamic Campaign." To emphasize the religious nature of his crusade, he constructed an "army of Islam" consisting of Ottoman soldiers and Azerbaijani Tartars. No Germans were allowed to join this army.[110]

Attitudinal and ethical problems

The Germans and the Turks represented two very remote ethical systems. As guests on Ottoman territory, the Germans realized they must accommodate themselves to the norms of the land. Many Germans who had served in Turkey for several years began to adopt Turkish ways of life. Some began to wear the fez; others smoked the water pipe. But there were also signs of moral decay among German officers. Those who adopted Turkish traits were labeled with an unfavorable German adjective, *verturkt,* which was invented to describe such an undesirable metamorphosis. But the biggest culture shock for foreigners living in Turkey was to learn how riddled the country was with corruption. One could not go very far in dealings with businessmen or government bureaucrats without resorting to bribery. Most Europeans were startled by the open manner such form of corruption was spoken about. *Bakshish* was so widely used that it appeared each public official, including judges, had a fixed price depending on his status.[111] In Germany, on the other hand, bribery was a practice punishable by law. However, the German government quickly realized the need for its representatives in Turkey to play by the rules of the host society. "There is no God but *bakshish,* and the Deutsche Bank is his prophet," German officials in Turkey jokingly paraphrased on Islam's most prominent verse.[112] When Liman's mission was sent to Turkey, the Kaiser insisted that he be given one million marks annually to bribe government officials. To promote its strategic and political goals in the region, the Germans were willing to compromise their norms and values and signal to their military and other diplomatic officials that norms unacceptable in Germany could be adopted under certain circumstances.[113]

What the Germans found more difficult to accept was the Turkish attitude toward life and the perception of self. Muslim religion and scholarship glorified the concept of martyrdom and encouraged the elevation of the afterlife above one's current life. Dying in a holy war was a religious obligation and source of honor. The caliph's declaration of Holy War appealed to the uneducated Anatolian soldier's desire for martyrdom:

> O Muhammedans, true servants of God! Those who will share in the Holy War and come back alive will enjoy a great felicity; those who will find in it their death will have the honor of martyrdom. In accordance with the promise

of God, those who will sacrifice themselves for the cause of right, will have glory and happiness here below as well as in Paradise.[114]

The promise of eternal life in paradise was an incentive for military excellence, increased motivation, courage and dedication. And indeed, the Ottoman soldier soon gained international recognition for his resolve and exceptional bravery as viewed by the allied forces in the battle of Gallipoli. Although he never associated himself with his men's beliefs, Mustafa Kemal, Turkey's most promising divisional commander during the war, acknowledged, in letter to a friend, the psychological and tactical effects of fighting in God's name as he witnessed among his troops:

> Our life here is truly hellish. Fortunately, my soldiers are very brave and tougher than the enemy. What is more, their private beliefs make it easier to carry out orders which send them to their death. They see only two supernatural outcomes: victory for the faith or martyrdom. Do you know what the second means? It is to go straight to heaven. There, God's most beautiful women, will meet them and will satisfy their desires for eternity. What great happiness![115]

Many Germans saw in the Turkish foot soldier a degree of courage and determination they had not seen before. When the Turkish officer was told to hold the line of defense and defend it to the last man that was exactly what he did, even if it meant losing all his troops. As much as the Germans benefited from being allied to extraordinarily courageous soldiers, they were bothered by the culture of indifference to casualties prevalent in the Ottoman Army. Commanders had no difficulty recruiting soldiers for missions considered suicidal and senseless by any Western judgment. The Germans were far more conservative and cautious in their decision-making. They were losing thousands of soldiers on the Western and Eastern fronts but were much less enthusiastic to exhaust their forces in the Ottoman Empire. They were calculated and methodical and resentful of the way Turkish generals unnecessarily wasted their troops. The Ottomans' attitude toward life expressed itself in other ways By and large, Turkish soldiers paid little attention to the treatment of the dead, even their own dead. In many battlefields, bodies of Turkish and Entente soldiers were left to rot in the field without concern for the ethical and hygienic implications. A clash of ethics revolved around the Turkish habit of robbing the bodies of dead soldiers for clothes, food or valuables, a practice alien to the Germans. It was perceived as barbaric and created a great deal of resentment. "The loosely donned garment of culture is quickly thrown aside by the Turkish soldier," complained von Sanders.[116] The Turks also differed from the Germans in their ethics of treating prisoners of war. German commanders in Turkey abdicated their responsibility to deal with allied prisoners. They transferred all prisoners to Turkish hands and, as mentioned before, transferred Muslim prisoners captured on other fronts to Turkish prisoner camps. We know, however, from their behavior in other theaters, that the German's treatment of POWs, especially officers, was fair. This was not the case among the Turks. The treatment of POWs by the Turks was not uniform, and there was no prescribed policy on the matter. It depended on the personality of the camp commander. In some camps, prisoners were treated as honored guests, while in others they were oppressed and tortured. All prisoners were treated by the Society of the Red Crescent, which inspected the camps, kept records of prisoners and provided for their welfare.[117] But the Turks had a habit incompatible with European norms and conduct. They used to march POWs through the streets of Constantinople to show them off to the infuriated masses. Many POWs were injured by the unruly behavior of the crowd. This humiliating display of human misery did not fit well with German *kultur*.[118]

Reflections on defeat

On November 4, 1918, on the shore of the Black Sea, Lt. General Hans von Seeckt, later the architect of the German armed forces in the inter-war period, summarized in a long document the causes for the German-Turkish defeat. He enumerated many reasons for the coalition's failure in the war: economic, strategic, political and personal.

Not once did he mention the word culture, nor did he allude to the fact that anything related to culture had any effect on the outcome of the coalition. But by ignoring the impact and lessons derived from the fact that the alliance was above all an encounter between the Occident and the Orient, Seeckt missed out on an important lesson that could have served him well in the preparation of the German military for its next challenge. Other German officers who wrote memoirs of their years in Turkey also scantily addressed the cultural gaps with their allies. The evidence detailed in this chapter shows that culture had a significant effect on daily operational work as well as on the conduct of the war on the strategic level.

The failure to internalize the impact of culture on military affairs could in itself be an indicator of a deeper problem in Germany's relations with non-European allies. Germany was a cultural monolith and so was its military. In addition, as a latecomer to the colonial race, Germany had little experience in cross-cultural relations. As a result, the German soldier was unprepared for his cross-cultural experience. He lacked the experiences his French and British colleagues had in their colonial adventures, and had very little awareness of the cultural sensitivities of non-European allies. Despite decades of prior cooperation with the Ottomans, there was no cadre of officers who could speak the vernacular or understand the nation's culture. Nor was there an infrastructure to qualify such men. Beyond bigoted tips about the country and its people, German military personnel received no meaningful preparation or guidance prior to their deployment. Furthermore, Germany's political and military leadership relied on the assumption that the Turks had boundless respect for the Germans and, therefore, there was no need for the officers sent to Turkey to have any knowledge of the country. Nor were they expected to make efforts to evoke Ottoman sympathy. In one of his letters, Wangenheim explained the German view of the desired qualities of the military advisor: "[The advisor] must be a strong figure, who knows how to force his views through. Knowledge of the language and culture is not necessarily required."[119] The result of this attitude was a coalition dominated by Germans with a flawed understanding of their Turkish ally. This, in turn, bred suspicion and misjudgment. "Germany is to be blamed for the lack of calm and clear judgment of what was within the powers of Turkey," Liman wrote. "It seems that thoughts of the tales of The Thousand and One Nights, or the fata morgana of the Arabian desert dimmed judgment at home."[120] But it was ironically Liman who was most responsible for the flawed communication between the Ottomans and the Germans. His selection as Germany's top soldier in Turkey reflected poor judgment and a lack of appreciation for the potential impact of culture. "It is inconceivable, that a man who was not fit to command an army corps was entrusted with the task of reforming the entire Turkish army," reflected von Seeckt.[121] Liman was not an easy man to deal with, even for people of his own kind. Unlike other coalition commanders that will be described in the coming chapters, he had no diplomatic experience, no knowledge of the region and no experience in cross-cultural relations. Only German naiveté could have hoped for him to befriend the pashas in Constantinople.

No less responsible for Germany's indifference to the cultural dimension was Kaiser Wilhelm II. The man who 15 years before the war instructed General Alfred von Waldersee, commander of the allied effort to crush the Boxer Rebellion, to become a modern version of Attila the Hun so that "never again will a Chinese dare to so much as look askance at a German," astonished the world several times by his callousness and insensitivity to other people's cultures.[123] The same insensitivity and reductionism also caused him to misjudge the disastrous implications of the manipulation of culture, especially religion, for political purposes.

The average Turkish soldier was also unaccustomed to working with soldiers unlike them and as a result did not understand the need for cultural sensitivity in order to effectively work with coalition partners. True, many Ottoman officers were familiar with the ways of the Occident, but their deep Islamic belief and their strong belief in their cultural superiority led them to deal with the Germans with a great deal of obstinacy and disdain. They resisted borrowing or adopting any of their partner's customs, norms or ornaments even when these proved to be superior to theirs.

Enver's difficult personality was a major source of tension in the coalition. His familiarity with Germany, its language and its culture was not enough to offset his pomposity, chauvinism, reck-lessness and immaturity. Remarkably, one could attribute the same qualities to Kaiser Wilhelm, and with two such leaders there is little wonder that relations developed the way they did.

Germany and the Ottoman Empire were two proud nations, self-absorbed with ideas of cultural superiority. Their difficulty in bridging cross-cultural gaps during the war was a result of the eth-nocentric sentiment so deeply rooted in the collective heritage of both their societies and armed forces. To assess how much of the ten-sion in the German-Turkish coalition was culturally driven it would be best to compare Germany's relations with the Ottomans to their relations with Austria-Hungary, an ally culturally much closer to Germany. Austria and Germany shared many cultural traits includ-ing language, religion, heritage, customs, philosophy, and artistic preferences. Despite that, their relations during World War I were characterized by endless complicity, diplomatic manipulations and personal animosity between the military leaders.[123] The history of Imperial Germany's participation in military coalitions shows that there was always something fundamentally wrong about its behav-ior vis-à-vis its allies, even those who spoke its language. Whether Germany's failure to develop solid relations with its coalition part-ners was a result of its obsession with *realpolitik* or some deeply rooted blemish in its strategic culture is a question meriting further study. But clearly whatever the problems were, they were only exac-erbated with the introduction of a culturally dissimilar coalition partner. The Ottomans were exactly such a partner. Many aspects of culture like language, customs and etiquette played minor roles in the German-Turkish relations, at times causing misunderstandings and bitterness. But other aspects of the cultural dimension affected the coalition in a profound way. Clashes of mentality and religion influenced the performance of the coalition not only on the tacti-cal and operational level but also on the diplomatic-strategic level. Germany and Turkey lost the war and parted ways. Both suffered political and economic instability. But whereas one was about to undergo a serious cultural and political transformation, the other was doomed to repeat the mistakes of the past. Following Turkey's War of Independence, it began a process of cultural revolution orchestrated by Mustafa Kemal. Militarily, Turkey withdrew into itself only to return to the international stage as one of the most cooperative and culturally adaptive members of the United Nations coalition forces in the Korean War. Germany, however, did very little to improve its cultural relations with potential allies. Its next partner in war, Japan, was no less remote and culturally challenging than Turkey. But this was an alliance of diplomats rather than a tightly knit military coalition. Separated by the Pacific Ocean, Germany and Japan were too distant to integrate their forces in any capacity, which is perhaps what spared Germany from repeating some of the errors it committed with the Turks.

3

TOMMY DRINKS SAKI: THE ANGLO-JAPANESE WORLD WAR I ALLIANCE

⌘ ⌘ ⌘

My one wish is that I may never have to fight them
A British officer in Tsingtau on his opinion on
the Japanese soldiers

English Army no use. Only Navy any good. Have
seen two hundred English Army.
No use.
The verdict of a Japanese military observer,
Rudyard Kipling's letters

Twice in fifteen years, the army of the empire of the rising sun fought alongside that of the empire on which the sun never set. The first collaboration took place in June 1900, as part of an expedition force, consisting of British, French, Japanese, Russian, German and American troops, sent to Peking to rescue a group of Europeans and Japanese civilians besieged by Chinese nationalist rebels, known by Westerners as Boxers. The Boxer Rebellion gave the Europeans the first opportunity to work closely with the Japanese Imperial Army and witness its combat capabilities. The Japanese contingent emerged as the largest and the most effective participant in the coalition. The Japanese soldiers, having many of the virtues European militaries appreciated, proved to be highly disciplined, courageous and dedicated fighters. "They marched fastest, they fought best, they were most amenable to discipline, they behaved most humanely toward the conquered," wrote one British observer.[1] Only four years passed before the Japanese army stunned the world with its overwhelming victory in the Russo-Japanese War culminating in the destruction of the Russian fleet in the Battle of Tsushima. The war, still considered by many to be the first time in modern history that a non-white nation defeated a European power, turned Japan into a world power that could not be ignored.[2]

The second military collaboration between Japan and Britain unfolded in a battle that despite its significance was neglected by most World War I historians. It was the siege and conquest of a small German colony, located in the southwest corner of the long Shantung peninsula protracted into the Yellow Sea, called Kiaochaw, also known as the "German Gibraltar of the East." Its main city, where the majority of the German population resided, was Tsingtau. The Battle of Tsingtau is meaningful in many respects. It was the first incursion in World War I by allied forces into German territory and the first defeat of the Germans in that war, a defeat that humiliated Germany and ended its colonial aspirations. So important was Tsingtau to the Germans that Kaiser Wilhelm II wrote to the German governor of the colony: "It would shame me more to surrender Kiaochaw to the Japanese than Berlin to the Russians."[3] It was also the first combined amphibious operation of the war, taking place months before the disastrous allied landing at the Dardanelles.[4] It was a battle that marked Japan's rise as the dominant power in East Asia, hence undermining the traditional supremacy of the Americans and Europeans in that region. Finally, its uniqueness was also due to the remarkable fact that the British contingent fought under Japanese command, setting the precedent of a "white" race army ceding its sovereignty to a non-white military. Considering the racial prejudices that prevailed in Europe at the time this was an extraordinary concession.

Built to meet the Russian threat common to Japan and Great Britain, the Anglo-Japanese Alliance was initially formed in January 1902.[5] Embroiled in a costly war in South Africa, Britain needed an ally to help defend its possessions in China and India. Japan was a willing partner. Hence, soon after the Russo-Japanese War, in 1905, the alliance was renewed for another ten years. In 1911, due to Germany's aggressive policies and rising tension between the European powers, Britain wanted to secure a tighter Japanese commitment, and a new treaty was drafted, stating that "the attack of any one power was to be the occasion of the operation of the alliance by the joint conduct of war on the part of England and Japan."[6] There were several reasons why the British were interested in allying themselves with the Japanese. They became increasingly aware of Japan's aspirations to dominate the region and wanted to supervise Japanese military activity in China. At the same time they hoped the Japanese would help them contain the expansionism of fellow European powers in Asia. The British were concerned that if a war broke out in Europe, Japan might be amenable to reaching a separate arrangement with Germany. Finally, the British were hoping that by joining forces with Japan in its endeavors in the East, they would create a moral obligation on the part of the Japanese to send forces to the Mediterranean and Europe if the need were to arise.

With the European militaries marching towards the Marne and Tannenberg, Japan's moment in the East arrived. A speech delivered by Prime Minister Marquis Okuma stated the objective: "to eliminate from the continent of China the root of the German influence, which forms a constant menace to peace of the Far East and thus to secure the aim of the alliance with Great Britain."[7] Hence, on August 15, 1914, Japan sent an ultimatum to Germany, demanding an answer within a week. It requested that Germany withdraw all naval vessels from the waters in the vicinity of Japan and China. In addition, it demanded that Germany surrender its territory in Kianchow. On August 23, the ultimatum expired without any response from the Germans. Japan and Germany were now officially at war with each other.[8]

From the very beginning it was clear that due to its strategic location, the city of Tsingtau would be Japan's prime target. In addition to its being one of the most fortified ports in the East, Tsingtau's strategic importance was rooted in its position on the railway connecting Peking to the Yellow Sea. The city was garrisoned by 4,000 German soldiers, 170 officers and a force of Chinese soldiers. It was surrounded by land mines, trenches, and 18 batteries with 130 guns. Sixteen vessels, including five cruisers, patrolled its waters. The stock of ammunition was not large, but food supplies were sufficient to endure a long siege.[9] Altogether, Tsingtau was a relatively easy prey. If the fortified city were to fall, it was clear that the German presence in the region would cease to exist.

Japan's strategic objective was, first of all, to promote its Asian interests and to establish a strong foothold in China by diminishing the presence of the Europeans in the region. While the European powers were heavily invested in the trench war back home and could not care much for the East, Japan sought to seize the moment and consolidate its power in China. Fearing European meddling in Asian affairs, the Japanese preferred to fight alone rather than as part of a coalition. Japanese Foreign Minister Kato Takaaki informed the British that Japan did not require British or any other European assistance to defeat the Germans.[10] Most of all, the Japanese disliked the idea that either French or Russian forces would join the coalition. A unilateral Japanese action was exactly what Britain wanted to prevent. Britain's participation in the campaign, the British held, was therefore diplomatically and strategically necessary. But its objectives were limited and its main motivation for taking an active part in the coalition was merely to be, as one historian put it, "the watchdog on the Japanese."[11]

On August 16, British military authorities decided to send to the front a brigade consisting of two British and two Indian battalions. This force was later trimmed to one battalion of 1,000 troops from the South Wales Borderers and half of the 36 Sikh Battalion (450 troops) deployed in China.[12] The force was accompanied by 350 horses, 300 Chinese auxiliaries, and a naval component of the battleship *Triumph* and the cruiser *Usk*. The British contingent was commanded by Brigadier Nathaniel W. Bernardiston, who was assigned the dubious honor of becoming the first white force commander to ever serve under Asiatic field command. Bernardiston was less than enthusiastic about his designation and tried to minimize his subordination to the Japanese by pressuring London to increase the size of the British contingent. He thought a token force would not suffice and sought to become an independent force with equal status to the Japanese.[13] His request met little sympathy in London. "British troops are only engaged to show that England is cooperating with Japan in this enterprise," was the curt response of the British High Command.[14] The small size of the British force and the great distance from British bases in the east meant that the British force would take part in a coalition in which Britain would not only be a minor power but also a power completely dependent on Japanese logistic and operational support. It was the Japanese army that was about to build the beachhead, clear the minefields at sea, lead the British ships to anchorage, disembark the British troops from the ships, and provide for their transportation, siege materials and food. To many British citizens accustomed to coalitions in the fashion of the Napoleonic Wars or the Crimean War in which Britain played a key role, this kind of dependency was hard to accept.

The Japanese were also less than thrilled. As much as they respected the British, they resented the fact that Britain had sent such a small contingent. They believed the British needed to decide one way or the other: cooperate or not. If the former, the Japanese felt they should take the field with a reasonable force self-sufficient in all its details and with a command large enough to play a role commensurate to Britain's imperial position in the world. If the British desired only token representation then why not simply send a diplomatic official with an escort? The Japanese opinion of the battalion-and-a-half of British infantry was, therefore, that in terms of number it was "negligible" and "more hindrance than a help."[15]

British troops arrive in Tsingtau, 1914

Japan's operational plan was to land two forces in the vicinity of the German territory, advance toward the city of Tsingtau and besiege it. The first force, consisting of the main forces of the Japanese 18th Division, was to land in Lungkow, outside the

Kianchaw territory, on the northern shore of the Shantung province some 100 miles from Tsingtau. The second force, consisting of heavy guns, various siege groups and heavy materiel was to land at Laoshan Bay, within the German zone. This plan harbored a politically explosive decision regarding the British role. Lungkow was a Chinese territory, and landing there would be considered a violation of China's neutrality. The British refused to become a party to a dispute with China and were opposed to landing there. But the Japanese refused to land all their forces at Laoshan Bay. Though geographically closer, the waters of Laoshan Bay were littered with mines, and it would take great efforts to secure the landing. In addition, it was monsoon season, and the bay was completely flooded and muddy. The Japanese resented the fact that the British, as a minor power, tried to limit their operational maneuverability and dictate the war plan. Britain's strategic imperative was viewed by Japan as merely an operational hazard.[16] On September 2, Japan landed 2,000 soldiers in Lungkow. But owing to unprecedented floods, roads became almost impassible for wheeled traffic and guns, and it was decided to make a second landing elsewhere - in Laoshan Bay. The British plan was thus vindicated. During the four days following September 2, the Japanese landed in Laoshan Bay the main force of 30,000 troops under the command of Major General Kamio Mitsuomi. Under heavy rain and floods, Japanese forces marched toward their positions north of Tsingtau. Their force buildup was interrupted September 18 by occasional German fire, which caused only a few casualties. On September 23, British forces disembarked from their ships at Laoshan Bay and took positions at the frontline. Their late arrival was not to their benefit. Although Bernardiston was received by the Japanese commander-in-chief very cordially, he was not provided with any detailed military intelligence or any information that could allow him to have meaningful influence on the operational planning. It was clear that the Japanese were trying to minimize the British involvement in the planning and execution of the campaign.[17] By the last week of October, the British-Japanese forces completed their preparations for attack while the British and Japanese navies were tightening their blockade. The attacking forces were based 1,200 to 2,000 yards from the German defenses, and the four Japanese siege artillery battalions were fully positioned and armed. The D-day for the attack was October 30, the birthday of the Japanese Emperor. In the morning, the Japanese opened their bombardment, and soon after they started the allied infantry attack on the German defenses. The British occupied a 600-yard portion of the first line of attack alongside a Japanese brigade. The coalition forces met an outnumbered, though resolute, defender. The Germans fought a hopeless battle inflicting on the allies almost 2,000 casualties, most of them Japanese.[18] But in early November, they ran out of ammunition and exhausted their capability to fight. Finally, on November 7, the white flag was hoisted over Tsingtau.

The success at Tsingtau whetted the appetite of many British officers for increased Anglo-Japanese cooperation. Throughout the war, the idea of involving Japanese troops and ships in the fighting in Mesopotamia and the Mediterranean fronts was constantly debated in the British cabinet and War Office. Senior British officials like members of the War Cabinet Lord Milner and Lord Curzon were very much in favor. In June 1918, General Edmond Allenby specifically requested Japanese divisions for Palestine. With them, he promised, "I could do big things."[19] Others, like Secretary of State for India, Austen Chamberlain, vehemently vetoed the idea, believing British prestige in Asia would be severely damaged if it resorted to seek the help of an Asian power.[20] A great debate was sparked in the British cabinet regarding the implications of participation of Japanese troop participation in the battle of Palestine. Most ministers agreed that the effect on the Christian world of Japanese troops capturing the holy city of Jerusalem could outweigh the operational advantages of their employment. There was a real concern that the news of Islam's holy places falling in the hands of Asian idolaters would "shock European public opinion."[21] At the same time such an event would agitate the Muslims much more than the threat of a Christian conquest. This could cause consternation and consolidation of the Muslim world against the Entente.[22] In a moment of strategic distress, considerations of culture and race took precedence over operational needs and the war ended without further Japanese military contribution on the ground. Cooperation at sea, on the other hand, continued in various capacities throughout the war. Japanese warships escorted Australian and New Zealand Army Corps (ANZAC) troops to the Middle East and French troops sailing from East Asia reinforcing units fighting in the western front. Japanese naval units deployed in Singapore to help the British hold the colony and fought along allied warships in the war against German U-boats in 1917 and 1918.[23] However, for the allies, Japan's contribution was never enough. Partly due to British hesitance to incorporate the Japanese in fighting in Europe and Mesopotamia and mainly due to Japanese dodging and procrastination, there was a feeling among many that Japan was not taking on a full share of the burden. Its aloofness regarding military fronts other than Asia prompted the title a "jackal state," a free rider that enjoyed the kill but assisted too little in the hunt. This produced resentment and mistrust in Britain that, in turn, led to the beginning of the decline of the Anglo-Japanese alliance.[24]

Major General Kamio Mitsuomi

The cross-cultural landscape: How did the Japanese view the British?

Up until the 1868 Meiji Restoration, Japan had almost no relations with the West. It was a feudal society ruled by the sword of the samurai and the power of the emperor. The Restoration brought with it an end to seclusion and a growing interest in the Western lifestyle. Japanese embassies to Europe and the United States brought back to Japan Western ideas, innovation and institutions. Japan went through a revolution that transformed the fabric of its society into that of a modern state. But despite the openness to the West and its economic promise, there was still little regard for its culture. The Japanese attitude toward European culture was entirely utilitarian. What could be used to promote Japan's progress was quickly adopted; the rest was regarded with contempt.[25] The West was viewed as the world of the barbarian, and its cultural imperialism had to be resisted. Furthermore, Western attempts to propagate Christianity or secular ideas among the Japanese were confronted with hostility, since they interfered with the effort to institute Shinto as the nation's predominant religion.[26] But close to the turn of the century, hostility toward the West began to ease, and its culture was treated with growing tolerance. Only seldom could one find evidence of Japanese xenophobia in the numerous reports of Western travelers, journalists and diplomats who visited Japan at the time.

Even more outward looking than Japanese society was the Japanese military, which by all accounts was receptive to the West's way of life. Since the mid-1860s, the Emperor's army was courting three major European militaries - the French, the German and the British - in an effort to transform itself into a modern armed force.[27] From the outset, France was the most willing facilitator among the European powers of Japan's military transformation. The French, more than the others, understood that linguistic infrastructure was a key factor in winning the contest between the Europeans for the hearts of Japan's brass. They developed an edge over the other European powers in language instruction by establishing a French school in Yokohama to qualify interpreters who later became officers in the army.[28] In 1869, the Germans began their military involvement in Japan when a German non-commissioned officer began training the Japanese utilizing to German methods.[29] Impressed by German precision and discipline, the Japanese became increasingly interested in German doctrine, which had secured impressive victories in Europe. By 1870, the Japanese army was divided between those who supported the adoption of French training doctrine and those who favored that of the Germans. Surprisingly, despite the French defeat in the Franco-Prussian War, the Japanese decided to go with the French doctrine. The simple reason was that very few Japanese knew German, and there was a dearth of interpreters who could work with the Germans. It was one of those occasions in which a cultural consideration determined the avenue that an entire army took.[30] Consequently, in 1872, a French military mission landed in Japan and stayed there for eight years. The French mission introduced drills, tactics, and doctrine. It also laid the foundation for the Japanese conscription system. Though French instructors often complained that "it is much harder to drill and discipline Japanese troops than Chinese or Indian soldiers," they got along well with the Japanese. They regarded the Japanese soldier as brave, energetic and dedicated.[31] The Germans held similar views. In 1885, the German Major Meckel arrived in Japan on a one-man mission to assume the role of Staff college lecturer and advisor to the Japanese Army General Staff. His ambition was to instill German training methods and emphasis on offensive tactics and maneuvering in the Japanese Army, some of which proved to be very useful in the subsequent wars against China and Russia.[32] Here too, in contrast to the German officers who trained the Ottoman army at the time, reports about the Japanese were nothing but commendatory.[33]

But of all the European powers, relations with the British army and navy were the most long lasting and fruitful. The British were involved since the 1860s in the effort to transform Japan into a modernized state. Among the members of the large British community in Japan were experts who helped develop the Japanese railway system, taught science and engineering, and established the Japanese telegraph system. A garrison of 1,500 British troops was stationed in Yokohama with Japanese permission to protect

British economic and strategic interests.[34] One side effect was that the Japanese were gradually exposed to the Victorian Army's military culture, the British recruitment system and its fighting experiences. The Japanese sent their officers to observe the British war in South Africa. They were impressed by the military performance and held the highest opinion of British soldiers.[35]

The most important British role was building the Japanese Imperial Navy. To accomplish this mission, British naval officers were stationed in Japan to instruct the Japanese navy, Japanese cadets were sent to Britain for training, and Japanese officers regularly sailed aboard Royal Navy vessels.[36] The British-Japanese alliance, signed in 1902, a source of great pride for the Japanese, made the British the most popular foreign force in Japan. British officers in Japan were treated with the highest respect. They enjoyed preferential treatment, were invited to exclusive social events and attended confidential military exercises from which all the other foreigners were excluded.[37]

The exposure of Japanese officers to European militaries contributed to their appreciation of Western habits, customs, values and beliefs. Unlike the Ottomans, trained by exactly the same European powers, who resisted any change in their military culture, the Japanese were receptive students. They adopted French and German dress codes, built comfortable barracks for their troops, fed them well, drilled them using European commands, regulated uncompromising disciplinary rules and increased awareness of cleanliness and personal hygiene. The Japanese were the ultimate borrowers, and in many aspects they surpassed their teachers.

By and large, Japanese soldiers felt equal among equals when dealing with the British and other Europeans. In November 1913, the same coalition members that crushed the Boxer Rebellion reunited to conduct an international maneuver at Tientsin in North China. British and Japanese contingents, alongside the French, Germans, Russians, Austrians and Americans conducted an exercise that tested their ability to work together. Major General Sato of the Imperial Japanese Army assumed the duties of Director and Umpire-in-Chief, a choice that demonstrated the great respect the Europeans and Americans had for Japanese judgment and military professionalism. The exercise was a success. It proved, among other things, that the Japanese troops were compatible with any other European military and that they were able to smoothly cooperate with the others despite cultural barriers. At the end of the exercise, General Sato delivered a speech reflecting Japan's readiness to fight alongside European allies:

> We have always thought that the combined action of the international troops would prove a difficult matter, as all have different languages and different forms of tactics. However, it appears from our experiences today that the difficulties are not so great as we had imagined, and our confidence in our combined power has increased proportionately. This happy issue is in a great measure due to the mutual friendship and cordial relationship existing among the international troops.[38]

The Gurkhas' cousins

By 1914, the British Empire covered 20 percent of the world's territory and ruled over almost 25 percent of its population. From Canada to the West Indies, from Sydney to the Cape Colony, from Calcutta to Hong Kong, the British imperial government administered the lives of people of almost every race and culture. No other nation had so many encounters with foreigners and so many opportunities to interact with them and learn about their cultures as did the British. Their diplomats, merchants, teachers, journalists and soldiers moved across the empire and interacted with people of different colors and cultures. Books and reports about their experiences became the main source of knowledge ordinary people had about alien cultures. English men and women of the Victorian and Edwardian period were known to hold ideas of racial hierarchy, cultural chauvinism and jingoism. It was a widespread belief among the British that they were, as Cecil Rhodes put it, "the finest race in the world and the more of the world they inhabit, the better it will be for mankind."[39] The British sense of supremacy stemmed from the subscription to the popular theory of social Darwinism.

Proponents of racial hierarchy saw the Anglo-Saxons as a super-race, explaining British dispersion across the globe in its inherent destiny to rule over what they considered to be inferior races, such as the Negroes, Indians and Orientals.[40]

Racial attitudes in the Victorian-Edwardian army were not very different from those of the British society. British soldiers who served in the colonies treated African, Indian and Asian locals with utter disdain. They viewed them as inferior races, incapable of equaling the West's military prowess. As late as 1896, a British general predicted that "the day is still very remote when the war-like races will be qualified to supply the place of the European officers."[41] To assert its regime throughout the empire, the Victorian army recruited and trained native soldiers placing them under the command of British officers. A handbook for young officers, published in 1833, advised them to show tolerance toward their men's religions but the use of terms such as "self venerating Hindu" and "the bigoted Mussulman" left no doubt that proper treatment of native soldiers was not a high priority in the British army.[42] In order to finally come to the realization that the most efficient use of native soldiers depended on an understanding and sensitivity to their cultural needs, the British armed forces had to undergo a long program of cultural education, at times with devastating consequences.

The classroom was the Indian subcontinent. There the British faced not only a unique social system of caste and segregation but also a cultural kaleidoscope with some of the most bizarre customs and traditions to the eyes of any European. British officers, addressed as sahibs, found themselves ruling the lives of tens of thousands of Brahmin, Muslim, Sikh, and Ghurka sepoys of whose cultures they knew very little. The degree of racial prejudices among the Victorian British is still a subject for debate among historians, but clearly among many of those deployed in India there was a strong sense that they were the masters of India. They believed they were "superior beings by nature to the Asiatic."[43] Racial bias bred insensitivity and disdain toward the dark-skinned Indians. Countless testimonies on the appalling treatment of the sepoys can be found not only in Indian historiography but also in many letters and memoirs by British soldiers. "The sepoy is regarded as an inferior creature. He is sworn at. He is treated roughly. He is spoken of as a 'nigger'. He is addressed as *'suar'* or pig, an epithet most opprobrious to a respectable native, especially the Mussulman, and which cuts him to the quick," wrote one witness. Another Englishman: "A great cause of complaint is the foul language which the officers use. I have heard the vilest language used on the parade ground, by a commanding officer while exercising the troops. High caste Brahmins and Mohammedans, such as we have in our regiments, writhe under abuse from a European."[44] Facing such indignities, resentment among the sepoys was only natural. Local opposition became frequent and often required military force to be brought against it. Every few years, the British Army was involved, somewhere in the empire and especially in Asia, in a continual series of border skirmishes, punitive expeditions, and rebellious attempts. Interestingly, most of the instability had culturally driven origins. The tension between the Raj and its Indian subordinates emerged as early as 1806, when Madras officers attempted to introduce a new, uniform appearance and dress code among the sepoys. Distinctive caste marks on the forehead as well as the impressive beards and moustaches were prohibited. The Indians were forced to trim their facial hear, a source of pride and manliness in their culture, to a more 'presentable' proportion. The traditional headdress, the turban, was to be replaced by one with a leather cockade suspected to be made from pig and cow skin, both highly objectionable materials to Muslim and Hindu soldiers. Additionally, in their ignorance, the British failed to understand the importance of daily ablutions and religious ceremonies to the lives of their indigenous troops.[45] Strict rituals of daily ablutions could not be performed during long military expeditions, one stark example of culture interfering with operational decisions. Age-old customs forbade the Hindus from sailing on sea voyages since they were obligated to cook their food on an open fire, something that was totally prohibited on the British Navy's wooden ships. In addition, strict rituals of daily ablutions could not be performed during long military expeditions. When war broke out with Burma in 1824, the British had to march their troops hundreds of miles through Assam and Arakan at high cost in order to avoid a short, relatively risk free sea voyage.[46] British refusal to provide the necessary logistics for the long march sparked the Barrackpore mutiny in which the 47th Native Infantry was virtually massacred for refusing to march. [47] Similar reasons caused the Hindu sepoys to refuse to cross the Indus during the first Afghan War.

In 1856, with utter disregard for the Indians' sensitivity, the British passed the General Service Enlistment Act. This stipulated that all recruits of the Bengal Army would agree to serve overseas if required to do so.[48] Several other laws including the one prohibiting Hindu wives from being burned to death on their husbands' funeral pyres were considered highly offensive. There were also incidents in which sahibs prevented their soldiers from celebrating their religious holidays. One of these cases resulted in the murder of a British colonel by his Muslim subordinate.[49] Simultaneously, British missionaries under the auspices of the army converted Indians to Christianity. Soldiers who converted to Christianity were immediately promoted.[50] By 1857, both Muslims and Hindus shared the same fear for their religions. There was a full belief that the Raj was about to attempt a forceful conversion of its subjects. In an atmosphere of anger and suspicion came the cartridge crisis, the last straw that brought about the 1857 Indian Mutiny, which rapidly became the greatest of all the imperial wars. It broke out in a rather peculiar way. The projectile for the new Enfield rifle included a paper cartridge that contained both ball and powder charge. British regulations required the paper to be bitten off before the cartridge was placed in the muzzle of the weapon. To facilitate this process the cartridge was greased with animal fat. Sepoys heard and quickly passed on the rumor that the grease was a mixture of cow and pig fat. Biting this cartridge would mean breaking the caste of the Hindu sepoys and defiling the Muslims. The rumors were not baseless. *The Times* of London published a report claiming that "The government ordered mutton fat for the purpose [but] some contractors, to save a few shillings, gave pigs' and bullocks' fat instead."[51] In the atmosphere of mistrust that prevailed in 1857, British denials of any use of objectionable material had very little chance of being accepted. On the contrary, more and more rumors circulated about how British merchants were mixing bone powder in the flour and how forceful conversions were taking place. The beginning of the mutiny occurred on May 10, when 85 sepoys refused to 'bite the bullet' and were sentenced to ten years imprisonment. Within days, a mutiny of monumental scale, dragging on for almost two years, erupted throughout the subcontinent. Women and children were butchered by both sides; cities and villages were devastated; acts of savagery and atrocity were committed.

The Indian Mutiny was one of the traumatic moments in the history of the British Empire. The racial and religious struggle for supremacy between dark-skinned and white and between Christians and non-Christians was a product of British cultural insensitivity, bigotry, and remoteness from their colonial subjects. Most historians of the Indian Mutiny agree that it only strengthened British racism. "Once betrayed by those whom they had trusted, the British could no longer bring themselves to trust anyone with a brown face," concluded one of them.[52] But the rebellion, which ended in a British victory, also forced the British to derive some important lessons about their relations with non-white residents of their Empire. It taught them that in order to work together with the local population they should know its culture and respect it. Hence, the distance between whites and Indians was gradually removed: legislation banning racial discrimination was introduced; in 1885, the British abolished the term "native" resented by the Indians; reforms to equate the status of Indian officers to that of the British were adopted; and laws prescribing white officers to respect religious holidays and ceremonies were passed.[53] In the years between the Indian Mutiny and World War I, the British Army was involved in no fewer than 150 mutinies, insurgencies, raids, expeditions and other small wars. British troops fought alongside Indian and Chinese soldiers, African tribesmen, and Central American warlords. They knew that effective cooperation necessitated good cross-cultural communication and the highest degree of sensitivity to the partner's cultural needs. As World War I raged, one of Britain's finest soldiers, Major General Sir George Younghusband, who served with the Indian army, was wrapping up his forty-year army career with an insight: "To get on with the native you have to understand him, and that understanding is the result of intimate knowledge of his prides and his prejudices, which only comes with long residence in the country and daily intercourse."[54] His contemporary, General Ian Hamilton, who is known for commanding the ill-fated Mediterranean Expeditionary Force during the Battle of Gallipoli, reached a similar conclusion: "Mutual understanding is the only bedrock upon which alliances, whether diplomatic or matrimonial, can find enduring foundations. Flatteries, cajoleries, exaggerations, insincerities, are the prelude to disillusionment, if not to divorce."[55]

This advice was fully heeded with regards to the Japanese. The events around the turn of the century, the stunning Japanese defeat of China in 1894-95 and the victory over the Russians in 1905, caused many Europeans to view Japan as a latent aggressor, a country that skillfully integrated the Bushido tradition with modern military technology and European doctrine. It was a civilized nation with an exotic culture very foreign to the West. But it was also a nation with an impressive military capability and a proven ability to prevail over a European power. The term, "the Yellow Peril," coined by the German Kaiser Wilhelm II, was adopted by many to describe the emerging Sino-Japanese civilization, a serious challenge to the white race's dominance of the world.[56] These expressions did not fall on deaf ears in Britain. In 1898, for example, British author Mathew P. Shiel published a popular fiction book, *The Yellow Danger*, describing a Sino-Japanese conspiracy to take over the world. The book popularized the image of the Oriental as a cruel barbarian.[57] Many ignorant social commentators and diplomats failed to see the cultural wedge that was forming between the Japanese and Sinic civilizations, thus treating the two as though they were cut from the same cloth. But this misperception was propagated not only by laymen. Senior British diplomats spoke about Japan in terms of a power that was about to "unite the yellow races and get too big for her boots."[58] The darling of the British military establishment, the American Anglophile Alfred Thayer Mahan, a man who wholeheartedly believed in Anglo-Saxon racial superiority and who was a card-carrying member of the "Yellow Peril" movement since 1890, consistently proliferated the idea of an imminent "struggle between the white and yellow races in the Pacific."[59] As a frequent contributor to *The Times* of London and an honorary member of England's most prestigious officer clubs and military academies, he had a receptive audience to which he portrayed the Japanese as "culturally static, racially inferior and intellectually backward."[60] Mahan and his like knew very little on the subject of their contempt. But there were others, like missionaries and travelers to the region during the pre-World War I period, who knew the Japanese people closely and conveyed a mostly positive picture of Japan's culture. Though some associated the Japanese with ruthlessness, vanity and incapacity to comprehend abstract ideas, almost everybody agreed that they were esthetic, polite, loyal and friendly.

Three people were responsible more than anyone for the interpretation and popularization of Japan's culture in the West. The first was a Greek-born writer, Lafcadio Hearn, who lived in Japan fourteen years and published many articles and books for Western consumption. Hearn was a Japanophile in the full sense of the word; he saw Japan as "a civilization full of charm."[61] His works, written from the perspective of a European, were instrumental to Western understanding of Japanese culture, especially its complex religion. Despite his sympathy to Japan, Hearn was an objective, highly credible observer who described both the grace and peculiarities of Japanese culture. Hearn's friend, Basil Hall Chamberlain, professor of Japanese at Tokyo University and the Imperial Naval School was another prominent Western interpreter of Japanese culture. His book, *Things Japanese*, published in 1905 was the most popular work on Japan. It introduced the Western readers to a wide array of topics, including Japan's cultural and social life. Particularly instructive was his essay about the Japanese people and their collective psyche. This essay presented not only the dominant characteristics of the Japanese but also how they viewed the Anglo-Saxons.[62] The third figure, Sir Ernest Satow, a diplomat and cultural commentator, was among the most distinguished Japanese linguists, widely known and respected among the educated class of Japan. He lived in Japan in the late 19th century and wrote books and articles on Japanese history, art, and rituals.[63] In a world deprived of mass media, the three fulfilled an important role educating the British public on a country that was an enigma to many. But they were not the only ones. Scholarly work on Japan was becoming increasingly popular, and, by and large, most of the works praised the Japanese people and their culture. The notorious British sense of cultural superiority was somewhat repressed when it came to portraying the Japanese. "Great talent, but little genius," concluded one European traveler. "They impress me as the most pleasing people I have ever seen," remarked another.[64]

When it came to Japan, the British soldiers deviated from their traditional parochialism. One writer influential in shaping the British public's view of the Japanese soldier at the end of the 19th century was Rudyard Kipling author of *The Jungle Book*, who had spent several months in Japan in 1889 and in 1892 and published articles about his impressions of the country and its people.[65] Kipling was fully aware of the dedication and courage of the Japanese soldier. His advice to the British was: "If you meet Japanese infantry, [...] commence firing early and often and at the longest ranges compatible with getting at them. They are bad little men who know too much."[66] Kipling's letters also touched on a sensitive racial idea about the Japanese that was privately shared by many British officers. Their physical appearance was ridiculed; they were described as an "undersized, spectacled, hollow backed and hump-shouldered" people.[67] To European observers the Japanese soldiers looked very small, often less than 5 feet tall. British soldiers were much taller. By 1898, for example, only four percent of British recruits were under 5 feet 3 inches.[68] It was a common British belief that the typical Japanese body structure impaired their ability to ride horses and develop a strong cavalry. "The Japanese as a nation are very long in the body and very short in the leg, a physical conformation dead against good horsemanship," explained one senior British officer.[69] In a military culture that held the highest admiration for the cavalry branch, short people hardly fit into the British concept of the ideal soldier's physique. But by the beginning of the 20th century, when the "short"-bodied Japanese soldiers proved able to defeat the "tall", robust Russians, these views began to change. General Hamilton, attached to the Japanese First Army during the

Russo-Japanese War, actually praised the physical condition of the Japanese soldiers claiming that they were, in fact, first cousins of the "gallant little Gurkha" who by then had already achieved recognition as the King's finest soldiers. "In the whole of Tokyo," he observed, "I have not seen a single soldier who is flat-footed, narrow-chested or slouching. [...] The army is the cream of the nation. How different from us!"[70]

The association with the Gurkhas, the revered "Martial Race" from Nepal, showed that despite their tendency to look down at those not like themselves, British soldiers held the Japanese in higher esteem than other the non-white nations with whom they interacted. Many British military experts were impressed by Japan's military culture. They held that Japan's military prowess was not due to its technology or doctrine but rather due to a tradition of honor and chivalry manifested by the spirit of Bushido as described in Inazo Nitobe's book *Bushido: The Soul of Japan*, which sold a number of English editions in Britain.[71] They saw them as noble, brave and disciplined soldiers. "The Japanese have behind them the moral character produced by mothers and fathers, who again are the product of generations of mothers and fathers nurtured in ideas of self-sacrifice and loyalty," wrote Hamilton.[72] The attachment of British officers to Japanese Army units became a popular and effective practice. It allowed British officers in line for promotion to become commanders of local soldiers and thus gain basic knowledge of the East and learn about foreign customs and languages. Hamilton wrote that "there can be no better discipline for officers destined to command Asiatics than, for one brief period in their lives, to study the Asiatic character from a subordinate instead of a superior position; as unconsidered underlings, instead of awe-inspiring, unapproachable Sahibs. [...] In India British officers are always busy imposing their views on an Eastern race; in Japan they learn to seek for what the East has got to give to the West."[73]

In sum, public opinion in Britain on Japan was almost equally shaped by the diametrically opposed views of Japanophobes and Japanophiles. The result was an ambivalent perception, a mixture of admiration and fear, affection and suspicion. But by all accounts, Japan and its people were viewed as far superior to the rest of the non-European ethnic and racial groups with which the British Empire interacted. With such attitudes, no wonder the soldiers who fought in Tsingtau had mixed feelings toward the Japanese. A very small minority embarked on the expedition with "such prejudice against the Japanese that even if the latter proved themselves to be angels there would have been no diminution of the detestation in which they were held," wrote one British observer.[74] Another senior British officer at Tsingtau reflected that "the British regarded the Japanese as inferior race, as coolies in uniforms whose good opinion it was quite unnecessary to win." Nevertheless, he acknowledged that such sentiments could have been due to the lack of popularity of the mission rather than the identity of the partner, and due to the fact that the British troops were completely dependent on the Japanese, rather than to a pure racial prejudice.[75] On the other hand, most people felt differently. Vice Consul Eckford reported of many British soldiers "in whose eyes the Japanese were the incarnation of superhuman excellence. For these they remained such to the end and the most glaring wrong was absolved with 'it is their custom.'"[76] Hence, the large bulk of the British force treated the Japanese with no great racial prejudice, providing them a fair chance to establish their virtues. For them, the Japanese were 'splendid soldiers,' 'tireless workers,' 'clever devils,' and 'the finest shrapnel bursting.'[77]

How did they communicate?

By and large, the Japanese exercised a great deal of tolerance and respect toward the British. On September 3, 1914, the Japanese General Staff gave the Japanese commander Kamio specific instructions to place maximum effort in obliging to British needs. He was advised to be attentive to issues like language, race, customs and religion[78] To make the British feel like equal partners, the Japanese commanders made sure British flags were placed alongside Japanese flags at coalition bases and positions. Kamio signed all documents as "commander-in-chief allied forces." Relations between the two force commanders were cordial and accommodating. Bernardiston fought with the 2nd Middlesex regiment in the South African War from 1901 until 1902. He then became military attaché in Brussels and The Hague and from 1906 until 1910 was assistant commandant of the Royal Military College at Sandhurst. Later he became assistant director of military training at the War Office. In this capacity he was a liaison officer with numerous foreign, including Asian, delegations. He had extensive diplomatic experience, a gracious personality, and good communication skills making him the perfect choice to work with the Japanese.[79] Kamio was also a fitting choice. Calm and charming, he enjoyed social activities and had many friends. He spoke English well and could easily communicate with the British. British intelligence reports portrayed him as one who is "calm, able and inspires confidence." He was also known to like foreigners.[80] His chief-of-staff Major General Hanzo Yamanashii also had a great deal of European experience. He lived in Germany several years and spoke German. Though flamboyant and at times emotional, he was also an easy person to deal with.[81] Throughout the coalition, only one incident strained the relations between the two commanders. Bernardiston demanded to have his name coupled with Kamio's on the permission for non-combatants to leave Tsingtau before bombardment. Kamio rejected the request so strongly that both commanders referred the matter to their respective governments with the result that the Japanese contention was upheld. This dispute caused some estrangement between the two commanders. Kamio was encouraged by being able to make a display of his superior authority and was insensitive to Bernardiston's sense of inadequacy as a dependent junior partner. But all things considered, relations between the commanders were as cooperative as one could expect in such situations.

From the launch of the coalition, it was clear that language and communication were likely to be a source of difficulty. Few Japanese officers could understand English, and the British could not communicate in Japanese.[82] Unlike the German-Turkish relations, there was no neutral language both sides could use. General Kamio was one of the few who could speak English, a fact that helped him communicate with Bernardiston without being dependent on interpreters. Naval cooperation was also smoothed by attaching Commander Kiyokawa, who spoke fluent English, to the British Naval attaché during the whole operation. It was largely

Brig. General Bernardiston and Maj. General Kamio

due to his tact and language abilities that cooperation was so successfully maintained.[83] But a good command of English among senior commanders was not enough. Channels of communication with those Japanese field commanders who could not understand English had to be established. The natural solution in this kind of case was to use the services of bilingual liaison officers. The British military system relied on a permanent staff of diplomats, defense attachés and language officers with good language skills who usually served in overseas embassies. When military operations in a region demanded speakers of a specific foreign language, those who could speak it were immediately seconded by the military to serve as liaison officers. From 1904, the British began to qualify Japanese-speaking language officers. These officers, usually in their thirties, were sent to Japan where they lived with Japanese families and studied the language intensively, many reaching a high level of proficiency.[84] When the British decided to join the Japanese campaign, the two sides decided to exchange liaison officers. But owing to a shortage of officers in the British army when the war broke out, all language officers had already been recalled back home.[85] To reinforce their linguistic team, the British recruited their military attaché in Peking, Major David Robertson, a linguist who served most of his career in diplomatic posts in Asia for the Tsingtau operation. Others summoned were naval attaché Captain Hubard Brand and Everard Calthrop, a brilliant linguist who translated Chinese and Japanese books and understood Asian culture. In addition, there were five other language officers at the embassy.[86] This staff of interpreters was sufficient - mainly due to the fact that the British force was so small - to bridge over language difficulties at the senior level. Nevertheless, for soldiers at the lower levels of command and in the trenches, the only means of communication was sign language. Despite the efforts invested in improving verbal communication, throughout the campaign the language gap proved to be an irritant that hindered the operational effectiveness of the coalition. Eckford described it as a source of "almost insuperable obstacles that much aggravated the inconvenience, already great enough, arising from fundamentally different systems of warlike organization."[87] And indeed, the inability to communicate often resulted in quarrels and misunderstandings, mainly between the Sikh soldiers and the Japanese engineers who were deployed next to each other. Several times, British forces patrolling at night were mistaken for Germans, fired upon and taken prisoner. On one occasion, a captain of the Sikh force was captured and mistreated.[88] This problem of friendly fire was solved once the British began to wear distinguishing marks and take along interpreters. Most of the interpreters, however, were of poor skills and found it difficult to understand the strong accents of the Welsh. But luckily for the allies, the limited scope of the campaign and their overwhelming superiority over their enemy allowed them to overcome the language problem without paying a heavy price.

Another problem in the relations had to do with trust. From the start of the campaign, the Japanese were distrustful of the British.

Their commanders were constantly withholding information and never informed the British about the next phase of the campaign plan. Fearing information leakage, the Japanese commander General Kamio did not allow Bernardiston to send signals to Peking or overseas. As a result, Bernardiston could only send London two dispatches throughout the duration of the six-week campaign with updates about his activities.[89] Japanese paranoia about intelligence leaks greatly affected their staff work. Contrary to British military culture, which emphasized the use of written orders, the Japanese relied on oral communication, using no written documents. A Japanese commander would deliver an oral briefing and then randomly select a subordinate officer to repeat the directives in order to ensure that the orders were fully understood. Japanese officers were used to this system and extremely attentive during the briefings. Failure to recite the orders was considered humiliating. British officers who attended the briefings and who were used to relying on written documents, failed to memorize the details of the battle plans as presented by the Japanese commander.[90]

Another interesting cultural gap the British complained about was related to the Japanese belief that it was undignified to show publicly that one is busy. In their meetings with the British and in other large gatherings, Japanese commanders pretended to be relaxed and undisturbed by the challenges facing them. They gladly discussed frivolous matters but never addressed work-related issues in large staff meetings. Instead, they limited dealing with work to small, intimate groups.[91] The British behaved differently. They were more business-like and were not embarrassed to be publicly seen as busy and even distressed. On the contrary, the harder one worked the more dedicated he was perceived to be.

Throughout the campaign, the British and the Japanese had daily interactions at the lowest levels. British forces marched together with the Japanese from the landing beach to their battle positions and shared the same roads for their supplies. British trenches were in close proximity to the Japanese lines, so they could observe their partners' way of life. Though both the British and the Japanese armies were considered among the most disciplined militaries of their time, there were clear differences in their priorities and emphases. Sharing the same muddy roads, the forces' distinct styles of marching were foreign to one another. The British marched in columns according to a fixed rhythm and paused only in groups. The Japanese were accustomed to marching in small groups, without specific order, leaving much more latitude to the individual soldier to maneuver himself. They also allowed individual pauses. The result was that Japanese soldiers often broke into the British lines, throwing soldiers off the road. The British were bitter about this Japanese behavior, a constant source of quarrels. They thought the Japanese were trying to deliberately undermine their participation in the campaign.[92]

Culture of the bayonet

In the early Meiji period, Japan was consumed by a wave of anti-Christian sentiment targeted mainly at Christian missionaries working hard to expand their circle of believers. It was a nation in a state of religious and intellectual disarray, as a set of religions competed for dominance. The struggle between Christianity and Asian religions bred hostility and often violence. Proponents of Japan's rapprochement with the West realized how damaging Buddhist intolerance was to relations with the Christian world. In a meeting with the heads of the Buddhist sects in Kyoto in September 1884, the city's governor warned his audience of the perils of religious fundamentalism and anti-Christian sentiments. "Any religion must be free for the people who dwell here," he proclaimed, and pleaded the clergy to do their outmost to prevent unlawful acts against non-Buddhists.[93] By 1889, despite pockets of resistance in some intellectual circles, the Japanese constitution assured freedom of religion for all Japanese. With the installation of Shinto as the country's leading religion, religious paranoia subsided. But those Europeans hoping that religious openness would allow them to turn Japan into a Christian nation were about to face deep disappointment. Despite feeling increased tolerance, Christian missionaries working in Japan failed to achieve mass conversion. The typical Japanese soldier ascribed to either Shinto or Buddhist religious ritual. Ceremonies of both religions were frequent and solemn. Shinto was better suited for military life since it emphasized patriotism and loyalty to the Emperor above any other virtue. Furthermore, it gave much more weight than did Buddhism to the virtue of personal sacrifice and suppressing the selfish side of one's character. It also glorified death as a soldier's ultimate achievement. To many Westerners invited to attend religious ceremonies and bow their heads to "strange" gods, Japan's religions were both fascinating and puzzling. It was clear, however, as Hamilton reported, that "Japanese officers don't seem to believe very much in their religion; are rather ashamed of it indeed, and anxious to make out that it is just a mere form; good for the private soldier; nothing more."[94] Similarly, among the ranks of the British, religion was not a major driving force. In his illustrative portrait of the British Army, Byron Farwell concluded that: "Most officers considered themselves good Christians, but they did not think too deeply or too often about their religion, and when they did, their thoughts were not likely to be profound. It is certain that religion was important in the lives of some officers and men, but the evidence seems to indicate that among the other ranks these were ever in the minority."[95]

As for the British, novelist Robert Graves who served with the royal Welsh Fusiliers noted that the British soldier was known for "his foul mouth, his love of drink and prostitutes, his irreligion, his rowdiness and his ignorance [...] Hardly one soldier in one hundred was inspired by religious feeling of even the crudest kind."[96] The British force in China was so religiously diverse that there was no place for the development of collective religious sentiment. One third of the servicemen were Sikhs, the others Anglicans, Roman Catholic and Protestants. Tsingtau was a unique coalition since both coalition partners fought away from their homeland and were thus not affected by religious and cultural sensitivities of their home societies. Unlike other coalitions examined here, there was no fear of religious contamination, nor were the invading armies at all interested in spreading their nation's religious beliefs.

Even if religion in its simple form was of little relevance to the operation at Tsingtau, there were deeper religious themes that directly affected Japan's military culture. The most important theme promulgated by the Japanese religion was the absolute loyalty to the Emperor and the sense of moral obligation to pay dues to society by sacrificing one's life for him. As a result, when it came to courage, the Japanese made no compromises. Display of cowardice and weakness were intolerable and inflicted shame not only on the soldier but also on his entire family. The Japanese army also retained many of the martial elements of the Samurai culture and Japanese soldiers were fascinated with the culture of the bayonet. They believed fighting means suffering casualties. They were eager to attack and charge forward with their bayonets and felt disdain toward those who fought more conservatively. This view was noted by the British during the Boxer Rebellion, as observed by the British military attaché in Japan, Colonel A.G. Churchill:

> The real reason for the Japanese opinion may be traced to their fixed idea that a 'good fight' is to suffer casualties, and their eagerness, amounting to rashness, to get in with the bayonet. The Indian troops, when under fire, assumed the extended formations they are taught to take up from the day of their enlistment, and this in conjunction with the tactical dispositions of a general experienced in savage warfare, resulted in our casualties being out of all proportion to those sustained by the Japanese, who presented their usual close targets to the enemy's fire. The Japanese apparently failed to understand this disparity in losses, and attributed it to the over-cautiousness of our general and to a want of dash in our troops.[97]

The 15 years that had lapsed since the Boxer Rebellion did not change that culture. Major E. F. Knox of the 36th Sikhs reported "the whole spirit of the Japanese training is devoted to getting near enough to use the bayonet, and certainly far more attention was paid to rendering each individual soldier proficient in the use of that arm than used to be the case in the Indian army."[98] This observation was correct. Since the Boer War, officers of the British Army were debating the merits of the use of bayonets. Many believed that face-to-face combat was obsolete and that too much time was devoted to bayonets drills. British infantry officers advocated an increased use of sharpshooters and machine guns in order to kill their enemy from afar. As a result, Japanese soldiers at Tsingtau showed extraordinary willingness to take personal risks and endanger themselves by moving closer than did the British to enemy lines. For them, precautions were unworthy. The result was a noticeable disparity in the sides' casualty rates. By the end of the battle, the Japanese had suffered 415 dead and 1,451 wounded, while the British toll was limited to 13 dead and 61 wounded. What was perceived by the British as an elementary measure of caution was interpreted by the Japanese as faint-heartedness. They had little appreciation for those who did not adhere to their risk-taking values, and expressed their disappointment at what they thought to be British poor performance.[99] British officers were viewed as spoiled and feeble, people who came from wealthy families and were, therefore, unfit for the hardships and dangers of a campaign.[100]

The Japanese also had a different view on the concept of capitulation. The Japanese soldier was highly averse to the idea of surrendering and becoming a prisoner of war. He saw capitulation in battle as a humiliating practice, an abdication of responsibility and betrayal of the emperor. Japanese soldiers were never prepared physically or mentally for such a contingency. Once reports on the battles in Europe began to arrive, the Japanese were struck by the great numbers of prisoners of war on both sides. They believed that their British counterparts were not wholeheartedly committed to the fighting and that they would not fight to the end. In a private letter, Calthorp, the military attaché in Tokyo, regretted the distorted view the Japanese formed of the fighting value of the British.

> They think that the fighting in Europe must be after all a rather tame affair, and they point a finger at the number of prisoners on either side, their impression being that few Japanese troops would settle the business. This is where they have the mistake, I think. They have the offensive spirit, but they lack staying power and the reserve of force that pulls us through a long and dreary campaign. They are

too excitable or emotional and they do not recognize the latent strength behind the lethargic British private.[101]

To the British, Japanese indifference to the lives of their men was puzzling. The British saw no point in sacrificing lives just for the sake of social obligation. For them, fighting was merely a utilitarian practice to fulfill a strategic purpose. The Japanese values of camaraderie were also foreign to the British. From their trenches they saw how wounded Japanese soldiers could lie in the field without attention or attempts to rescue them. To the Japanese they were, as Ruth Benedict later described, "damaged goods."[102] But in British military culture, saving a comrade's life under fire was one of the greatest virtues for which soldiers were highly decorated. The British abhorred Japanese indifference to the pain and suffering of their comrades, and worse, had no faith in Japanese aid in case they were caught under fire.[103]

Happy marriage

It is hard to place the Battle of Tsingtau in the same class as other World War I epics such as Verdun, the Somme or Tannenberg. Despite its symbolism, the battle has never gained much interest or glory even in the countries that won it. For the Japanese, a defeat over a defender outnumbered by almost ten to one was not perceived as a victory in which one should take great pride. Their demonstration of force, leading a coalition with British participation, was a reaffirmation of the fact that Japan could no longer be treated as a second rate power. For His Majesty's soldiers the expedition in China was a trying experience. They had to march and fight under severe weather conditions, with short supplies and detached from anything European but their German enemy. In addition, they hated the fact they were under Japanese command. They viewed their participation in the battle as a humiliating experience in which they proved to be "a toothless bulldog" in their relations with Japan and her military leaders.[104] Despite the occasional bitterness, the Anglo-Japanese coalition in China was one of the more successful coalitions of the 20th century. It was an endeavor carried out elegantly by two technologically compatible powers bound together by an alliance commitment and, yet, by mutual interest to check each other's imperial aspirations in East Asia. All evidence shows that the two partners made considerable efforts to minimize operational and cross-cultural friction. They had no dispute about the allocation of forces or the hierarchy of command, they were doctrinally compatible, and their commanders treated each other cordially. A British senior official who visited Tsingtau wrote, "the Japanese were most anxious to conduct their operations with the outmost correctness. The meticulous trammels of Japanese regulations were perhaps a little galling to some of our men, but on the whole, cooperation between the two armies was most cordial and complete, and no contretemps had marred the harmony."[105] "The Japanese," wrote another British officer, "have been splendid over this show, and my opinion of them has gone right up to the top."[106] It would be no exaggeration to describe naval relations between the Japanese and British fleets in the Chinese theater of operations as harmonious. A report of the naval attaché in the British Embassy in Tokyo said that cooperation was excellent. "There was no friction whatsoever. The Japanese Commander-in-Chief, and all naval authorities, did their utmost to make things run smoothly, and every convenience was placed at the disposal of British ships."[107]

Throughout the campaign, British and Japanese commanders treated each other with grace and cordiality. Their mutual gestures were sincere and respectful. First Lord of the Admiralty, Winston Churchill, expressed the British enthusiasm about working in conjunction with the Japanese: "The officers and men of Great Britain rejoice in fighting the common enemy on the side of the loyal officers and men of the Imperial Japanese Navy."[108] Japanese officers, on their side, sent valuable presents to their counterparts to show their gratitude for Britain's support. Even the Emperor himself insisted on sending his aide-de-camp to personally inquire about the state of the British expeditionary force and present them with Saki and cigarettes. The British found the offering "unsmokable and undrinkable" but were deeply moved by the Emperor's token of appreciation.[109] Like any joint venture, the coalition was not free of mishaps. However, when they occurred, as in cases of friendly fire, the Japanese went out of their way to apologize. In one case the Japanese even made a battalion involved in capturing and mistreating a British captain parade before the British and offer them a formal apology.[110]

Why were the relations so good? Why were powers so culturally remote able to work together so smoothly? Perhaps the first answer that comes to mind is that there were many social and cultural similarities between the British and the Japanese. Both peoples came from aristocratic societies that emphasized to a large degree hierarchy and social distance between men. Both had utmost loyalty to their rulers. Militarily the British and the Japanese were both disciplined, professional forces that shared many doctrinal commonalities. As early as 1904, a British naval attaché in Japan complained that the Japanese Navy "is so like our own in almost all respects that there are few salient points to attract attention."[111] British complacency toward the Japanese could also be explained by the fact that the Tsingtau coalition was a very unbalanced one. The disparity in size of the two allies and the high degree of British dependency on the Japanese army made the British a minor power. As such, the British were in no position to offend their Japanese hosts, ignore their cultural sensitivities or raise any obstacles or preconditions. The British War Office indicated clearly to General Bernardiston that his role was plainly to participate in the campaign as a token force and that Britain had no intention to divert more forces from other fronts to China. This compelled the British contingency at Tsingtau to defer to the Japanese and avoid any operational, political and cultural friction with them. But what could explain the Japanese treating the British so favorably even though they were the senior partner? If Japan was indeed such a dominant power in the coalition, then why did it refrain from taking advantage of its weaker ally? What is the explanation for Japanese officers' sensitivity and receptiveness toward their British partners? One should not overlook the fact that such a power sharing arrangement was made possible *only* due to the remarkable British decision to place its troops in the hands of Japanese command. As early as March 1913, the Director of Military Operations in the British War Office had detailed operational plans for an independent capture of Tsingtau without any participation of Japanese soldiers.[112] Had the British wanted, there is no doubt that they could have achieved the same victory alone by diverting more forces from India. Even so, they decided not to go alone but rather fight in a coalition with Japan, letting Japan be the senior partner. This was, in itself, a sign of British recognition of Japan's military capability. But more than that, it was a sign of British acknowledgment of its high regard for Japanese civilization.

To grasp the significance of the British decision to join the coalition as a junior partner, one should look at it in the context of the Edwardian period when the British Empire was still at its zenith. The Anglo-Japanese coalition symbolized more than anything a British change of attitude toward non-Western people. Students of the period are perhaps the first to understand the leap England took since the days of the Raj, when non-white people were viewed as inferior to the British master race. The thought of British soldiers submitting to the command of Asians during such times was inconceivable. But by 1914, this attitude clearly changed. The transformation in cultural attitudes in British society and army was a result of a series of experiences in its colonial endeavors in which British cultural insensitivity had caused instability and at times calamities that rocked the foundations of the empire. The British learned not only to coexist with other cultures but also to appreciate them. The military establishment's attitude toward the Japanese coalition counterpart was derived from the dominant societal views and attitudes toward Japanese culture. Japan held a unique place in the British collective attitude toward non-European cultures. Though they couldn't quite force themselves to equate Japan to European cultures, the British did view the Japanese as culturally superior to other non-white peoples. Unlike the Germans who looked down on their Turkish colleagues, most British soldiers in Tsingtau held the highest admiration for their Japanese counterparts. This admiration was not exclusively due to Japan's military prowess but due to an appreciation and sometimes infatuation with Japan's exotic culture. If Japan had any sense of racial inferiority, it ended when the King of England entrusted his forces in the hands of the Emperor of Japan. Japan's gracious behavior toward the British at Tsingtau was to a large extent an expression of its gratitude for the British show of confidence.

Prior cross-cultural exposure was also a key factor contributing to the ability of the British and the Japanese to understand each other. Their armies and navies were well exposed to alien cultures. Contrary to the German Army, which had very little colonial experience, the Victorian-Edwardian Army was the most experienced army in the world in cross-cultural cooperation. Its units were spread throughout the empire; a large part of its enlisted personnel were indigenous to the colonies; and there was acute awareness to cultural sensitivities of alien cultures derived from lessons learned from past colonial debacles. The Japanese, for their part, were also highly exposed to foreign cultures. Although, their enlisted personnel were racially and culturally homogeneous, they were not foreign to Western customs, language and thought. Most Japanese army and naval officers had first-hand experience in working with European and American counterparts, and a large group of them was trained in European countries or in the U.S. Japanese units participated in joint military exercises, and their doctrine manuals advised them on how to overcome cultural barriers.

The British experience with the Japanese was a harbinger of other instances of successful multiracial and multicultural cooperation during World War I. British soldiers fought alongside 1.4 million Indian troops in Mesopotamia and the Western Front; the African colonies produced 57,000 soldiers and nearly a million porters and laborers for service in the campaign against Germany in East Africa; more than 300,000 Arab soldiers and laborers worked with the British in Arabia and Egypt; and a whole regiment of Jewish soldiers contributed to the war effort in Gallipoli. In all of those cases, cooperation was successful and free of significant cross-cultural problems. This is not to say that the racial prejudice which largely characterized the British ceased to exist. It was still very much alive, but along with it emerged a growing appreciation for the virtues of the non-European soldier. The abhorred Indian sepoy of the 19th century was suddenly viewed as "a first class soldier and nature's gentleman."[113] Other allies received similar compliments. But high above all the others stood the soldier of the sun, courageous, robust and wrapped in the allure of an ancient warrior culture.

Japan emerged from the war as the strongest power on the Asian side of the Pacific. It was more than anything the Battle of Tsingtau that significantly enhanced Japan's sense of military superiority over the Europeans. After defeating the Russians in 1905, witnessing the poor defense of Tsingtau by the Germans, and seeing a sample of British military endeavors, Japan perceived itself capable of prevailing over any one of them, if not perhaps to all three combined. One could only speculate on the extent to which this mindset contributed to the emergence of subsequent Japanese aggressive policies in the inter-war period. But in 1918, only few people were able to see through Japan's imperial aspirations. For the British soldiers who fought alongside the Japanese at Tsingtau, this reality was much clearer. American military personnel arriving at the scene of the battle shortly after the German defeat questioned their British colleagues about the nature of their Japanese ally. They received a chilling and prophetic assessment that Japan's masterful attack and siege of Tsingtau is but an example of the ultimate fate of Manila.[114]

4

GI's IN THE LAND OF THE MANDARIN: U.S. MILITARY MISSION IN CHINA 1941-1945

⌘ ⌘ ⌘

We knew how to handle horses and machines, but not {other} humans.
John P. Davies to General Stilwell, March 1943[1]

When I first went to China I think I imagined in my short stay that I would gradually change the simple Chinese. I used to rant and rave about this and that, and try to show the house-boys better and more efficient ways to do things. But they never changed, and finally I realized that they were changing me.
Colonel Robert L. Scott [2]

Shortly after the Japanese attack on Pearl Harbor, a public opinion poll in the U.S. revealed that approximately sixty percent of Americans could not locate China on a world map.[3] Despite that, Americans in 1942 had very solid opinions of the 400 million people of the land about whom they knew so little. They viewed them as a faceless mass of polite, stoic, submissive, inert, at times cruel people who were very difficult to understand. Their prejudices about the Chinese were formed mainly through superficial relations with members of the Chinese-American community rather than through an intimate knowledge of the indigenous population of the Chinese mainland.[4] The Americans that *did* get a feel for the real China were those who served in the forbidding China-Burma-India (CBI) Theater in 1941-45. Of the 16 million Americans in uniform during World War II, only a quarter of a million passed through CBI. Sixty thousand of them served in China itself. They were observers, advisors, instructors, Lend-Lease administrators, and other members of General Joseph Stilwell's Military Mission. There were the air and ground crews of Clair Chennault's American Volunteer Group, later the Fourteenth Air Force, which performed the biggest airlift of the war over the portion of the Himalayas called the Hump. There were also the 3,000 infantrymen known as Merrill's Marauders, who collaborated with the Chinese to recover northern Burma and allow the construction of the Ledo Road, which linked India to the old Burma Road. Finally, there were the members of the Office of Strategic Services (OSS), the predecessor of the CIA, and even the U.S. Navy officers who opened training camps for Chinese guerrillas, spies and saboteurs. Their goals were to prevent the Japanese steamroller from reaching the Indian frontier, to open China's only outlet to the world, the Burma Road, and to weld the demoralized Chinese forces into an effective fighting force capable of driving the Japanese out of China.

Many writers describing Sino-American relations in the Chinese theater chose to personalize the nations' difficult relations by focusing on the feud between General Stilwell and China's leader, Generalissimo Chiang Kai-shek, a feud that finally brought about the former's recall in October 1944.[5] There was, however, much more to U.S.-Chinese relations than the Stilwell Crisis. This was a historical encounter between two very different civil and military cultures that were called upon to work together for a common goal. It was also the U.S.' first major coalition experience with non-Western partners. The CBI Theater was a cultural mosaic of national and cultural groups. There were fighting forces from Britain, India and Africa as well as many local Burmese tribesmen - Nagas, Karens, Shans, Kachins, and others. But for the U.S. the most challenging partners were the Chinese. True, years of American deployment in Hawaii and the Philippines exposed U.S. troops to Asian cultures. China, though, was an entirely different world. Unlike the primarily Catholic Filipinos, exposed to Western civilization over centuries, the Chinese, a product of Confucian ideology and Buddhist religion, were far more insular. Their language, customs, traditions, ethics, and family values were like nothing the

Americans had ever witnessed. A stark cultural gap was caused by diametrically opposed attitudes on issues like the value of life, time, accuracy and authority. This culture gap stood at the core of almost every operational, logistical and organizational decision taken during the four-year Sino-American coalition, the most burdened, tense and racially charged coalition in which the U.S. has ever taken part.

From a very early stage in the war it was clear that the CBI Theater would be the stepchild of America's overall war effort. Europe, the Pacific and North Africa were theaters of far greater strategic importance. That said, the situation in China was perhaps the gravest of all. By 1941, China's strategic posture was abysmal. It was economically ruined; some thirty percent of its territory was occupied by the Japanese; its access to the South China Sea was blocked, as were the land routes connecting it to its neighbors. With the Japanese occupation of Burma, China's last outlet to the world, the Burma Road, was closed. Chiang Kai-shek's government fled from the capital, Nanking, up the Yangtze River to Chungking in Szechuan Province. Nature's punishment - famine, floods and disease - ravaged what the Japanese missed. To make things worse, China had also been engaged since the early 1930's in a civil war with the Chinese Communists under Mao Tse-tung. The Japanese invasion in 1937 forced Chiang to mobilize his country's resources to fight both the challenge from within and that from outside. On both fronts China paid a very high price in blood and treasure.

America's entry into the war in December 1941 inspired a great deal of hope among the Chinese. Many of them saw Pearl Harbor Day in America as Armistice Day in China.[6] Whereas the U.S. was embarking on a massive war to defeat the Japanese in the Philippines, the exhausted Chinese, unaware that their struggle was only beginning, were already preoccupied with the domestic order of the post-war era. For a country besieged and occupied by an aggressor that had committed some of the worst atrocities in history, the Chinese showed remarkable lack of enthusiasm to fight the Japanese. It was as if they thought: "time is on our side, let the Americans and the British win the war. We have already done our share of the fighting."[7] Forcing the Chinese to fight was one of the

U.S.' main challenges. China was interested in fighting a cheap war, and many of its officers believed they could win the war without fighting it at all.[8] Military analysts in the West attributed Chinese battle aversion to their pacifist culture and lack of military tradition. "The character of the Chinese people is such that they could never become militaristic. [...] They are essentially a peace loving people," wrote one.[9] Others saw their pacifism as mere cowardice.

Fearing the loss of China to the Japanese, the U.S. embarked on a massive campaign to assist the Chinese. It made clear, however, that it would not fight the war for them. Just like the arrangement with the British prior to Pearl Harbor, the U.S. provided the tools, and the Chinese were expected to do the work. The U.S. opened its arsenals to the Chinese and supplied them with Lend-Lease military articles. A military mission headed by Brig. General John Magruder arrived in China in October 1941 to facilitate the transfer of military aid. "Money no object," wrote Stilwell about assistance to China three months later, when he assumed the role of senior U.S. commander there.[10] For the Chinese, Uncle Sam's money was also no object, and for this reason they made extravagant demands for military articles they could not even use, showing utmost disregard for the monumental logistical problems involved in flying tens-of-thousands of tons of equipment over the Hump. American generosity was not received with Chinese gratitude. On the contrary, the Chinese were full of grievances about the slow inflow of military aid and about the fact that the Americans did not allow them to decide on the content of military articles supplied whereas the British had such a prerogative.

The war itself was much more than China could handle, for its military capability in 1941 was close to nil. The Chinese Army may have been strong in number but it was hollow by any military yardstick. It was a tired, neglected army with no leadership; poorly trained, poorly equipped, badly organized, and worst of all, despised by the people. In fact, it was not so much an army as a cluster of feudalistic military forces loosely bound by personal loyalties under the leadership of Chiang Kai-shek.[11]

Accustomed to a strict, highly organized military organization where the soldier was the most valued asset, U.S. soldiers deployed

in the theater were shocked by the deplorable conditions in which
the Chinese soldier lived. The well-fed, well-clothed, well-equipped
and well-trained GI discovered a partner who was none of the above.
In November 1941, members of the mission conducted an inspection tour in Chinese units. One of the visitors reported:

> The officer personnel [...] is poor. How poor is difficult to
> visualize without seeing. In the battery specially selected
> for our inspection at Laolokow the battery commander was
> not of a very high intelligence. He was barefooted except
> for sandals. It would probably be very difficult to teach
> modern artillery methods to men of this type.[12]

It was a well-grounded observation. By and large, Chinese military commanders were corrupt, insensitive to the needs of their
troops, and hardly interested in fighting the Japanese. "Division
and Army commanders are a great problem," wrote Stilwell in a
report to Chiang in May 1942:

> Very few of them are efficient. They seldom get up to the
> front and they very rarely supervise the execution of their
> orders. Reports from the front are accepted without check,
> and very often prove exaggerated or entirely false. The vital
> necessity of continuous reconnaissance and security is com-
> monly ignored, often with fatal consequences. The aver-
> age division commander seems to feel that issuing an order
> from a point sometimes 50 miles from the front is all that is
> required of him. Many of these officers are personally brave,
> but most of them lack moral courage. [...] Without clear-
> ing out the inefficient, the Army will continue to go down
> hill, no matter how much materiel is supplied for it.[13]

The other great problem of the Chinese Army was malnutrition. Chinese troops were so starved that they sometimes stole
pets from the Americans and ate them.[14] Most of the soldiers suffered from vitamin deficiency diseases, and the almost nonexistent
medical care was primitive. Americans who complained about the

lethargy and laziness of the Chinese soldiers who they were supposed to train, realized that one of the reasons for malnutrition was that the commanders were never held responsible for their soldiers' welfare.[15] After great efforts were made to feed and medically treat the soldiers, they became fit for training. Plans to train Chinese troops included two groups of 30 divisions each. This ambitious plan never fully materialized. The tens-of-thousands of Chinese that did receive American training during war were divided into three groups. One group consisted of the divisions being trained in India, separately referred to as X-Force. The Americans established a training camp in Ramgarh, in the Bihar province, where more than 53,000 Chinese officers and soldiers, most of them flown in from China, were trained between August 1942 and October 1944.[16] The second group, termed Y-Force, was organized in Yunnan Province in southwest China where a field artillery training center was established. The third group, called Z-Force, was assembled and trained in an infantry-training center near Kweilin in Eastern China.

Lt. General Lo Cho ying and General Stilwell inspect
Chinese troops in Ramgarh

American personnel acted as instructors, liaison officers and military advisors operating closely with the Chinese. By 1944, some 4,000 American liaison officers were assisting the headquarters of four Chinese army groups, 12 armies and 36 divisions. They worked in small teams of four or five men commanded by an officer and spread between Chinese regiments and divisional headquarters. Each team had a Chinese interpreter. Though they were forced to live and share the miserable conditions as the Chinese Army, most of them were not fond of their students. "The one abiding sentiment that almost all American enlisted personnel and most of the officers shared was contempt and dislike for China," observed American reporters.[17] This antipathy between the Chinese and the Americans pervaded not only the junior levels of command but, as described later, also characterized the relations between American and Chinese generals at the most senior level. The Chinese felt that the Americans were not treating them as equal partners, such as U.S. refusal to admit Chinese representatives into the Combined Chiefs of Staff conferences. They were right. The Chinese military mission to Washington, headed by General Hsiung, was ignored by the Pacific War Council after which its insulted members decided to head home.[18] When Chiang shared his frustrations about America's discriminatory treatment with Mahatma Gandhi, the latter flatly declared that "the West will never voluntarily treat us Orientals as equals."[19]

In late June 1942, the first major crisis occurred between the U.S. and Chiang when American air units were withdrawn from the CBI Theater to assist the fighting in the Mediterranean. Chiang laid down his famous Three Demands: dispatch of three American divisions in Burma, 500 new planes, and increased quantities of airborne supplies over the Hump. If China's demands were not addressed, a defection from the alliance would be seriously considered. The U.S. flatly rejected Chiang's demands and laid down demands of its own. Ultimately, cool heads prevailed and the alliance survived.

The most important American goal was to see the Chinese do what they had been trained and equipped to do: fight the Japanese. The essence of Stilwell's strategy in 1943 and 1944 was a combined, two-pronged attack on Japanese-held Burma. Stilwell saw the Chinese army in India as the spearhead of the Chinese offensive across northern Burma which would open the line of communication into China. This effort should have been supplemented by another attack from Yunnan, carried out exclusively by Chinese units. But the Chinese were reluctant to fight.

By the beginning of 1944, as the British were facing a strong Japanese threat to their lines of communication to China, President Roosevelt became impatient with what he saw as Chiang's procrastination and incompetence. He demanded immediate action by the Chinese or else Lend-Lease shipments to China would be suspended.[20] But the Generalissimo refused to send his 71st Army Group against the Japanese 56th Division, deployed west of the Salween River. The official excuse was that China was too weak. A Chinese attack was conditioned on an additional American loan of one billion dollars. If not paid, Chiang stunned the Americans, the U.S. would have to pay all expenses incurred by its army in China. Chiang's outrageous conditions brought the U.S. and China to the lowest point in their relations, and a series of discussions took place in Washington as to whether to continue the relations with the Nationalists or not. The crisis over the Salween Campaign was finally resolved due to the back channel intervention of low level officials who quietly resumed cooperation in such a way that neither side lost face.[21] The American flirtation with the Chinese Communists in North China also harmed relations with Chungking. Believing that China's disunity hindered its capacity to win the war, the U.S. tried to force Chiang into an agreement with the Communists. But for Chiang, the presence of Americans in the north was a destabilizing factor and a challenge to his authority as the undisputed leader of Nationalist China. He was hyper sensitive to any challenge to his authority, but American observers soon leaned that his obsession with power was a result of inherent weakness. Stilwell's political advisor John P. Davis who proposed the cultivation of relations with an alternative Chinese leadership in the north argued that "The Generalissimo is probably the only Chinese who shares the popular American misconception that Chiang Kai-shek is China."[22]

By the spring of 1944 the Japanese had launched their massive attack through Hankow toward Chungking and the Hump airbases. A Chinese army of 300,000 evaporated and with it Stilwell's position and prestige. His recall in October 1944, and the appointment of General Albert Coady Wedemeyer as commander of the China Theater marked a positive turn in Sino-American relations. Wedemeyer was more tactful and friendlier than Stilwell. His personality was disarming, and he knew how to make his advice palatable, creating more positive relations with Chiang. Furthermore, American investment in the Chinese Army began to bear fruit. By early 1944, at least 30,000 Americans arrived in China, and by the end of the year the U.S. began transferring well-trained, well-equipped Chinese troops back into China. These units showed some impressive achievements against the Japanese. The stock of the Chinese soldier began to rise in the eyes of many American officers. But this was too late and too little. The positive turn hardly offset months of exasperation U.S. commanders had endured in China. Wedemeyer himself, despite improved rapport with Chiang, was highly critical of Chinese manners. He saw them as "apathetic and unintelligent." The Generalissimo and his staff were "impotent and confounded."

> Psychologically they are not prepared to cope with the situation because of political intrigue, false pride, and mistrust of leaders' honesty and motives. [...] Frankly, I think that the Chinese officials surrounding the Generalissimo are actually afraid to report accurately conditions for two reasons, their stupidity and inefficiency revealed, and further the Generalissimo might order them to take positive action and they are incompetent to issue directives, make plans, and fail completely in obtaining execution by field commanders.[23]

The strategic and technological incompatibility between the Americans and their Chinese counterparts was stark and produced a coalition that suffered from almost every possible handicap: divergence of war aims, poor logistic coordination, lack of trust, and operational disagreements. All this was topped by intense personal hatred between the American and Chinese commanders. This hatred led to a point in which an assassination attempt against Chiang was seriously considered. Stilwell's trusted deputy Frank Dorn provided a detailed description of an order to devise an assassination plan that came from the "very top" of the U.S. administration during the Cairo conference. The plan was to cause a mechanical malfunction in the Generalissimo's plane as it flew over the Hump and force him and his entourage to abandon the plane. Chiang's parachute would be sabotaged so it would not open. With such relations, the ground was ripe for cultural gaps between the Allies to only make things worse.[24]

American attitudes toward the Chinese

In August 1942, while American marines were throwing themselves on the beaches of Guadalcanal, President Franklin D. Roosevelt was presented with the findings of a project he had commissioned to find the effects of racial crossing in order to improve and tame the Japanese race. "The President's thought is that an Indo-Asian or Euroasian or better Euro-Indi-Asian race could be developed which would be good and produce a good civilization and Far East order," reported one of the people involved in the project.[25] American society during World War II, from the President downward, had very little compunction about dealing publicly with racial issues, as was the academic study of eugenics. The U.S. was still a racially segregated country, where ideas of white supremacy and racial hierarchy were widely espoused and openly discussed. In addition, it was a society fighting a fierce war with Japan, a war at least as much about racial supremacy as political rivalry.[26]

The history of the Chinese people in the U.S. is paved with shameful episodes of anti-Oriental race hatred, discrimination, abuse and ill treatment on both popular and institutional levels. In the 1890s, cultural icons such as Robert Lewis Stevenson offered a gloomy picture of American hatred and ill treatment of the "despised race" of China.[27] His observation was correct. Missionaries and travelers in the 19th century conveyed a very negative view of the Chinese. They described them as dirty, immoral, dishonest, repulsive, and ignorant. A.T. Mahan, one of the intellectual leaders of the Yellow Peril movement in America, referred to them as pitifully inert and dangerously barbaric. American 'China experts' such as Arthur Smith, Rodney Gilbert, and Carl Crow published books portraying the Chinese national character in unfavorable terms and describing the Chinese as children who needed to be disciplined.[28] On Capitol Hill, the Chinese community was also under attack. It was the perpetual target for a series of discriminatory anti-immigration laws passed in the Congress from 1880 into the 1920s. By the beginning of the 20th century, Chinese in the U.S. were derogatorily referred to as "coolies" and "chinks" who lived in ghettoes. Americans saw Chinese as villains in popular movies; offensive cartoons in American popular magazines portrayed the Chinese as ugly, pig-tailed, robe-wearing creatures; college students surveyed in the 1930s saw the Chinese as uncivilized, peculiar and treacherous people; American children grew to believe that the Chinese were rat eaters.[29] In the racial hierarchy most Americans believed in, the Orientals were ranked midway with the Latinos above the Indians and the blacks. These racial stereotypes about Asians not only affected communal relations but also burdened the U.S.' foreign relations with China.[30]

The 1920s brought about a positive change in American attitudes toward the Chinese. Harold Isaacs viewed this change as a shift from "the age of contempt" to "the age of benevolence."[31] Side by side with the general dislike of the Chinese, there was a growing trend of Sinophilia, and a search for the beauty and the promise of China's ancient and great culture. Some American cultural figures began to present the Chinese as a people of great promise who could, if only helped, shake off a stagnant cultural tradition. Charlie Chan, a cultural icon created in the 1920s by Earl Derr Biggers was a Hawaiian-based Chinese detective with outstanding characteristics who became the most significant Chinese character in American fiction. Charlie Chan books and films had a positive influence on the image of the Chinese in the U.S.[32] Pearl Buck, author of *The Good Earth,* who was awarded the Noble Prize for literature in 1938, helped popularize China's culture for millions of Americans, creating a tide of respect for the long-suffering people of China. Instead of the image of the Chinese as dangerous, cunning, and brutal, emerged a new, positive image of a Chinese character that was wise, human, trustworthy, cheerful, humorous and industrious. The Japanese invasion of China in 1937 helped boost support for China, and growing parts of the American public expressed admiration and overwhelming sympathy for the gallant resistance of the Chinese people against the Japanese.[33] Similar to the mixed sentiment the British had toward the Japanese prior to World War I, the American public had love-hate relations with China, relations of pity and disdain, contempt and infatuation, fear and admiration. As in the British case, the sentiments held by society in general were also espoused by the U.S. military as its commitments in China broadened.

The U.S. military in China

U.S. military presence in China began in the aftermath of the Boxer Rebellion out of a need to secure the lives of the growing number of Americans residing there. Over the years, a garrison of approximately 1,000 troops was deployed in Tientsin, Peking, Shanghai and other parts of northern China.[34] In 1927, after a wave of attacks by unruly Nationalist troops against foreign citizens, the U.S. deployed in Shanghai an additional force of 1,500 Marines.[35] The garrison in China soon became the most attractive station the U.S. Army could offer in the thirties.[36] For the officers and soldiers serving in the 15th Infantry Regiment in China until 1938, life was characterized by a stress-free environment, parties, shopping, drinking and lots of sport.[37] Even the aloof Lieutenant Colonel George C. Marshall, who served three years in China, learned to indulge in the amenities life in China offered, admitting it was "one very delightful period."[38] U.S. personnel in China had little interaction with the indigenous population. Most of the Chinese with whom Americans came in touch were manual laborers and servants. American officers enjoyed the personal services of the Chinese staff, which took care of their daily needs and those of their families. It was not rare to see Chinese coolies coming onto the drill field during inspections to dust off their master's shoes.[39] Americans stationed in China viewed the Chinese as subhuman, an inferior race with which they preferred not to mix. It was not rare to see American clubs and other gathering places with signs in Chinese and English: "Chinese and dogs not allowed."[40] It was no surprise then, that from the very beginning of the American deployment in China in World War II, GIs had little respect for the Chinese. They looked down on them and were nauseated by the horrible living conditions and filth of the people with whom they had to work.[41] They referred to them as 'chinks' and when use of the derogatory term was prohibited by the military, as "slope headed-bastards" or, in short, "slopies."[42] In many cases American servicemen used physical force and abused the Chinese until American headquarters were forced to issue an order prohibiting U.S. personnel from beating, kicking, or maltreating Chinese personnel under any circumstances.[43] A survey of American servicemen in China showed almost all of them harbored personal distaste and bitterness, if not hatred, toward the Chinese. Such attitudes toward the Chinese were explained by the fact that the American GI was exposed mainly to the lower class and "little can be done to change the feeling."[44] It was also said that the hostility was due to the Americans' frustrations with serving on a far from home front and dealing with an ungrateful ally. The problem was not only at the GI level; there are very few good words about the Chinese in the memoirs of the generals who served in CBI. Vice Admiral Milton Miles who trained Chinese guerrillas during the war claimed that *all* senior American commanders in China, including alleged Sinophiles like Stilwell, Magruder and Dorn, "commonly and outspokenly rated themselves superior to *all* Chinese," and that the colonels and other officers in the intermediate level took their guidance from their superiors.[45]

Chinese attitudes toward Americans

China's relations with the outside world have always been complicated and, yet, fascinating. For most of its history, China was cut off from Western influence. "White men have gone to China with three motives: to fight, to make money and to convert the Chinese to our religion," said British philosopher Bertrand Russell to a Chinese audience in Nanking, telling them what they had already known.[46] This did not leave much to be liked about the West. And indeed, before 1898, China had very little desire to interact with the outside world. There was not even a foreign ministry, because relations with foreign countries were deemed unnecessary. Besides harboring fear of Western exploitation, China was hostile to the West due to its own views about race, this xenophobia rooted in its history. China was the Middle Kingdom, a civilization engulfed by barbarians who constantly tried to assault it and destroy its culture. Western attempts to subjugate and humiliate the Chinese, as during the Opium Wars and the Boxer Rebellion, only reinforced feelings of contempt toward foreigners. Like the Americans, the Chinese also believed in racial hierarchy. Whereas the Americans ranked the yellow people somewhere between whites and blacks, the Chinese viewed themselves as racially superior to both. Chinese literature contains many references to the racial superiority of its people. They viewed their physical features, such as little body hair and lightly pigmented skin as evidence of their superiority vis-à-vis the neighboring races, which were hairy and either dark or white skinned.[47] It was also a widely held view that by virtue of their long history and the achievements of their ancient civilization, they were far better equipped to work around the problems of the world than was the emerging civilization of the West. Toward the U.S., the Chinese had a specific grievance. They were highly resentful of the discriminatory manner in which Chinese immigrants in the U.S were treated and that even though China was an ally, American anti-Chinese immigration laws were not repealed. One witness in a congressional hearing warned that the resentment in China about anti-Chinese legislation was worth twenty divisions to the Japanese Army.[48] The Chinese who lived on the West Coast of the U.S. harbored similar sentiments toward the Americans. An FBI report in December 1942 on Chinese activities in San Francisco revealed that approximately fifty percent of the Chinese community in the U.S. actually felt hatred and contempt toward Americans. The report, based on discussions with Chinese informers, also revealed that despite their suffering under the Japanese, most Chinese preferred

Japanese rule in China over intrusion by Western nations. They felt a war to achieve supremacy in the Pacific between the Oriental people under the leadership of China and the West under U.S. leadership was inevitable.[49]

The race card quickly played into the hands of the Japanese who understood the Chinese mindset better than the Westerners. From the outset of the war in the Pacific, Japanese propaganda, designed to impress upon the Chinese that Japan was fighting the Western nations only and had no hostile feelings toward China, exploited the racial and cultural issue in an attempt to turn the war into a clash between white and Asian civilizations.[50] Indeed, talk about a global union of the darker race was a popular topic in the West, and many saw the main reason for keeping China in the war as a way to prevent such a scenario from materializing. Caught between racial and strategic expediencies, the Chinese government did not play down Japanese attempts to provoke anti-Americanism. Just like the resentment in the Muslim world 60 years later toward U.S. President George W. Bush's miserable choice of the word "crusade" to describe the war against terrorism, the Chinese were enraged by the use of crusading terms by British Foreign Secretary Lord Halifax when he portrayed the Allies' endeavor in Asia as a struggle to save Christian civilization. Both the Chinese and the Americans knew very well that their alliance was insurance against a great race war between the whites and the Asians.[51] Ultimately, just as the German-Ottoman attempt to create pan-Islamic solidarity against the Entente powers failed, so did the Japanese attempt to lure the Chinese into buying the pan-Asiatic idea. After five years of atrocious Japanese behavior on their soil, the Chinese could see through Japan's bid for racial solidarity and preferred to focus on rebuilding their scourged land.

The arrival of U.S. soldiers in China during World War II evoked mixed feelings among the Chinese.[52] On the one hand, they had an appreciation for the Americans who fought for their freedom. They admired the heroism of the "Flying Tigers" and the GIs who supplied China with essential food and ammunition and trained the army for its missions. On the other hand, many Chinese saw the Americans as an unwelcome element. Chinese who came in contact with American troops thought of them as noisy, stupid and impolite. "Our reputation," concluded a report from the U.S. Embassy in Chungking, "is not good."[53] According to the report, most Chinese, knowing very little about the Americans, suffered from a "tinge of anti-foreignism."[54] American intelligence agents, diplomats and travelers also reported a strong undercurrent of dislike and suspicion of Americans. Americans walking down the street often heard derisive shouts directed at them, the favorite of which meant barbarian dogs.[55] In his visit in China in November 1944, U.S. Representative Michael J. Mansfield was surprised to witness scenes of Chinese throwing rocks and tomatoes at the Americans.[56] Intrinsic Chinese dislike for foreigners was exacerbated by rumors of American misconduct. In April 1944, reports of American troops misbehaving in Kweilin, Kunming and Chengtu began to arrive at the U.S. Embassy in China. The second secretary warned that the people of Chengtu were "shocked by the increasing rowdiness of American troops on leave in the city." It was also noted that rumors of American drunkenness and wild behavior, plus reports of large numbers of American troops arriving in these areas, angered the local population.[57] In some cases, American presence was used as a target to deflect popular animosity toward the regime. Graham Peck, for example, described how Chinese Air Force officers spread nasty rumors about U.S. planes deliberately bombing Chinese peasants. These rumors were ludicrous, but once spread, they were difficult to disprove.[58] It seemed the only people the Chinese disliked more than Americans in general were African-Americans. Black-skinned people were very rare in China, and for some reason many of the Chinese feared and resented them.[59] Thus, the introduction of African-American troops to China presented the Americans with an unexpected problem. From the outset of the deployment, the Chinese government refused to allow the free movement of black U.S. troops in China. In fact, they hesitated to admit them into the country at all. This created a problem, since many American servicemen in India, especially logistic support staff, were African-Americans. They were badly needed.[60] After debates and persuasion, Chiang Kai-shek permitted the entrance of these soldiers into China but only as far as the Hump terminals in Kunming. Only in early 1945 was Chiang ready to let black troops east of Kunming in on condition they be admitted to China in small numbers.[61] What Chiang's reason was for discriminating against black soldiers remains an open question. The official excuse was that it was hard enough for Chinese to deal with the influx of whites, and he, therefore, did not want to add more excitement by allowing the presence of blacks.

Besides their views on race, the Chinese attitude toward Americans had a sexual dimension. Many Americans deployed to China arrived with the preconceived notion that Chinese women were sexually loose and racially inferior and thus fair prey. This created a feeling among the hosts that they were subject to some form of sexual imperialism, that their women were defiled, their honor tarnished and their much cherished system of family values was under attack. Personal accounts of Americans in China at the time reveal sex was very much an issue between the two peoples. Oliver Caldwell, an OSS operative in China during the war, went even as far as claiming sex to be "the chief source of difficulty between American and Chinese."[62] The root of the problem was that most American soldiers did not understand that the free and easy relations between men and women in the U.S. were not socially acceptable in other cultures. They also failed to understand the explosiveness of publicly humiliating, sometimes in the presence of their husbands and fathers, upper-class Chinese women by making salacious proposition to them. Reports about U.S. troops' misbehavior enhanced by Japanese propaganda emphasizing the dangers of American intercourse with Asian women severely damaged the relations between Americans and the local population in places like Chengtu. This was one of the places the U.S. planned to build airfields, and the prospect of an influx of Americans into the region dismayed the Chinese, generating strong opposition to the project.[63] Prostitution has always been a widely accepted practice in China. American soldiers deployed in China prior to the war took advantage of the pleasures the country offered. Marshall's characterization of China as a place of "cheap liqueur and cheaper women" appealed to many of the GI's who viewed it as the "Paris of the Orient".[64] Consequently, the 15th Infantry Regiment in China for years led the U.S. Army's venereal disease rate.[65] The Chinese easily differentiated between "good women" and "bad women." Americans could not, or perhaps did not want to, distinguish between prostitutes and decent women. Part of the problem had to do with the stereotype of the Chinese females in the U.S. in pre-war years. Until 1930, immigration laws allowed in only 150 Chinese women a year. One result of the lack of Chinese females was that the great majority of them were forced to work as prostitutes.[66] In the 1930's the situation improved considerably, but the image of the Chinese woman as a cheap sexual commodity in the eyes of many Americans was already deeply embedded. Armed with this stereotype brought from home, many Americans came to China with the impression that most Chinese women were sexually receptive. In many cases they made sexual advances and insulted respectable women, forging unnecessary enemies among the local population. The sexually driven tension in Sino-American relations was exploited by some of the opposition forces struggling to destroy the alliance with the U.S. They launched an anti-American propaganda campaign directed toward Chinese women who were warned against American men who allegedly had "certain horrifying biological peculiarities that made them different from other men."[67]

As the number of American soldiers in China grew, so did popular sentiment against them. In early 1945, Chinese government-controlled press opened a campaign against those Chinese women who 'misbehaved' with Americans. Relations between Chinese women and American personnel became a social taboo, and in many cases Americans walking with Chinese girls were threatened and stoned.[68] The behavior viewed by the Chinese as proof of "the Ugly American" did not help establish friendly relations with the Chinese population. Though the pleasure seeking GI's wore out their welcome, luckily, the relatively small number of U.S. personnel overall in China prevented the problem from bearing on operational implications. The U.S. military failed to address the sexual aspect of host-guest relations, and many of the problems described above repeated themselves in greater intensity once U.S. forces in much greater numbers were deployed in other Asian countries such as Japan, South Korea and Vietnam.

Communication and perceptual problems

To fulfill the role of a military advisory mission, the advisor must be able to communicate his knowledge and ideas to the trainee. But the fact that so few Americans spoke Chinese and so few Chinese spoke English made the task of both the advisors and their trainees much more difficult. Chinese is a complex, rich language which takes years to master. One of the implications of American foreign policy in Asia, keeping the "Open Door" to China open, was the need to maintain a constant number of personnel with linguistic skills ready for a time the U.S. would have to deploy its forces in the region. Since 1919, the U.S. Army had run a Chinese Language Officer Program to qualify Chinese speakers.[69] American officers, among them captain Joseph Stilwell, studied at the North China Union Language School in a three to four year program where they gained a solid command of Mandarin.[70] After graduating, many of these officers were stationed at the American Legation in Nangking or in the War Department, translating dispatches and Chinese requests for aid.[71] In addition, from 1924 to 1938, U.S. personnel serving in the 15th Infantry Regiment in China were required to study the vernacular. As a result, American officers and servicemen picked up many Chinese words, and some even became fluent. They were the only foreign officers in China who could make themselves understood.[72]

When the war started, it quickly became apparent that almost none of the Chinese generals had knowledge of English and that the cadre of U.S. language officers was not sufficient to provide advisory services at the low levels of command. There was therefore an urgent need for Chinese interpreters. Despite the Chinese commitment to furnish all units working with American advisors with a sufficient number of interpreters, there was always a shortage, creating a major source of trouble in Chinese divisions.[73] Besides the shortage, not all interpreters were effective in their jobs. The official language of China, spoken in Peking and in the provinces north of the Yangtze, was Mandarin. There were many other dialects, the most important of which was Cantonese. One of the main problems with the interpreters was that though they came from all parts of China, they were mostly from the central and the southern provinces. In many cases, they were not fluent in Mandarin and had difficulty making themselves understood due to differences in dialect.[74] Some senior American officers had their own American interpreters, who understood only Mandarin. Most Chinese generals could speak the Chiangshan dialect, a little known language used in the district where Chiang grew up. When they wanted to conceal information from the Americans, they could converse freely in their presence without being understood by the American interpreters.[75] In 1944, it was apparent that the growing number of American advisors was leading to a growing need for interpreters. The problem was addressed by the establishment of a special section for interpreter affairs under the headquarters of the China Theater. It was not easy to attract young, educated English-speaking Chinese to serve in the military. To encourage them, the U.S. offered incentives such as ranks, high pay, and fellowships for overseas studies after the war. In 1945, there were more than 2,000 Foreign Affairs Bureau interpreting officers on duty in the China Theater.

A Chinese phrase book used by U.S. military personnel in China

The role of the interpreters was crucial. Without them the only alternative was an improvised sign language. In addition to translating language they were a cultural bridge between the Americans and their Chinese trainees. Their role was not only to translate but also to intentionally misinterpret and retouch common uncomplimentary remarks. Interpretation of orders was a particular source of problems, involving not only the literal meaning of the message but also its spirit. Like other languages, Chinese reflected China's culture and social structure, manifesting the long history of authoritarianism as a way of life. As a result, one spoke to a subordinate differently than to his superior. Saying "No" to a superior was almost a taboo; therefore questions had to be framed in such a way as to circumvent the problem. Americans also had to learn to reinforce their sentences with parallel phrases so that at least one clause of the sentence would be understood.[76] Indispensable as the interpreters were, they were also the Chinese soldiers most difficult to get along with. They were, as one American general testified, "a constant source of trouble."[77] One of the sources of difficulty in dealing with the interpreters was the ranks that colleagues believed they were undeservedly awarded. They were young and inexperienced but crucial to the functioning of the coalition. They knew it and, often their status went into their heads. At one point, in Ramgarh, they even mutinied and the American commander in charge threatened to execute them.[78]

As far as communication itself, in many cases, Chinese and English versions of directives had different meanings. Chinese documents were translated into English and then back into Chinese but with a different interpreter. The results were surprisingly unintelligible.[79] But altogether, considering the number of soldiers involved, the proliferation of dialects, the cultural barriers and, in some cases, the lack of prior knowledge of each other's language, the Sino-American cooperation is an example of a success in bridging over what could have been a major impediment to fruitful cooperation. Even when not literally understood, American advisors taught by example, and their students excelled in imitation. "Thank God we don't speak Chinese and we don't have interpreters. We demonstrate and they copy. They are the greatest mimics in the world," reflected one American instructor in Ramgarh.[80]

Time perception

It is no coincidence that the two most popular works published before the war about the Chinese national character dedicated an entire chapter to their indifference to time.[81] China's rugged topography, lack of adequate means of internal communication and slow bureaucracy all contributed to the formation of a society which beat to a different rhythm than that of America, where time was treated as an asset to be managed, saved or wasted. The Chinese had their own unique sense of time and an unparalleled patience. They saw "no more reason to boast about the accuracy of a watch than of a thermometer," observed Carl Crow.[82] A popular Chinese proverb said: if you continuously grind a bar of iron, you can make a needle of it, reflecting the belief among Chinese that patience and perseverance were very important virtues. Obliviousness to punctuality and timetables was so common that it was immediately felt by every foreigner that had to work with the Chinese. American officers and servicemen were trained to follow strict timetables and schedules. They became easily frustrated when things did not happen at the time they expected them to happen. Claire Chennault wrote that he had frequent clashes with Chiang and other Chinese officials due to his impatience contrasted with their loose sense of time. "They could think in terms of decades and dynasties when days and weeks seemed so vital to me."[83] Chinese commanders who carried out American plans failed to appreciate the importance of complying with the time frames allocated. Their indifference to time was a cause for waste and inefficiency in the view of the Americans. In the end, the Chinese rhythm was contagious. The Americans quickly learned to understand the Chinese attitude toward time and became more lenient in their planning. Many of them adapted to the Chinese slowness. "If you are a Westerner in a desperate hurry to get somewhere to do some important work, Chinese time is infuriating but its powers of influence are very strong. After a while you begin to wonder whether your work is quite so important after all and why you are in such a hurry," wrote one of them.[84]

Squeeze and watermelons

One of the principle ideas of Confucianism, China's philosophical foundation, is the elevation of the family unit above all other social structures.[85] Family bonds were the central fiber of Chinese society and economy, a phenomenon that resulted in the neglect of all other non-familial institutions. Chinese first loyalty was to the family, not to the state; the Chinese lacked patriotism and showed little willingness to make sacrifices for the state. Over generations, this trend had worsened. Families grew bigger and along with them grew the responsibility and the commitment to provide for the welfare of their members. In periods of adversity, Chinese families would close ranks; then, anything that served the benefit of the family was justified. The inevitable outcome was a declining level of reciprocity among unrelated people. This, in turn, brought to a decline in public morality and a deep-rooted corruption and nepotism infecting every stratum of Chinese society.[86] "The Chinese peasant produces two things," wrote Theodore White in *Life* magazine in 1944, "He produces food and he produces sons. [He is] the raw material of war in China [...] There is corruption in the collection of his grain tax and corruption in the recruitment of his sons. Today the [Chinese] Nationalist Party is dominated by a corrupt political clique that combines some of the worst features of Tammany Hall and the Spanish Inquisition." White's article was extremely controversial when it appeared. It revealed to the American people one of the darkest sides of their ally, a side many preferred to overlook.[87] But to Americans in China this reality was as apparent as the sun in a clear sky. Of all the impressions they gathered in China, the strongest one was that of a society extremely corrupt in its practices. Every U.S. soldier who served in the country was quickly introduced to the concept of the "squeeze," the word used to describe the illicit profit made in almost every transaction, and especially those involving government officials. The Occidental eye often found it hard to discern between an ordinary "squeeze" and large-scale corruption leading Americans to come to the incorrect conclusion that all Chinese were corrupt.[88]

Chinese society condoned the use of public office to take care of families' economic needs, and the senior military officers were the first to take advantage of the system. The typical Chinese commander received money he was supposed to appropriate as he deemed proper for food, salaries and medical expenses. Money was allocated according to the unit's table of organization. The more soldiers on the payroll, the more money the commander received. Commanders frequently inflated their rosters in order to receive more money. Often, a division reported to number 10,000 would really have only half that number. In many cases, the actual size of a unit was a third or a fourth of the paper strength. The commanders pocketed the difference.[89] This situation caused several operational problems for the Chinese Army, and likewise to American planners and instructors. First, it was hard to assess the real strength of Chinese military units and plan their employment accordingly. Second, generals of the Chinese armies were so involved in their trade and smuggling of narcotics that the interest in making money surpassed their interest in fighting the war. The entire military system was built on personal loyalties. This meant that Chinese officers trained to serve in one unit could not be transferred to other units as is done in the U.S. military. There was no system of replacement. A commander who lost soldiers would have to do without them. Taking casualties, therefore, meant a reduction in the size of the unit and, in turn, less money for the commander to pocket.[90] Contrary to the popular view that Nationalist officers were indifferent to wholesale human losses, the typical Chinese commander was averse to casualties, though for the wrong reasons, and thus reluctant to participate in fighting activity that might reduce his forces and hence his wealth. Third, the greediness of Chinese generals came at the expense of their soldiers and hence affected morale. Soldiers never got money for the food they needed. The money passed through so many hands that only a fraction of it actually reached its destination. The Chinese soldier was, therefore, deprived of the money and equipment designed to increase his welfare and his ability to fight. Much of the equipment that belonged to the troops found its way to the black market. "The whole of China was one black market," observed one American.[91] The Americans were angered to see the supplies they risked their lives to move through the Burma Road and fly across the Hump sold to the black market by corrupt officers.[92] In one incident, enraged American servicemen wrecked luggage waiting to be loaded on a dangerous flight across the Hump after discovering that the "strategic supplies" they risked their lives transferring were cosmetics, lingerie, fur coats and fancy groceries belonging to none other than Madame Chiang Kai-shek.[93] Many Chinese generals had no compunctions selling military equipment and state secrets even to the Japanese enemy.[94] The Americans, for their part, felt they were physically endangered by this practice after a few cases in which Chinese officers working for the Japanese sold intelligence on the location of the Americans.[95]

Perhaps most frustrating for Americans was the tendency among Chinese officers to deflect blame for their soldiers' shortages to the Americans, when the shortage was clearly caused by their own deliberate misconduct. An American Air Travel Officer at an airfield in Szechuan province described how when he went to the field where a number of Chinese soldiers were about to board an American plane for India, he found himself attacked by stones. An interpreter explained that the Chinese were furious, because their officers were charging them too high a fare to India. As it turned out, the soldiers received an allowance to finance their travel expenses, but when their officers learned about this they attempted to take the money from them under the pretext that the Americans were overcharging them.[96]

There were only two ways to deal with corruption: resist it or adopt the practices of the host society. The Chinese expected the Americans to play by the rules of the place. Lieutenant General Claire Chennault, the most popular American in China, wrote that "bribery was a tremendous problem in dealing with the Chinese." He was surprised to receive access from Chiang to a drawing account to finance "gifts" to ease his way in governmental circles.[97] He refused to conform. Unlike German officers who adapted their morals when faced with a similar challenge in Turkey, the Americans were not willing to compromise what they thought to be their superior ethics. Both Stilwell and later Wedemeyer understood that they had to attack the problem and apply their authority and control over resources to protect Chinese troops from their commanders. They were willing to resist corruption in matters related directly to the execution of their missions even if it meant clashing with Chiang and his officials. They decided that Chinese commanders would not receive any lump sums from which to pay their troops. There would be stringent control over money, and it would be allocated to the soldiers without middlemen. Naturally this caused tension with the Chinese commanders, including Chiang Kai-shek.[98] But it improved the welfare of the soldiers and made them more fit to fight.

Another aspect of Chinese familism was an inherent distrust toward anybody outside the family body or what Max Weber described as "universal distrust."[99] This deep-rooted feeling made Chinese society, in the words of Francis Fukuyama, a low-trust society, with all the social and economic implications.[100] The most apparent institutional characteristic of such a low trust society was an abuse of power and a high degree of centralization in government bodies. Chinese culture had a profound effect on its social structure, government bureaucracy and ethics. The combination of a diffuse, clannish society, institutional distrust and the commander-in-chief's personal paranoia produced a highly centralized military culture in the Chinese military. Centralism was symptomatic throughout the army's entire command echelon. The Chinese staff in Chungking under the Generalissimo tried to control everything: the movement and disposition of the smallest units, appointments of junior commanders and the minutest details of logistics. Since they were remote, their orders did not fit reality. They showed little trust for intermediate commanders and violated the principle of subordinate command authority. One example that demonstrates the problematic command relationship was an order issued in March 1942 by Chiang and sent to Stilwell's headquarters in Burma: "All Chinese should be buried with their ancestors. Therefore the bodies of all men who were killed or died in Burma will be shipped back to China in pine-board coffins."[101] The order reflected Chiang's detachment from the reality of life in Burma. There were no pine trees there, nor were there any sawmills or available carpenters to make the coffins, not to mention the logistical difficulties involved in shipping thousands of bodies across the Himalayas at a time when food and ammunition could hardly pass through. Naturally, such an order could never have been obeyed. Chiang's habit of sending his subordinates tactical orders across the mountains and hence circumventing intermediate commanders had a profound effect on relations with Stilwell. Chiang would bombard Stilwell's headquarters with orders regarding the most petty issues. "Burma is a hot place," the Generalissimo reminded his perspiring men one hot day as if they had not noticed. "Watermelons are good for the morale of thirsty troops. Stilwell will provide one watermelon for every four Chinese soldiers," he added.[102] "Nothing in the course of Stilwell's theater command was to have a more baleful effect," wrote Barbara Tuchman as she described the ups and downs of Sino-American relations. "Coming at the darkest time in Allied fortunes, when Burma was crashing about his ears [...] the watermelon order clinched his contempt for Chiang Kai-shek. [...] The mutual effect was far-reaching."[103] Chiang's distrust was not limited to Stilwell but extended to virtually anybody working under him. Wedemeyer saw the Generalissimo's insistence on conducting the war from Chungking and his refusal to decentralize power to his subordinates as one of China's greatest problems. "The management of affairs of state in itself," he reported, "would require a Disraeli, Churchill and Machiavelli all combined in one."[104] But Chiang's sin was greater. His conduct set a bad example and was adopted by Chinese commanders at all levels of command. An unhealthy military culture characterized by timidity, apathy and lack of enterprise emerged in the Chinese army at a time when the exact opposite traits were desperately needed.

Losing the head to save the face

Face is the "key to the combination lock of many of the most important characteristics of the Chinese," wrote Arthur Smith in *Chinese Characteristics.*[105] John P. Davies, who grew up in China, described face as "something like status, but even more cherished and much more easily bruised. You could have it, not have it, lose it, acquire it, make it or save it."[106] The idea of face, or rather the fear of losing face, is a cultural trait that has deep origins and is strongly emphasized in Confucian ideology.[107] Any action that is perceived as humiliating involves the loss of face and has strong social repercussions. "In dealing with Chinese don't take away their face from them unless you do not care if you make enemies," warned Stilwell to an American audience as early as 1929 in a lecture titled "The Psychology of the Oriental."[108] And indeed, the Chinese were known to be willing to go to great lengths to protect their honor and save face. Chinese folklore offered stories about people who had lost their head in order to save their face. Great emphasis was placed in Chinese culture on self-control as a way to ensure saving face. The issue of face defined relations among people in all walks of life but above all in the military, a male dominated environment as well as highly hierarchical, stratified and authoritative. The typical Chinese citizen did not appreciate directness and frankness the way many Americans did. These characteristics were considered to be barbaric and unsubtle. Chinese behavior was much more tactful. Their concern was how to make the other fellow feel as comfortable as possible and give him face. This came many times at the expense of telling the truth. Many foreigners who came in contact with the Chinese found their tactfulness irritating and incomprehensible.

Chinese obsession with face posed great challenges to cooperation with the Americans. The main problem was to get the Chinese officers to acknowledge and accept the advice and instructions of their American colleagues. Just like the Ottoman tendency to refuse taking orders or advice from non-believers, the Chinese, due to deep-rooted anti-foreignism and obsession with face, found it difficult to accept advice from foreigners. One historian compared the American experience with training Chinese troops to that of a man who led his horse to water, but could not make it drink.[109] The Chinese did not cooperate with American requests and recommendations and when they did, they refused to lose face in the eyes of their subordinates by being bossed around by people whom they perceived to be less civilized than they.[110] The Chinese also rejected American plans when they felt that the Americans were dictating to them what to do. Chinese officers felt that that they must assert their authority in contradiction to that of their

American advisors. Not doing so would be perceived as loss of face. American liaison officers reported that the higher the rank of Chinese officers, the more serious the obsession with face and hence the more difficult the relations. Americans were annoyed by the need to exercise extreme caution when dealing with the Chinese. They felt Chinese officers were vain and in some cases even narcissistic. Instead of showing gratitude for American assistance, the Chinese were complicating the lives of their allies with their obsession with face issues. For the duration of the mission, U.S. advisors grappled with the dilemma of how to make the Chinese take their advice without causing them to lose face. In the beginning of 1945, Wedemeyer and Chiang agreed on some guidelines on how relations between the advisor and the advised should be conducted. They agreed that if the Chinese commander refused to accept the suggestions offered by the American advisors, it would have to be brought before both the Generalissimo and Wedemeyer. "Any Chinese commander who continually fails to follow the well considered advice of his U.S. advisor will be replaced or have U.S. assistance withdrawn from his unit."[111]

The obsession with face was not only an irritant; it was a serious issue with implications for the overall operational conduct of the war. At times, it even brought tragic consequences. Three incidents are particularly enlightening. The first occurred in March 1944, when the U.S. and China quarreled over the Salween Campaign. As mentioned before, the Americans demanded that Chiang order his Yunnan forces with their American equipment to advance against the Japanese 56th Division in northern Burma. President Roosevelt issued an ultimatum to Chiang threatening to terminate arms supplies if the Generalissimo refused to commit his forces. The ultimatum reflected FDR's frustration with Chinese intransigence, but issuing an ultimatum was hardly the way to achieve Chinese cooperation. The President and his military advisors failed to understand the cultural implications of such a threat. Surrendering to the American ultimatum would be humiliating, and Chiang's only way of saving face was to reject the American demands, posing a counter-ultimatum threatening to sever his relations with the U.S. unless a loan of one billion dollars was approved. With the two sides refusing to budge, on April 7, George Marshall advised Stilwell to cease Lend-Lease supplies. The coalition was on the verge of collapse. A week later, Brigadier General Frank "Pinky" Dorn, responsible for American forces in Yunnan, invited a group of high level guests including Chief of Staff and Minister of War General Ho Ying-ch'in to a dinner party in order to mend some fences. Chinese wine lubricated the wheels of the coalition, and two days later Ho officially ordered the Chinese forces to move against the Japanese. His letter to Marshall indicated that the decision was made "on the initiative of the Chinese without influence or outside pressure."[112] Clearly, a hardball approach was not the way to increase Chinese cooperation. On the contrary, for the sake of saving face, China's leaders proved willing to compromise national security considerations. It was the same Pinky Dorn who stood at the center of another face-related episode. Dorn was the American advisor to Marshal Wei Li-huang, also known as "Hundred Victories Wei," one of the most respected officers in the Chinese Army. In October 1944, an opportunity was created to evict the remaining Japanese forces from northern Burma, which would, in turn, permit an uninterrupted construction of the Ledo Road. As usual, the Chinese were procrastinating, and Wedemeyer was called to intervene. Both Dorn and Wedemeyer flew to Wei's headquarters near Kunming in order to pressure him to launch the attack. Bluntly, Wedemeyer ordered the marshal, in front of his entire staff, to attack the Japanese at a specific hour on a certain date. "I gave these instructions exactly as I would have given them to a group of American officers," wrote Wedemeyer.[113] But treating a Chinese marshal as if he were an American officer was the wrong way to go. Outside the marshal's tent, Dorn criticized Wedemeyer for his callous treatment of Wei and predicted that the marshal would not carry out the order just for the sake of saving face. Wedemeyer was not open to such criticism and, instead, lashed out at Dorn for adopting the Chinese gesture to cup hands and bow when taking leave of a senior official. "If the cupped-hands, bow-out-backward method had been successful, perhaps I would not have been ordered to China to succeed Stilwell. In the future," he added, "don't you ever let me see you kowtowing to any Chinese official. I expect all officers to be courteous, tactful and completely honest in their contacts with Chinese, but I want them always to be so in the American tradition."[114] But as Dorn predicted, the marshal did not attack, at least not at the date and hour ordered. A marshal's face could not be blemished. A similar case occurred in early December 1944, when two Japanese divisions were moving toward the Kweiyang area. The Hump terminals were only 200 miles away, and the Americans believed that if they were lost that would probably mean the end of the war in China. In his direct manner, General Wedemeyer ordered three armies to move toward the vital area and prepare for a Japanese assault. The U.S. liaison officer in the 57th Army reported that its commander, General Liu was refusing to move. The General's explanation was that it would be a loss of face to take orders from an American liaison officer. The Chinese doctrine of command, he claimed, specified that commanders should take orders only from their superior officers and not from liaison or staff officers. Therefore, although the marching orders were issued by Wedemeyer with the Generalissimo's blessing, they were not binding, because they did not come through the proper channel.[115] Again, this incident shows that even at the gravest moment, when the future of the entire war was at stake, Chinese commanders were preoccupied with formalities, face saving and power games. Furthermore, these were not isolated incidents. Secret OSS memoranda reported countless incidents where carefully planned attacks were either cancelled or foiled due to high ranking Chinese officers making sudden changes in the orders issued by the Americans simply because they refused to be seen as lackeys. Such occurrences often ended in a needless loss of life. However, face was saved.[116]

World of make-believe

Another source of cultural tension was the different attitude Americans and Chinese had toward facts and accuracy. Unlike the meticulous, methodical and organized American soldiers, the Chinese paid very little attention to planning, precision and order. It was pointless to plan, since things never turned out according to plan. Facts and figures did not mean much to them. The Chinese,

General Wedemeyer (center) confers with Chinese and American officers

for example, reported about recaptured towns while they were still held by the Japanese.[117] A constant challenge for the Americans was to figure out the strength of Chinese units in terms of their roster and supply levels. Without accurate figures, they could not plan the distribution of Lend-Lease supplies among Chinese units and make sound operational decisions. The Chinese control of their supply levels was abysmal. They used to request military articles and other supplies like food, blankets, and medical supplies without knowing that tons of these articles were rotting in their own storehouses. In short, the right hand did not know what the left hand was doing. Another problem was the Chinese tendency to inflate numbers of enemy casualties and spin exaggerated stories about their military achievements. By exaggerating the strength of the Japanese Army, Chinese officers hoped to impress upon the U.S. their contribution to the war.[118] "According to Chunking estimates, the entire Japanese army should have been wiped out," wrote war historians Theodore H. White and Annalee Jacoby.[119] But the Japanese army was far less hurt than Chinese generals reported. American planners counting on these reports underestimated the threat facing them and launched hopeless attacks against formidable Japanese units.[120] With time, the Americans learned to take Chinese reports with great skepticism. U.S. liaison officers always double-checked Chinese reports and in many events even risked their lives by taking dangerous trips to the frontline in order to verify them. The head of the first American military mission in Chungking, Brig. General John Magruder, described what he saw as Chinese perception of reality:

> It is a known fact that the Chinese are great believers in the world of make-believe, and that they frequently shut their eyes to the hard and unpleasant actualities, preferring rather to indulge their fancy in flattering but fictitious symbols, which they regard as more real than cold facts. Manifestations of this national escape-psychology have been clearly discernable in China's international relations. She has consciously given free rein to her native penchant for alluring fiction in Chinese propaganda abroad. People in other countries swallow such glib untruths whole without realizing that they are being deceived. As instances of this deceptive symbolism, I may adduce many reports emanating from Chinese diplomatic sources abroad referring to the marvelous achievements and abilities of the Chinese Army. Such reports are absolutely without foundation. They are largely due to the above mentioned Chinese love of symbolism, or else can be attributed to nothing other than a downright desire to achieve certain specific objectives by clever deception.[121]

Not everything was bad about the different approach the Chinese had toward what the Americans believed to be fact. The Chinese, for example, were superb in deception and evasion tactics. Ancient Chinese military writings had always praised the merits of deception as an effective tool to weaken the enemy, and most Chinese generals were more mindful of that than their American counterparts. Elusiveness also served Chinese soldiers at the lower level. Armed with century-long experience in smuggling, concealing of goods, evading taxes and getting around government regulations, the Chinese showed an impressive ability to gather and distribute intelligence. They also knew how to conceal and operate a great number of secret wireless stations in Japanese occupied areas. These stations supplied important, timely intelligence usually shared with the Americans.[122]

From General Hospital to General Reserve

Perhaps more than anything, Americans who served in China were struck by the cruelty, callousness and utter disrespect for human life shown by most Chinese officers. Reports of harsh treatment, physical punishment and capricious executions of soldiers without trial appear in most books describing the period. By and large, Chinese officers treated their troops like animals.[123] In fact, in some cases, animals were treated better than soldiers. American liaison officers learned, for example, that Chinese company commanders could execute a soldier with less bureaucratic complications than if they shot a horse or a mule.[124] Commanders could hit, torture and kill their subordinates on a whim. If a soldier failed to obey an order, he was instantly taken out and shot.[125] There was no investigation and no accountability. American soldiers, learning of one practice where Chinese officers would crop their soldiers' ears, were revolted by the inhumane treatment.[126] Barbara Tuchman described how at one staff meeting, an American officer was shocked when a Chinese commander callously threw to the wastebasket reports he had handed him moments before on the number of Chinese soldiers who had died of sickness and exhaustion en route to Ramgarh.[127] More chilling was Fred Eldridge's tale of an American plane flying a load of Chinese soldiers over the mountains. The Chinese, who had never before flown, were fascinated by the scenery below. One soldier approached the opening left by the removal of the plane's door to watch the view. Another Chinese soldier sneaked behind him, and, looking back at his companions, made pushing motions with his hands. The passengers immediately responded with similar gestures egging him on. The jokester then calmly pushed his comrade out of the door to his death. "The plane rocked with Chinese laughter," wrote Eldridge.[128]

Due to this insensitivity to casualties, officers had no problem sacrificing their troops as long as they knew that they would be replaced.Nor were Chinese commanders concerned at all with the welfare of their soldiers. An American report on health conditions in the Chinese Army noted, "the basic reason for the poor health of soldiers appears to be the continued wrong attitude toward them shown by their leaders."[129] The Chinese soldier knew that he was not likely to be treated for wounds he may suffer. His concern was well-founded. Many soldiers had to wait up to thirty days before their wounds were treated. Even when they happened to arrive at a hospital, treatment was not assured. Due to the diffuse nature of the Chinese Army, the soldier of one unit could not enter the hospital of another unit.[130] The Chinese also differed from their American partners in their attitude toward rescue. For the Americans, saving someone's life was a virtue, an act of great valor in which one took pride. Soldiers received the highest decorations and honors for saving the life of another individual or for risking their lives to retrieve the body of a comrade. For the Chinese, there was no credit given for saving a life. On the contrary, it was commonly believed that if you save a life you become responsible for that person, including feeding, clothing and curing him, all, of course, at high cost. Retrieval of dead bodies was also uncommon since, again, it involved covering the expensive funeral and burial costs.[131] Thus, the Chinese soldier lived under the notion that there was nobody out there to save his life, attend to his wounds, or bring him to burial if he was killed. This was hardly a mindset conducive to the development of fighting spirit and strong morale.

Conscription was another sore point between the U.S. military and the Chinese Army. Unlike the Americans who selected the best men to serve in the military, in China, the best and the brightest were left at home to continue their civilian responsibilities leaving the poor and less educated to fill the military ranks. It was believed that by protecting the upper social crust, the race would only improve. "You in America take the best men out to get killed and leave the weaklings at home to propagate the race," thought the Chinese of their allies.[132] The Chinese public had a long tradition of despising the military profession.[133] The peasants despised the corrupt regime of Chiang Kai-shek and his warlords and loathed fighting for them. Ferocious as the Japanese were, Chinese peasants felt so alienated from their army that they thought the enemy was better.[134] Army units going through towns and villages raped, murdered, looted and set fire. When the villagers wanted to return to their homes, the army charged them money to pass.[135] "The Chinese were wonderful at looting," wrote one U.S veteran adding, "Sometimes, I think, looting was the prime aim of the Chinese army."[136] Other American soldiers reported how the Chinese warned villagers that the Japanese were advancing and, when the villagers fled, they looted their property. In another case, Chinese troops were so busy looting that they failed to see the Japanese who then annihilated them. As a result, very few Chinese citizens volunteered to serve their nation. To fill the ranks, the majority of the soldiers had to be forcefully conscripted. But the recruitment process was carried out in a brutal and insensitive manner.[137] A report sent to Chiang by General Wedemeyer in August 1945 described the deplorable conscription system in China:

> Conscription comes to the Chinese peasant like famine or flood, only more regularly - every year twice - and claims more victims. Famine, flood and drought compare with conscription like chicken pox with plague. [...] You are working in the field looking after your rice [...] [there come] a number of uniformed men who tie your hands behind your back and take you with them. [...] Hoe and plough rust in the field, the wife runs to the magistrate to cry and beg for her husband, the children starve. [...] The conscription officers make their money in collaboration with the officials and through their press gangs. They extort big sums of money from conscripts which have been turned over to them by the officials. [...] Having been segregated and herded together the conscripts are driven to the training camps. They are marched from Shensi to Szechuan and from Szechuan to Yunnan.[...] They are too weak to

run away. Those who are caught [running] are cruelly beaten. They will be carried along with broken limbs and with wounds in maimed flesh in which infection turns quickly into blood poisoning and blood poisoning into death. [...] If somebody dies his body is left behind. His name on the list is carried along. As long as his death is not reported he continues to be a source of income, increased by the fact that he has ceased to consume. His rice and pay become a long-lasting token of memory in the pocket of his commanding officer. His family will have to forget him.[138]

Horrifying as it sounds, this method of conscription was broadly used throughout the war in all of China's provinces. No wonder the fighting morale of the Chinese soldier was so low. "Going into the army was usually a death sentence," wrote White and Jacoby. And indeed, more soldiers died on their way to the army and in the training camps than due to enemy action.[139]

How did that affect the relations? The sight of district magistrates throwing a rope around the neck of an unwilling peasant seen walking dawn a street was a frequent occurrence that could not escape the eye of Americans in China.[140] Many American soldiers resented the conduct and were unhappy about collaborating with an ally capable of treating human beings in such a harsh manner. Operationally, the condition of Chinese soldiers arriving at the training centers was so bad that most of them were found unfit to serve at all. On their arrival to base, Wedemeyer claimed, the recruits were "ready for General Hospital rather than the General Reserve."[141] Furthermore, the inhumane way Chinese soldiers were recruited prompted many of them to desert at the first opportunity. Desertion became such a common practice that American instructors felt their efforts to upgrade the Chinese military were in vain.

Command problems

The case of Chiang Kai-shek and General Stilwell provides us with one of the most contentious relations between commanders in a coalition setting. The quarrel between the two men and its effect on the American assistance to China inspired many historians, and its details need not be repeated here. How much of the tension was due to culture and personality and how much due to differences in policy or doctrine is in the eyes of the beholder. One thing is clear: with Chiang struggling to bring about Stilwell's deposal and the American general plotting to assassinate the Generalissimo, there was little hope for Sino-American relations to flourish. From the outset, there was disagreement between the U.S. and China regarding the type of people who should become American military commanders in China. A January 1942 letter from China's foreign minister, T.V. Soong, to U.S. Assistant Secretary of War John J. McCloy asked the U.S. not to send officers to China who were experts on the Far East. Both Chiang and he were suspicious of those Americans who had knowledge of the methods and the norms existing in China. They believed those people would come with preexisting anti-Chinese bias and try to enforce changes on the military.[142] The Americans thought otherwise. They believed that the more familiar the candidate was with the country, the people and the culture, the more suitable he would be to fulfill the role of military advisor or to command a military mission. According to this logic, they appointed officers like Magruder, Stilwell, Dorn and Wedemeyer who were not strangers to China. Some of them were considered China experts in the U.S. Army. Magruder had served eight years in China as attaché and spoke Chinese. Stilwell had served ten years in China and was also fluent in the language. But to what extent did they really understand the culture and the sensitivities of their allies? On the surface, Stilwell's resume demonstrated that he was a fitting choice, but his case showed that familiarity with the land and the language did not necessarily guarantee cross-cultural sophistication. "Though he had traveled extensively into various provinces and the interior of China, Stilwell lacked true appreciation of the culture of the Chinese race and the spirit of the age, and was poor in evaluating people," wrote Chin-tung Liang.[143] This view was also held by non-Chinese writers. Military analyst Hanson Baldwin wrote, for example, that Stilwell's appointment had been one of the great mistakes of the war: "Stilwell was a lovable character and a fine soldier, but his nickname, 'Vinegar Joe,' the difficulty he had in working with the British, and his natural

tendency to give primacy to military, rather than political considerations did not make him the ideal theater commander in the most
difficult theater of the war: one where toughness needed to be combined with urbanity and with greater political *savoir faire*."[144]

Armed with Liman von-Sanders' memoirs, Stilwell went to
China to repeat the same mistakes his German role model committed in Turkey. His main mistake was his insistence on imposing
organizational and cultural changes on the Chinese military in an
attempt to turn it into what he viewed as an effective force. His
ideas to merge Chinese divisions to bring them to full strength,
to purge inefficient commanders so that every Chinese Army rank
of colonel and above would be filled by American officers, and to
have complete authority over the Chinese, were insensitive and
imposing.[145] His attempts to remove corrupt and the incompetent
commanders and transform Chiang Kai-shek and his army into a
full-fledged Westernized military were doomed to fail and had a
great impact on the chain of events that subsequently led to his
removal. He was also impatient, wanting fast results in a country
where nothing happened fast. It was naïve of him to think that a
few weeks of training could neutralize the cumulative effects of
centuries. Stilwell failed to heed the advice given to him by Chiang
in June 1942:

> There is a secret for the direction of the Chinese troops
> unlike the direction of foreign troops. I am well aware of
> the fact that our senior officers do not possess enough edu-
> cation and sufficient capacity for work. [...] Knowing their
> limited capacity I plan ahead for them. [...] The German
> officers who had been employed by China for their training
> were unable to get along with Chinese officers. It would
> be necessary to think in terms of their mentality. If you
> are with me closely for few months, you will understand
> the psychology of Chinese officers, and I will tell you more
> about their peculiarities.[146]

Shortly after Stilwell's recall, Harold Isaacs in a *Newsweek* article
described Stilwell's term in China as "One Man's Fight Against

Corruption." The down-to-earth general did not have the patience to let the Chinese win the war in their own way. "Stilwell," Isaacs concluded, "fought a losing battle against inertia, corruption, inefficiency, and questionable motives." Even so, his failure to accept the Chinese as they were brought to his downfall.[147] The American attempt to reform Chiang and his regime, as propagated by Stilwell, bred trouble. Some Americans realized it soon enough. As early as February 1943, John P. Davies wrote in his diary: "one of our major mistakes is attempting the impossible - command over the Chinese. We have the weapons [...] we have our ideas of command and organization. We want to impose them on the Chinese because we consider the Chinese inefficient and incompetent. We are approaching them with the mentality of Gordon and Ward during the latter half of the 19th century. And it doesn't go down."[148] Forcing a coalition partner to adopt a new military culture proved to be futile and often counterproductive. The notion that people could change if just handed the material aid required to implement a change was flawed. It ignored the tradition of non-cooperation and the deep-rooted cultural and social heritage that had shaped the minds of the Chinese centuries before the U.S. was even conceived. Furthermore, the attempts to impose new norms and regulations on a reluctant client for whom face preservation played such a crucial role were perceived as patronizing and were a cause for antagonism. It took the American commanders in China almost three years to realize that changing the Chinese and fighting their idiosyncrasies were impossible missions and their only option was to learn to accept them as they were. General Wedemeyer's ability to maintain good working relations with Chiang was mainly due to this approach. The directive accompanying the assumption of his command stated that the U.S. was no longer hoping to reform the Chinese army. The mission was strictly to assist. To help the Chinese help themselves. Assistance became the key word, not reform.[149]

Lessons from the East

When the U.S. made its commitment to join China's war for survival, very few Americans could truly lay claim to a comprehensive knowledge of the characteristics of the Chinese. China presented the Occidentals with a grim combination of a dire military situation and cultural remoteness. It was a nation that brought suffering to a new frontier. Fifteen million Chinese perished in the war from military action, disease and starvation. China was a place where, as one American morbidly described it, "the dogs ate the soldiers when they were dead, and the soldiers, when they were alive, ate the dogs."[150] To help the Chinese help themselves, the U.S. military had to collaborate with an army that was handicapped in almost every sense. Corruption, neglect of training and discipline, lack of food and medical care, incompetent leadership, mismanagement, personal allegiances, oppression of the people, and low morale were all unfamiliar problems that could cause even the most indifferent American soldier a culture shock. From the outset of the Sino-American coalition, it was clear that China was at the mercy of the U.S. in almost every respect. Unlike the strategically balanced alliance between the Germans and the Turks or between the Japanese and the British, the Chinese had neither the doctrinal nor logistical infrastructure to fight and win the war by themselves. Their rudimentary air force was a product of Chennault's initiative and industriousness, and their infantry divisions became effective only due to Stilwell's rigorous training. The U.S. was China's savior and its only chance to defeat the Japanese. The Chinese dependency was fully exploited by the U.S., which forced the reluctant Chinese into active engagement in the fighting. The threat of halting arms transfers was dangled several times by the U.S. in order to prod the Chinese into compliance with the norms of modern military organization. The U.S. was not shy about asserting its will and preferences on its ally, even at the cost of a clash, nor did it avoid challenging Chinese norms and customs. It was reluctant to send combat forces to China, and was, thus dependent on the leadership of Chiang Kai-shek and on China's full cooperation on the ground. The dependence on the Chinese soldier to fight and win the war was often forgotten by some American commanders. The power disparity between the U.S. and China allowed them to treat their allies with paternalistic condescension that did not fit well with the Chinese obsession with face.

A major part of the Sino-American incompatibility stemmed from the fact that the U.S. and China were not very exposed to each other in the years prior to the war. The Chinese knew very little about American culture and lifestyle. Their main source of information was reports from relatives who lived in the U.S. Those Westerners who lived in China, including missionaries, businessmen, diplomats and members of the U.S. garrison were isolated and had too little interaction with the indigenous population to make any impression on the Chinese. The Chinese military was very insular. Most Chinese officers had never left the country and unlike the Ottomans and Japanese had no interaction with foreign militaries. The small number of Chinese officers who had studied in Japan, Europe or the U.S. were the most cooperative and receptive to change.[151] There were also small foreign military missions from Russia and Germany that had tried to modernize the Chinese army and failed. The German military mission had worked in China between 1928 and 1938 and had focused only on the training of Chiang's own units; its impact on the overall Chinese understanding of the West was miniscule.[152] The U.S. Army, for its part, was more exposed to foreign militaries, including its Chinese partner. An American presence in China since 1901 had helped introduce many of America's sons to the culture of the East. The Chinese Language Officer Program of the U.S. Army produced a cadre of officers with strong language skills, most of whom served several years in China. There was an impressive group of fine officers with China experience - among them Generals Marshall, Stilwell and Wedemeyer - who had made their way up to senior positions in the U.S. military. Though the U.S. military was still segregated, its enlisted personnel were distinctively multicultural. Black, Hispanic, and Asian soldiers fought alongside Caucasian soldiers in almost every American unit. Another difference between American and Chinese coalition behavior was in the willingness to learn about the other as relations progressed. Although Americans were guests in China and therefore had more responsibility for educating their troops about the host society, there is very little evidence of Chinese reciprocity in educating their troops about the nature of the strange people risking their lives for them. There was no systematic effort to improve familiarity of troops with the Western way of life or to make a special effort to show Americans signs that the Chinese appreciated their culture. The only cross-cultural effort in which the Chinese invested was the effort to educate the Americans about China's cultural eminence and the wonders of the Middle Kingdom. The U.S. for its part invested considerable efforts in cultural relations. It granted fellowships for Chinese students to study in the U.S., screened American films, and produced radio programs in Mandarin and other dialects designed to introduce the Chinese to different aspects of American culture. The U.S. Department of State also launched a comprehensive program of cultural exchange with China designed to narrow the cultural gaps between the two powers.[153] In addition, there were also efforts to educate the GIs and increase their cultural sensitivity in dealing with the Chinese. U.S. commanders were instructed to teach their soldiers about the culture of the host. In 1943, the OSS issued a twenty-page illustrated booklet for American soldiers about to fly to China. In addition, a book, *Here's How,* was distributed to the servicemen immediately upon arrival. The War Department issued another booklet called *Our Chinese Ally,* which offered a good background on the land and its people.[154]

As in other cases of cross-cultural coalition relations, the effect of mutual racial antipathy cannot be discounted. The Sino-American cooperation in World War II was hindered by a strong mutual racial prejudice. Most Chinese and Americans viewed each other as inferior races and had a low regard for their partner's culture. The feeling was prevalent in all levels of command, up to the very top. The perception of Chinese powerlessness and racial inferiority among many key U.S. commanders caused them to treat the Chinese in a patrician manner, viewing them as mentally incapable of dealing with the problems they faced. The only remedy Americans could offer for the acute problems of the Chinese army was to impose change on the Chinese and reform their military establishment as the war progressed.

Interestingly, influential as culture was, there was one important cultural trait that played a very small role in the Sino-American coalition: religion. Throughout the coalition, not the slightest tension was generated by the fact that the U.S. was a Christian power while the majority of Chinese were followers of the Asian religions, Buddhism and Taoism. This could be explained by the same reason religion was negligible in the Anglo-Japanese case, namely, the religious tolerance of both parties. Most Chinese drew spiritual guidance and comfort from Confucian ideology, which lacked the notion that men are assigned a different value according to their religion.[155] Confucius conveyed an ambiguous attitude toward religion. Asked by one of his pupils about gods and spirits, his comment was: "respect gods and spirits, but keep them at a distance."[156] Many Chinese and Western scholars arrived at the conclusion that in China religion played an important role in consolidating the family body and providing comfort, but the Chinese people were less bound by religion than most other cultural groups. Furthermore, they had a tradition of being far more tolerant in comparison to the great monotheistic religions.[157] Perhaps as a result of their unique attitude toward religion, the Chinese, like the Japanese vis-à-vis the British in Tsingtau, showed no attempt to impose religious beliefs or practices on their guests or to in any way limit them from practicing their religious rituals on Chinese land. This was also the way they treated the four million Christians and twenty million Muslims who lived in China at the time.

Religion aside, the overall effect of culture on the Sino-American coalition was profound. Culture was an exacerbating element in a relationship already burdened by so many other incompatibilities. But unlike cases of military cooperation impaired by religious tension or language barriers, in this case the cultural gap was manifested through two opposing systems of ethics. Chinese culture espoused norms, behaviors and attitudes that were completely unacceptable in the U.S. and in many cases contested fundamental human rights most Americans took for granted. Ethical differences were in degree as well as in kind. Predominant values of the U.S. military like responsibility toward subordinates, candor, punctuality, public morality, camaraderie and patriotism were seen in a different light by the Chinese. This led to numerous operational difficulties.

The American experience in China was the debut of a series of subsequent experiences of military cooperation with fellow Asian nations. A year after the U.S. 'lost' China, it was embroiled in a war to salvage the Republic of Korea from the Communists. A decade later, the U.S. was involved in Vietnam, Cambodia and Laos, all predominantly Buddhist nations. The period between World War II and the Vietnam War was an important time of social transformation and cultural change in the U.S. including a gradual process of desegregation. Racial barriers were removed, and civil rights were granted to formerly discriminated against minorities. And indeed, one could notice a gradual change between the Korean War and the Vietnam War in the attitudes of U.S. servicemen toward their Asian counterparts. In Korea, the American GI approached and treated his Asian counterpart with a similar attitude he had shown toward the Chinese in 1941-45. Americans, by and large, viewed the South Koreans with contempt, often treating them as "subhuman cannon fodder."[158] As one historian put it, Americans "did not regard the Koreans as fellow human beings who deserve human treatment but near animals."[159] They were appalled by their corruption, lack of respect for human life, obsession with face, and treatment of POWs and civilian population. They were annoyed by what they perceived as their partners' inefficiency, backwardness and indifference to time. A plan to improve relations with the ROK by augmenting U.S. Army units with Korean soldiers was instituted in August 1950. Hundreds of Korean recruits were attached to American units in what was referred to as the "buddy system." But within a few months it became clear the plan was a failure. Americans had little appreciation for Korean soldiers, and used them for little more than carrying ammunition and rations. The "buddy system" was abandoned by winter.[160]

But the lesson China taught the Americans about working with culturally dissimilar people, namely, don't change your partner, was learned and implemented. The mission assigned to American advisors of the U.S. Military Advisory Group in the ROK captures the scope of the attitudinal change: "Your mission is to organize and train, in a democratic way, a small but efficient organization, loyal to the government of the Republic of Korea, and capable of maintaining internal sovereignty. Your mission is NOT to convert the Korean into an American," said the advisor's handbook.[161]

In the years since Korea, American society changed dramatically, taking major steps to remove cultural barriers and prejudices left among ethnic, cultural and racial groups both domestically and internationally. During the Vietnam War these changes were still in progress, but one could see signs of increased appreciation of the Asian counterpart and greater understanding that it should be treated with respect and sensitivity. General Westmoreland made it a high priority to instill among his troops respect for South Vietnamese culture and sovereignty ordering every American troop to carry at all times a card listing the do's and don't of dealing with the Vietnamese.[162] His relations with fellow ARVN generals were absent of the intrigue and squabbles that characterized the relations of his predecessors in China and Korea with their Asian colleagues. His juniors from all services of the U.S. military also grew to view the Vietnamese as equal human beings who deserved treatment as partners, not subordinates. In the years since Vietnam further progress was made in America's core society. A culture of political correctness and hypersensitivity to other people's cultural needs replaced the long-standing ethnocentric sentiment. The new spirit of cultural tolerance pervaded every part of American society including the military. Minorities were fully integrated in the military and in 1990, when 500,000 U.S. troops went to fight the Gulf War, America's number one soldier, Chairman of the Joint Chiefs General Colin Powell, was a man of color. The coalition in the Gulf, this time with mainly Muslim partners, gave the U.S. an opportunity to show an unparalleled degree of respect for the culture of non-Western fellow coalition counterparts. This, as we shall see in the next chapter, raised new, no less challenging, problems.

5

COALITION OF PROHIBITION:
U.S. AND SAUDI ARABIA
IN THE GULF WAR

⌘ ⌘ ⌘

My kingdom will survive only insofar as it remains a country
difficult of access, where the foreigner will have no other aim,
with his task fulfilled, but to get out.
King Ibn Saud[1]

The Saudis eliminated the main causes of most problems, namely wine,
women and song. Without them there ain't much left to get in trouble over.
An American military policeman in the Gulf[2]

If the coalition with China was a harbinger for a series of
American coalitions with Asian nations during the Cold War, the
post-Cold War era has so far been rich in American military collab-
orations with members of the Islamic civilization stretching from
the Balkans to Central Asia. Working with Muslims, whether Arab
or non-Arab, presents the Westerner with an entirely different set
of cultural challenges than those presented to the British by the
Japanese in World War I or to the Americans by the Chinese in
World War II. The key difference between the Asian and Islamic
civilizations is the role religion plays in shaping social structure,
family values and the attitude toward foreigners. Whereas members
of Asian cultures showed a remarkable degree of religious tolerance
toward their Western coalition partners, coalitions between Muslim
and Western counterparts have always exhibited religiously driven
tension. From the Germans in Istanbul to the Americans in Kabul
the Westerner has been a savior, a facilitator for military victory but
at the same time an infidel, a contaminating agent and a threat to

the delicate fabric of the indigenous Islamic society. The 1990-91 Gulf War coalition to liberate Kuwait from the Iraqi grip was the starkest expression of this dissonance. It was one of the most culturally challenging coalition endeavors, since it coupled the U.S., the epitome of liberalism and pluralism, and Saudi Arabia, a country governed by Wahhabism, the most extreme, rigid and puritanical manifestation of Islam.

Founded in the late 18th century by Ibn Abd al-Wahab, Wahhabism rejects the innovations and compromises that have been adopted by other branches of Islam. It preaches an ascetic lifestyle, rejecting all luxury, dancing, gambling, music, and the use of tobacco and alcohol. Islamic law, *sharia*, is observed and enforced throughout the kingdom without compromise. In 1932, after generations of tribal wars, the Arabian Peninsula was finally united by King Abdul Aziz ibn Saud, the founder of the Saudi monarchy. Wahhabism became the hallmark and source of legitimacy for the House of Saud. One after the another, Ibn Saud's sons ascended the throne, each having to deal in his own fashion with the almost impossible challenge of balancing between tribal rivalries, quelling political dissent, preserving the royal family's religious legitimacy and protecting the oil treasure that lies under Saudi Arabia's soil from outside predators. To do so, they have always needed the support of a great power such as the U.S.

Since the February 1945 meeting between President Franklin D. Roosevelt and Ibn Saud on board the USS *Quincy* in Egypt's Great Bitter Lake, the U.S. became the unofficial guardian of the guardian of Mecca. It supplied advice and state-of-the-art weapons to defend the country from neighbors like Yemen, Iran and Iraq and from Islamic fundamentalists who struggled to undermine the regime from within. But the Saudi-American friendship has never been an easy one. It has been, in the words of author Said Aburish, "a brutal friendship."[3] In the eyes of many Muslims, the U.S. was not only the land of the infidel, a decadent, morally corrupt country and the protector of the Zionist enemy but also, by virtue of its military presence in the Middle East, a lightening rod, attracting the wrath of Islamic militants at home and throughout the Arab world. American military advisory groups were invited to train and organize the Saudi military, only to be expelled in royal fits of rage whenever their presence in the kingdom became more dangerous to the Saudi rulers than the outside enemy.

Between 1949 and 1951, King Ibn Saud failed to persuade Washington to sign a defense agreement with Saudi Arabia. The U.S. agreed, however, to keep a small advisory mission in the kingdom to instruct the nascent Saudi armed forces. When King Saud took over in 1953, he was apprehensive of relations with the U.S., and in early 1954, he instructed the American military mission to leave the country. Three years later, during a state visit, Saud instructed to renew military cooperation, and the U.S. gained permission to use the Dhahran air base for five years in exchange for substantial military and economic aid. A training mission commanded by a U.S. Air Force brigadier general arrived in the kingdom to modernize the Saudi military. In 1961, Saud expelled the Americans again from the kingdom, but with the outbreak of the Yemeni civil war Saudi Arabia faced danger, leading Crown Prince Faisal to restore military ties. In 1965, a joint Anglo-American Commission was founded to develop the kingdom's armed forces and enable it to defend itself. However, the 1967 war with Israel increased anti-Western sentiments in Saudi Arabia due to the fact that the U.S. was siding with the Jewish state. This resulted in anti-American demonstrations and an attack on the American airbase. The deterioration in Saudi relations with Iran in the early 1970s drove the Saudis, again, to seek military assistance from the U.S. From then on, there has been an uninterrupted, increasingly growing military cooperation.

In 1970, military purchases from the U.S. totaled only $45 million; three years later the total was $1.2 billion. In 1981, the Reagan administration approved a controversial deal to sell the Saudis of the Airborne Warning and Control System (AWACS) and other advanced weapons. Despite Saudi military modernization the country has always been inherently weak and militarily unable to defend itself.[4] It has depended on the American military umbrella but, at the same time, to avoid the appearance of a vassal state, the Saudis have striven to minimize the presence of Americans in the kingdom, to make them invisible. The strategy worked.

Over the years, the feeble monarchy survived the turmoil of the Yemeni Civil War, the Iranian Revolution, and the subsequent 1979 attack on the Grand Mosque in Mecca by Saudi radicals. The August 2, 1990 invasion by Saddam Hussein's Iraqi army into neighboring Kuwait, however, introduced a clear and immediate danger to the existence of the House of Saud. The King and his ruling elite saw how, within hours, defenseless Kuwait was crushed under Iraqi tanks and how its ruling family became refugees overnight. With this in mind, it did not take much convincing for King Fahd to open his country to an unprecedented deployment of American forces and make it a launching ground for a military operation against Iraq.[5]

The coalition against Saddam Hussein's army included 33 nations from five continents, most sending token forces as a sign of mere solidarity. As the host nation, Saudi Arabia carried a heavy burden to provide for the needs of 750,000 guests who came to its assistance. It supplied bases, tents, water, fuel, food, transportation, and communications equipment. Being the host nation granted it an important seat around the decision makers' table and a say on matters related to the strategy and conduct of both Operations Desert Shield and Desert Storm. At the same time, hosting the war presented the Saudis with a cultural challenge: how to deal with the influx of non-Muslims and how to control contact with the closed, puritan, suspicious, at times xenophobic, society. Many Saudis viewed the foreign deployment on their sacred land as sacrilegious. They spoke about the foreign presence in terms of "cultural contamination" and "religious pollution." They saw the non-believers as a greater danger to the survival of the desert kingdom than Saddam's Republican Guards. Prominent mainstream Saudis spoke out against "winning the war and losing our country." The Islamic opposition was incensed and openly challenged the deal the royal family had struck with the "devil." These pressures from within had a significant impact on coalition relations and, at times, on important operational decisions taken during the war. "My special duty," wrote the commander of Saudi and Arab forces General Khaled bin Sultan, "was to protect the sovereignty of the Kingdom, as well as our religion, culture and tradition, from any infringement by the forces which came to our aid. [...] If I had not stamped immediately on infringements, the whole relations between Saudi Arabia and the U.S. [...] would have broken down."[6]

Being a guest in another country, as U.S. commanders and soldiers quickly realized, was no easier task than playing host. To preserve good relations with the Saudis, American and European soldiers deployed in the desert had to abide by the law of the land and exercise an unparalleled degree of modesty, restraint and self-denial of the most basic needs soldiers have in a combat environment: the need for spiritual and religious comfort, the need for entertainment, sex and alcohol and the need to interact freely with the people of the country they came to defend. All of these needs were denied. Saudi policy was to minimize the interaction between the people of the land and the coalition soldiers. Americans, whose national character is marked, as Hans Morgenthau once observed, by self-reliance, individual initiative, spontaneous manipulation of social change and mistrust of government dictation, could have been a bad influence on the society that exhibited the exact opposite traits.[7] Furthermore, the restrictions applied to members of open, egalitarian American society serving in Saudi Arabia raised questions and dilemmas regarding the civil and constitutional status of soldiers deployed in foreign countries as part of a coalition endeavor. The nature of the coalition demanded that American soldiers give up upon landing on Saudi soil some of the freedoms granted by the U.S. Constitution: the freedom to openly express religious beliefs, the freedom to eat and drink whatever one liked, the freedom to wear clothing of one's choice. The biggest sacrifice of freedoms was demanded of the thousands of female U.S. soldiers who found themselves caught between their desire to serve their country in the best manner possible and their need to protect their sovereignty as humans of equal status in a society that clearly viewed women as second-class citizens.

One difficulty in writing about the Gulf War coalition is observing the interplay between culture and politics in the Middle East and the difficulty in telling them apart. The war forced Saudi Arabia, as well as other Arab countries such as Egypt, Morocco and Syria, to participate in a military campaign against a fellow

Arab country. This presented them with a cultural, political and moral quandary. Their cultural affinity toward Iraq clearly exceeded their sentiments toward their Western allies, but their anger with Saddam Hussein's aggression led them to act in contrary to their pan-Arab sentiment. This sentiment may seem to many as purely political, but in the Middle East it has a deep cultural aspect. The Arab identity is derived no less from cultural and traditional bonds than from political commonality. Arabism, in other words, is first and foremost a cultural affiliation and only then a political alignment. Throughout history, Arabs fought each other many times, but their wars were always perceived as family feuds. A popular Arab proverb says "my brother and I against my cousin, but my cousin and I against the stranger." The Gulf War coalition broke this rule. The Saudis were called to fight their cousins *alongside* strangers, and they did so with anguish. Therefore, many of the issues related to the fact that Arabs fought Arabs and the implications on the coalition will be presented in this chapter in a cultural context, though they could also rightly be presented as purely political.

The strategic landscape

The decision to allow foreign troops in Saudi Arabia was not easy. Two major issues concerned the Saudis. First, they feared the U.S. might not be fully committed to defend the kingdom. They had good reasons to suspect American half-heartedness. A decade earlier, following the revolution in Iran, President Jimmy Carter had sent American F-15s to deter a potential Iranian aggression against the kingdom. When the planes were already in the air, he revealed to the Saudis that they were unarmed. The Saudis were humiliated.[8] In 1990, the Saudis believed that if the Americans, again, sent insufficient force or pulled out before Saddam was defeated, the kingdom would be in even greater danger. The second fear was that U.S. forces would remain in Saudi Arabia after the completion of the mission, thus irritating the Islamic establishment and undermining the legitimacy of the regime. From the outset of the crisis, the Saudis followed public opinion polls in the U.S. which revealed that 50 percent of Americans thought that the U.S. should keep its military forces in the region on a permanent basis even if the Iraqis got out of Kuwait.[9] To the Saudis, this was unacceptable.

According to a prophetic tradition, *hadith*, non-Muslims are not permitted on holy Islamic soil, *dar al Islam*. From the outset of the crisis, there was a heated debate between the kingdom's Islamists and the liberals about the collaboration with the non-Muslims. The Islamists harshly denounced the invitation of foreigners, seeing the act as un-Islamic. An entire debate sparked among Saudi clergy over the definition of 'Islamic soil.' Some Saudis suggested that not all of Saudi Arabia is holy and that the oilfields in the east of the country are not part of the sacred land of Mecca and Medina. Granting the decision religious legitimacy, Saudi Arabia's foremost religious leader, the senior *'alim* Shaykh 'Abd al-'Aziz bin Baz, on August 13, 1990, issued a *fatwa* endorsing the presence of non-Muslim troops on Islam's holy soil during the war. The *fatwa* even specified that "atheists, Christians, and women deserve appreciation and will be rewarded by God for coming to the defense of the kingdom and its holy places."[10] King Fahd was very sensitive to any decline in his legitimacy and status due to the controversial decision. To confer even more legitimacy, during Desert Shield he adopted the ancient Islamic title "Custodian of the Two Holy Mosques, Mecca and Medina." His main obligation was to make sure these two mosques were forever accessible to the Islamic world. If he failed to be a proper custodian of these mosques, he would have lost legitimacy as a ruler, and his regime could face the prospect of downfall. In September, the King invited 350 Islamic leaders and scholars to Mecca to discuss the theological implications of the alliance with the West. The purpose of the gathering was to demonstrate to the kingdom's religious elite that Islam's holiest place was free of infidel troops, contrary to what had been reported in fundamentalist propaganda.[11] But not everybody was satisfied. Many radical Sunni fundamentalists harshly criticized the decision to invite the foreigners. "Muslims should not join with infidels to fight other Muslims. [...] It is not the world against Iraq. It is the West against Islam," said one of the radical scholars.[12]

Saddam Hussein, for his part, viewed the Saudi-American alliance as a tool to de-legitimize the religious authority of the Saudi monarchy. Just as the Japanese tried in World War II to manipulate cultural and racial aspects in order to split the U.S. from the Chinese, Saddam launched a propaganda campaign to incite the Muslim world against the foreign presence in Arabia. Iraqi propaganda described American soldiers who allegedly went to Mecca, entered Islam's most sacred places and desecrated them.[13] Saddam called on the Arab masses to rise up against pro-Western Arab leaders whom he accused of betraying Islam by opening their gates to Western forces. In a radio address from Baghdad, he said: "Oh Arabs, Oh Muslims and faithful everywhere, this is your day to rise and defend Mecca, which is captured by the spears of the Americans and the Zionists. Burn the soil under the feet of the aggressors and invaders."[14] The main target for Iraqi propaganda was the Saudi population, which was called upon to resist the foreign invasion. Audiocassettes with sermons describing the war as a Western conspiracy to take over Saudi Arabia's oil and destroy its culture were distributed throughout the kingdom.[15] Saudi laymen were told horror stories about pro-Zionist agents working covertly in the kingdom in order to destroy it from within. The Iraqi gambit failed just as its Japanese predecessor did half a century before.

Contrary to the radicals, many liberal Saudis saw the American deployment as blessing in disguise, a harbinger of a new era of openness, liberalization and greater religious freedom. Many tried to challenge the status quo by ignoring some of the old prohibitions, hoping to create new social norms and take advantage of the turmoil the war created to create new facts on the ground. The sudden appearance of thousands of satellite dishes on the rooftops of many of the kingdom's dwellings was one of the signs of such popular sentiment.[16]

Caught between the two opposing forces of the liberals and the radicals, and yet, empowered by the determination of the international community to confront Saddam, the Saudi leadership was now fully committed to the war effort. In late November 1990, King Fahd reassured his worried nation that he would not allow the permanent stationing of foreign forces in the kingdom. The Americans, for their part, were sympathetic to Saudi concerns. They pledged to deploy a substantial force, to act quickly and to withdraw at the king's request.[17]

If there were no choice but to invite foreigners to fight the Arabs' war, it would at least have to be done in such a manner that the Saudis would not be seen as their lackeys. Saudi insistence on maintaining their sovereignty became an important theme that defined command relations with the Americans. In his memoirs, *Desert Warrior*, Khaled bin Sultan wrote that the preservation of Saudi control was one of his main objectives as a force commander:

> I did not want a repeat in Saudi Arabia of what had happened in Vietnam and Korea, where an American was the all-powerful supreme commander who could do what he liked. I believed my King and my country would not forgive me if history were to record that we had been commanded or controlled by a foreigner on our own soil.[18]

Closely guarding their sovereignty, there was no way Saudi troops could serve under American command; alternatively, the American contingent, by far the largest force contributor, could not serve under Saudi command. A unique command system, referred to as 'parallel command,' had to be invented. Under the system of parallel command the Saudi commander, Khaled, and the American commander of the U.S. Central Command (CENTCOM), General Norman Schwarzkopf, each commanded his own separate headquarters and his own designated units. Each of the smaller coalition counterparts could choose under which command it preferred to serve. The American command included all of the American units as well as the British and the Canadians. The Joint Forces Command (JFC) headed by Khaled was responsible for all of the Arab parties - the Egyptian and the Syrian contingents were the largest contingents - as well as forces from France, Senegal and Czechoslovakia.[19] The two headquarters were coordinated by a Coalition Coordination, Communications and Integration Cell (C³IC) where American and Saudi liaison teams worked together to ensure unity of effort and intelligence exchange. It was also the place where all disputes and miscommunication between CENTCOM and JFC were sorted out.[20] The C³IC was also where American and Saudi officers could together overcome some of the cultural differences. According to

Maj. General Paul Schwartz "the most important function of the C³IC was to act as a 'reduction gear,' to prevent 'Type A' American hard chargers from overwhelming the less compulsive Saudis."[21]

The invention of the parallel command system was dictated by cultural and political considerations. It was designed to demonstrate to the Arab world that the Saudis were sovereign in their land and that the protection of Islam's holiest sites was not being compromised. Khaled wrote:

> I wanted Schwarzkopf to understand that it was necessary to assure Saudi and Arab opinion that we were exercising control over these Westerners arriving in the heart of Islam. Without such control, it would have been seen as an invasion by stealth, an occupation by the backdoor, an overturning of our most cherished values. Hence the need for people to see that I was up there with the American commander in a parallel command.[22]

Despite the formal command arrangement, there was no parity between the American and the Saudi forces. Against the 300 planes, two mechanized divisions and four additional brigades the Saudis deployed, the U.S. contributed a massive force of 2,200 planes, two Army corps, a Marine expeditionary force and numerous support units. The Saudis were overwhelmed by the might of the American military, its superior technological infrastructure and the high motivation of its troops. All this made them even more sensitive to any sign that might indicate that they were in an inferior position to the Americans. In his memoirs, Khaled described how he had done everything he could do to guard his position as, at least, an equal partner to Schwarzkopf. To him, being perceived as Schwarzkopf's subordinate was unthinkable. Khaled, for example, could not bear the fact that Schwarzkopf's public appearance was more impressive than his:

> If a Saudi in the street saw Schwarzkopf's armed escort and then saw me with just one or two guards, he could immediately conclude that Schwarzkopf was the supreme commander. That I could not allow. My public appearance had

to be as impressive as his, down to the smallest detail. If he had men with guns, I had to have men with guns. So I formed a bodyguard to match Schwarzkopf's and even sent a few men abroad for training.[23]

He also took pride in the fact that throughout the war his daily appointments with Schwarzkopf always took take place in his office. For him, this was a "nonnegotiable item." He felt that if he went to Schwarzkopf's office, people would suppose that he was under an American command.[24]

General Khaled bin Sultan

Though the two pillars of the coalition were in accord about the principal objectives of the war, namely the liberation of Kuwait, the defense of Saudi Arabia and denying Saddam the ability to attack his neighbors and develop weapons of mass destruction, there were some profound strategic and operational problems in the relations between the two militaries. The first dispute was over how the two counterparts interpreted what it meant to „defend the kingdom." The King ordered Khaled that under no circumstances was he to give up one square inch of Saudi Arabia. Any tactical withdrawal or Iraqi incursion would be humiliating and would indicate that the Saudis could not defend their homeland. To accomplish absolute defense, Khaled had to ring military forces around towns along the Saudi border with Iraq and Kuwait, such as Khafji, Hafar al Batin and Nisab.[25] He expected the U.S. to do the same. But for the U.S., the objective of protecting Saudi Arabia did not entail guarding every yard of its territory. The Americans were unwilling to invest military effort in guarding empty sand dunes or even small localities along the border. They were interested mainly in defending strategic targets such as oilfields, airfields, main transportation routes and, of course, the big cities, Riyadh, Dhahran and King Khaled Military City. Furthermore, an Iraqi incursion into Saudi Arabia was a tactically welcome move that could allow the Americans to annihilate the invader more easily.

There was another bone of contention. From the beginning of the crisis, it was apparent that the Americans and Saudis did not see eye to eye on the amount of time available to deal with Saddam. The Saudis wanted the war, and with it the foreign presence in their country, to end as quickly as possible. By the first week of November 1990, there was a considerable increase in the activity and popularity of the domestic militant opposition due to a common belief that the foreign presence was undermining the morals and values of the Saudi nation. Simultaneously, President Bush announced that the U.S. would double its forces in Saudi Arabia by transferring the VII Army Corps from Germany. This meant a significant delay in the readiness of the coalition to launch the air and ground campaign. For the Saudis, this was an unsettling development. Leading Saudi military and political figures were concerned about how long Saudi public opinion would tolerate the foreign presence. They were also anxious about the possibility that the campaign would not end before the arrival of religious festivals likely to increase the undercurrent of hostility toward Western forces. The holy month of Ramadan, supposed to begin around March 17, had other implications for the Saudi leadership. As the custodian of holy places, the kingdom is traditionally host to approximately one million Muslim pilgrims arriving in Saudi Arabia to perform the religious duty of the *Hajj*. In addition to expenses and organizational efforts involved in hosting such an influx of visitors from all parts of the Muslim world, there was also a self-imposed duty to project an image of piousness and holiness meant to impress upon the Muslims that Saudi Arabia is rightfully the center of Islam. For the kingdom, the arrival of the pilgrims during the time that the country was flooded with foreigners was a problem. The Saudis, therefore, wanted to ensure that the kingdom was free of foreigners by Ramadan. Khaled bin Sultan wrote: "I could not pretend that the presence of nearly 750,000 foreign troops in the Kingdom - including half a million Americans - was not a cause for concern. I was uncertain about their impact on our local Saudi population, and this was a major reason why I regretted the long delay in resolving the crisis."[26]

They were also concerned that if the crisis dragged on, there would be a risk of turmoil on other fronts - such as along the Yemeni and Jordanian borders - or of subversive operations by Iraqi intelligence agents against the regime.[27] In a series of meetings, Saudi Defense Minister Prince Sultan, Khaled's father, tried to convince Western officials to expedite preparations for the campaign, believing that delays would affect the cohesion of the coalition.[28] The U.S., however, wanted to take the extra time needed to complete military buildup and detailed planning before the first shot was fired. The better readiness, the easier it would be to win the war. The Americans also believed that sanctions were effectively weakening the Iraqis, and the longer Iraq suffered from them, the weaker it would be on the battlefield.[29] Saudi haste was contrary to the kingdom's strategic interests and could have complicated the coalition performance. Saudi complaints about the long duration of the air campaign - in the eyes of the Americans - reflected impatience and an inability to comprehend the merits of sufficient preparation prior to the ground attack.[30] The Saudis were willing to compromise the success of the coalition for domestic and political considerations, thought U.S. military leaders.

As mentioned earlier, it was difficult for the Saudis to reconcile themselves to an attack on a fellow Arab country. One way to mitigate their anxiety and provide political legitimacy to an alliance with the West was to include many Arab countries in the coalition, especially Egypt and Morocco.[31] It was important for the Saudis to present the war as a pan-Arab endeavor rather than being viewed as proxies of the West in its war against an Arab country. Nevertheless, the Saudis never overcame their distaste for the idea that their country would be a launching ground for an attack against Iraq. During the months preceding Desert Storm, they repeatedly tried to influence the operational planning headed by the U.S. Joint Chiefs of Staff, advocating that the best way to liberate Kuwait was to launch an attack against Iraq through Turkey. The attempts to alter the plan caused the most severe crisis in the relations between Schwarzkopf and Khaled during the war.

Soon after U.S. planners drafted the plan for Operation Desert Storm, it was sent to Khaled. He responded with a memorandum written in Arabic reflecting his views and suggestions to the operation. He recommended that the U.S. exploit its airborne capabilities more and suggested different locations for Saudi forces. What irked Schwarzkopf most were Khaled's insistence that the operation be launched from Turkey into northern Iraq rather than from Saudi Arabia. Khaled's questioning the campaign's most fundamental aspect while tens-of-thousands of troops and vehicles were already gearing up to attack southern Iraq infuriated Schwarzkopf. He saw the Saudi memorandum as ludicrous and unprofessional. The two generals clashed on the same evening in a meeting that caused them to stop speaking for two days. Khaled was surprised by Schwarzkopf's angry response. He claimed his memorandum was just an attempt to provide American planners some food for thought and present them with a new, perhaps better, strategy. He was also quick to blame Rick Francona, Schwarzkopf's interpreter who translated the memorandum, saying that by writing "the main attack from Turkey" he had actually referred to the air campaign rather than the ground assault. Both Francona and Schwarzkopf saw Khaled's proposal as a Saudi attempt to remove the kingdom from the burden of being a staging ground for an attack on a fellow Arab country.[32]

The Saudi concern was not as unwarranted as many Americans thought. There were many signs of unrest and displeasure over the war aims among the ranks of the Saudi Army and the Saudi National Guards. Several Royal Saudi Air Force pilots deserted along with their planes to Sudan, Jordan and Yemen rather than fighting against Iraq.[33] Saudi servicemen began growing beards as a sign of solidarity with the fundamentalists. Anti-regime pamphlets began to appear in Saudi military units, and there were several incidents of shots being fired at U.S. soldiers by unidentified Saudis.[34] In one case, on February 2, 1991, a group of Saudis, protesting against the government's pro-American policy, fired on a bus full of American servicemen slightly wounding two of them. The Saudi government's response was harsh. Hundreds were arrested and tortured.[35] For the Saudi regime, losing the loyalty of the armed forces - the main instrument of its preservation - was a nightmare. They wanted to fight the war and, yet, keep it out of the public eye. At one point in September, Schwarzkopf pointed out to Khaled how unprepared the Saudi Ministry of Defense in Riyadh was for an Iraqi attack. Drawing on his experience from Vietnam, he proposed fortifying the bunkers surrounding the building with sandbags. He wrote: "The prince almost choked. *"Sandbags?* We can't put sandbags in the streets! It would alarm the people." "What's wrong with the people getting alarmed?" asked Schwarzkopf. "Oh, no, you don't understand, my friend. We've never done anything like that, and the people would be afraid."[36]

General Norman Schwartzkopf

The operational cooperation between the U.S. and the Saudi armed forces depended largely on the nature of the units involved. The Royal Saudi Air Force, for example, was very compatible with the American. The Saudis had similar equipment, and their pilots had all been trained by American instructors. American pilots who worked with them complemented their performance and trusted them enough to send them on 6,852 out of the 36,250 sorties during Operation Desert Storm.[37] The readiness of the ground forces was quite a different story. They were, as Khaled admitted, "in terrible shape."[38] The Saudi ground forces consisted of a 40,000-man Royal Army and the 30,000-man Saudi National Guard, the force deemed necessary to defend the kingdom against a military coup. The National Guard was considered a much better force, and its officers were personally selected for their loyalty to the regime.[39] The Saudi Army was sluggish and its officers spoiled. It operated like a "garrison army, highly dependent on Filipino bottle washers and Pakistani mechanics," reported the *Washington Post*.[40] The army units were well equipped with sophisticated weapons but had very little sense of how to effectively utilize their equipment or how to train their forces in the best manner. Even worse, they had little regard for maintenance, and their equipment was rapidly deteriorating.[41] Saudi soldiers had a poor work ethic and were averse to any form of manual labor. They relied on civilian contractors to do the work for them. Schwarzkopf recalled how one day a Saudi tank battalion commander complained after 24 of his 28 tanks were declared out of order, explaining that "the Americans have sold us defective equipment." American technicians who examined the tanks were surprised to discover how simple the problem was - dirty air filters. The Saudi tank operators, it appeared, did not even know how to perform the simplest maintenance routine. Blaming the Americans was much easier.[42] This anecdote was indicative of the culture of the Saudi armed forces, if not of Saudi society in general. It reflected the inability or lack of will at all levels to pursue solutions to simple problems. It also demonstrated apathy, a lack of initiative and a tendency to deflect responsibility for one's incompetence to others.[43]

The differences between American and Saudi military cultures were immediately apparent. American military personnel reported remoteness between soldiers, NCOs and officers in the Saudi military. Unlike American servicemen who are highly regarded by the American public, Saudi ground troops enjoyed very little respect for their work. Those who joined the armed forces were, by and large, people who could not accomplish much in civilian life.[44] They were meagerly paid, poorly treated and slowly promoted. U.S. military officers were expected to give highest priority to the well-being of their men. Saudi officers, on the other hand, seemed to hardly care about their troops and in many cases did not become personally familiar with them. Furthermore, there was no concept of teamwork. Soldiers did not feel part of a team working for a common goal. They did not share information and showed little initiative to improve the system's performance. Saudi officers were motivated by greed and self-indulgence and were frequently involved in corrupt practices at the expense of their units' preparedness.[45] Promotion was a function of nepotism rather than merit.

Arab culture places great emphasis on personal honor and pride. This was a dominating factor in the Saudi military. When a Saudi officer's honor was injured, the damage was irreparable. Officers were so protective of their prestige and honor that they were willing to compromise tactical considerations to save face. Such pride considerations often skewed their military judgment. The Saudis were too proud, for example, to allow foreign blood to be the first blood shed in defense of the kingdom. This meant that no foreign units could be deployed along the first line of contact with the enemy. The Saudis, ordered to defend their positions to the death, preferred to spread their forces in an ineffective thin line of defense along their border rather than cede a sector of the border to the other coalition forces. The Saudi forces were too scattered to withstand an Iraqi attack, and it was clear that they would have been annihilated had the Iraqis attacked through their sector. Their disposition of forces was clearly designed to satisfy political rather than military concerns.[46] After the Iraqi invasion of Khafji in January 1991, King Fahd requested that the Americans destroy the city rather than let a piece of Saudi Arabian soil fall into the hands of the enemy. Schwarzkopf told the Saudis that that this was not the way the Americans did business and that the best way to go was to take the city with a counter-attack. The American refusal to adopt the Saudi problem-solving recommendation saved the city from destruction.[47]

Another pride-related incident affected plans to retake Kuwait City, approximately 60 miles up the coastal road from the Saudi border. The U.S. Marines were assigned to plan the attack. The plan proposed by Lt. General Walter Boomer, commander of the Marine forces in the Gulf, outlined a Marine assault originating from the eastern sector of Saudi Arabia, an area otherwise manned by troops belonging to Khaled's Joint Forces Command. The plan made sense in every respect. The Marines were the most capable force in breaching obstacles and mine clearing; they could receive fire support from American battleships anchored in the Gulf; logistically, it provided short and accessible supply routes. The only problem was convincing Khaled to yield his sector to the Americans and let them do the job they were more qualified to do. Boomer, however, had uneasy relations with the Arabs. He had a low opinion of them and did not want to invest too much in cultivating relations with the Saudis. As a result, there was a considerable lack of trust between the Saudis and the Marines.[48] Furthermore, due to the personal distrust between Boomer and Khaled, it was decided that Schwarzkopf would take on the challenge of convincing Khaled to accept Boomer's plan. But Khaled vetoed the Marine plan out of hand. He explained that his reasons for rejecting the plan could be expressed in one word: "Pride."[49] Though from a tactical point of view the Marine plan was the right way to go, considerations of pride prevailed. He could not allow himself to compromise his royal status by ceding his sector.

Saudi attitude toward Western culture

Perhaps the bluntest expression of Wahhabism was its rejection of the way of life, family values and traditions of the non-believer. As the home of Mecca and Medina, the center of Muslim prayer and pilgrimage, Saudis believed in the sacredness of their land and in the need to protect it from being defiled by non-Muslims. At the core of the Saudi mindset stood the belief that the infidel was an inferior being whose presence on Saudi soil was destructive. Upon the arrival to the kingdom of the first American forces, the Saudis asked that Americans remove all sewage generated by their troops out of the country so that Saudi soil would not be contaminated.[50] Even more infuriating to the Americans was the Saudi demand that blood rations of Muslim and Christians in military hospitals be kept separate so that Christian blood would not be transfused into a Muslim vein.[51] They also made clear that Christian soldiers killed in battle could not be buried in Saudi Arabia, and no provisions were made for the handling of non-Muslim bodies.[52] These positions, some of them taken all the way to the king, outraged and insulted many of the foreign servicemen who felt that they were risking their lives for an ungrateful ally. Saudi xenophobia could be attributed to an inherent sense of insecurity as well as to the delicate equilibrium formed over the years between the people and the ruling class which viewed any outside influence as a destabilizing challenge.

To minimize inflow of foreign ideas into the kingdom, the ruling elite collaborated over the years with the religious establishment in an effort to close the country to Western influence. Consequently, the country never developed a tourist industry, allowing non-Muslims a glimpse into its people's lives. To prevent Saudis from absorbing non-traditional values that could destabilize the existing social system, the small number of foreigners admitted to the country, such as military personnel, contractors, diplomats and employees of the big oil companies, were usually confined to restricted areas and were discouraged from mingling with Saudi society. Saudi religion and family values were guarded by self-appointed morality policemen called *muttawwa'in*, who patrolled the streets and punished Saudis and foreigners for any violation of the country's strict religious and moral laws. Women could be beaten for exposing their bare arms, hair or face; merchants were harassed for failing to close their shops during prayer time. Ordinary Saudis became apprehensive of any public display of affection between a man and a woman even if there were legally married. There was also suspicion of the marvels of modern technology. Gadgets such as cameras, CD players, and computer games were taboo among traditional Saudis. To the ordinary Western visitor, such an environment was unwelcoming, and it was not surprising that by pursuing such policies Saudi Arabia succeeded in keeping itself insular. Hence, Saudis lacked the exposure to other ways of life as well as the knowledge of other foreign cultures needed to establish good working relations with foreigners. Despite the country's oil wealth, over thirty percent of its adult population was illiterate and knew nothing about the West. Most people could speak no foreign language. The education system focused mainly on religious themes with no attention to world history, geography, culture or philosophy. American officers were surprised by how little Saudis knew even about the history of their own country. They claimed that most American Foreign Area Officers knew more about it than did the Saudis.[53]

Whereas the above characterizations applied to the greater majority of the Saudi people, members of the kingdom's ruling elite were far less xenophobic. Saudi Arabia's upper class was more immersed in the life and culture of the West. Upper class Saudis traveled the world, were educated in European and American universities, learned to enjoy Western comforts and technology and even occasionally sinned by indulging in a glass of whiskey. Most Saudi generals received their military education in Western military academies and were aware of the technological developments and the latest changes in doctrine and military thought. By and large, the Saudi upper class was pro-American and its members cultivated close personal and business relations with Americans. It was this group of 15,000 to 20,000 influential Saudis who have been responsible for the conduct and the preservation of U.S.-Saudi diplomatic, military and economic relations over the years.

American attitude toward Arab culture

To most Americans before the Gulf War, knowledge of the Arabian Peninsula was limited to the tales of the Arabian Nights and the adventures of Lawrence of Arabia, both popularized in books and films. A 1988 National Geographic survey revealed that 75 percent of American adults could not locate the Persian Gulf, an important source of their energy, on a world map.[54] American elementary and secondary school education put little emphasis on the history and geography of the Arab world. A survey by the Middle East Outreach Council, a national group of educators trying to promote education about the area, showed that 50 percent of American high school graduates had been taught nothing about the region.[55] Since over 90 percent of the enlisted personnel in the Gulf had never attended college, it is safe to assume that the troops' level of knowledge of the region was generally on a par with that of the rest of the population.

Over the years, American perceptions of Arabs have been mostly negative. There was little appreciation of their culture and a tendency to view it as backward and inferior to Western culture.[56] This attitude was shaped in the mind of Americans from a young age. Data about American students' perceptions of the Middle East showed discriminatory tendencies toward Middle Eastern countries and culture. Opinions about the region were mainly derived from stereotypes such as: "the Middle East is anti-American," the Arabs are "devious," "lascivious," "terrorists" and "religious fanatics," "Arab men oppress women," "the Middle East is a backward, wealthy area fraught with violence."[57] One American Middle East educator commented on the upbringing of the soldiers sent to the desert: "All these soldiers have spent their childhood in a society that has regularly depicted the Arab as a greasy person with a long headdress and a big nose."[58] However, there was something fundamentally different about the attitude the Americans had toward their new coalition partners in comparison with past partnerships. The attitude toward the Arabs, at least publicly, was neither patronizing nor were there any illusions of reforming the non-Westerners, converting them or intervening in their way of life. The U.S. of the 1990s was a multicultural, pluralistic society in which respect for the culture of the other was a pivotal value. Though the Muslim population in the U.S. did not exceed four percent, there was a strong social convention against any public expression of anti-Muslim prejudice. Even if there were some who held racial or ethnic biases, the implicit regime of political correctness ensured these ideas could not be disseminated. Instead, Americans were geared up to go to their libraries and improve their knowledge about the region their sons were heading to defend.

Aboard U.S. ships and planes, American troops consumed the available popular literature about life in Saudi Arabia and in the Middle East in general.[59] American commanders were fully aware of Saudi anxiety over the foreign 'invasion' into their territory and wanted to do everything possible to minimize cultural friction generated from their soldiers' ignorance. A pamphlet published by CENTCOM titled *The Military Guide to Arab Culture* was distributed among every U.S. troop deployed in the region. It included information on Arab customs, behavior, language, body language, the role of women and other useful tips. Drawing on lessons from Vietnam and Korea, the cultural preparation emphasized the issue of personal space and physical closeness. American soldiers, accustomed not to invade each other's personal space, were advised that Arabs touched each other during conversation and that they should not be offended if touched by members of the same sex. All U.S officers had to undergo a program of cultural acclimatization before their deployment in the Gulf. The 15-hour program of cultural training included lectures, films and simulations. Each unit commander was responsible for holding a similar briefing with his soldiers. Servicewomen were handed a booklet called *A Woman in Islam,* which prepared them for the encounter with a society in which women are treated very differently than in the U.S. [60]

How did they communicate?

A Western professor who spent years in Saudi universities observed that many Saudis were averse to studying the English language because it symbolized secularism and westernization, both of which make traditional Saudis uncomfortable.[61] As a result, only a small percentage of Saudi soldiers were conversant in English. An even smaller percentage of Americans spoke Arabic. And yet, the Gulf War turned out to be the first modern war in which no major incidents of miscommunication due to language gaps were recorded. How did this come about?

Liaison between Saudi and U.S. forces was made possible by both Saudi and American bilingual coordinators and interpreters positioned in key units. Kuwaiti students also volunteered to help the Saudis and Americans bridge the language gap.[62] Since the 1960s, the U.S. military recognized the importance of qualifying a sufficient number of language officers to be used for liaison with potential Arab coalition partners. Many of these officers were graduates of the Foreign Area Officer Program of the U.S. Army and Air Force. They specialized in the Middle East region and went through intensive Arabic language training at the Defense Language Institute Foreign Language Center, the primary foreign language training institution within the Department of Defense. These officers were familiar with Arabic culture and customs, and even though most of them had not previously served in Saudi Arabia, they quickly learned to apply the experience gained during their service in other Arab countries. Most of these officers were much more than just interpreters. They received specialized training in fire support routines and could assist Saudi units with air and artillery support when needed.[63] On the more senior level of command, communication was in English since most Saudi generals were conversant in English. Despite their sensitivity to being considered equals with their American counterparts, Saudis had no problem ceding the use of Arabic when conducting military operations. This spared the sides the hassles involved with translation and bilingual documentation. Documents directed to smaller units where commanders could not read English were normally drafted in English and distributed to the liaison officers in Saudi units where they were translated into Arabic. The Gulf War produced many more English language documents than Arabic. This reflected one of the differences in American and Saudi military cultures. Arabs have a tradition of oral communication and a low regard for documentation. Prince Khaled explained: "we believe in discussing our problems and working them out face-to-face, with few of the memos common in the West."[64]

Though language hardly hindered cooperation, smooth communication with the Saudis required a thorough understanding of all of the non-verbal aspects and sensitivities of Arab culture.

It was "an ongoing educational experience," wrote Lt. General Gus Pagonis, CENTCOM's chief of logistics who conducted a great deal of business with the Saudis.[65] Pagonis' introduction to Arab culture is a typical example of the difficult learning process some American commanders had to undergo before they were seasoned enough to do business with the Saudis. They were prepared well enough to know that Saudi society was a high-contact society; like other Arabs, Saudis stand or sit closer to each other and touch people of the same sex in casual conversation. They also knew the do's and don'ts of Arab culture such as the taboos of exposing the sole of one's shoe when seated, giving a "thumbs-up" and the "OK" hand gesture. But there were always habits, such as backslapping or using one's left hand to offer something to an Arab, that were "hard to shake off" and could spoil relations.[66] Arabs were also averse to the direct, no-nonsense American approach to doing business. Before conducting business, one was usually expected to engage in an extensive session of small talk in which sensitive issues such as religion, politics, or any inquiry about the wife or other females in the family of their Saudi conversation partner could not be touched. Such small talk could take a long time and required a great deal of patience. "I am a blunt person, and I'm not known as a paragon of patience," wrote Pagonis, "but soon I learned that in the Middle East, you have to go slow to go fast. And so I did."[67] Schwarzkopf, who was known among his subordinates for his impatience and quick temper, also had to conform to the new cultural environment. He recalled how he was forced to spend hours every night sipping coffee and philosophizing with Khaled. "Decisions that would require fifteen minutes in Tampa or Washington would often consume three hours in Riyadh," he complained.[68]

Like in many of the Asian cultures, saying "no" was difficult for the typical Saudi. When a foreigner asked a Saudi for help, even for help that the Saudi was unable to provide, the answer would rarely be negative. To spare both parties any immediate embarrassment, no answer would be given at all. Americans who worked with Saudis often complained that due to their lack of directness, it was hard to know what was really on their mind. They also noticed that Saudis responded negatively to deadlines and that their perception of time was very different from the Americans'. Whenever an American specified to a Saudi that something had to be done by a certain day or a specific hour it was taken as if the American was patronizing his Saudi colleague. Americans also noted that they always had to expect interruptions in meetings, delay in schedules and endless changes in plans.

Besides interacting with the Saudi military, the deployment in the kingdom created a need to conduct many business transactions with Saudi civilian vendors and businessmen from whom the Americans purchased food, leased vehicles and obtained other supplies. This required them to master the art of bargaining, the bread and butter of the Middle Eastern bazaar. Some felt that adopting the habits of the locals, such as holding a string of worry beads or exchanging small presents, could change their status in the eyes of the locals and hence bring better deals.[69] Others were astonished how business transactions worth tens or hundreds-of-thousands-of-dollars were closed verbally without any registration or proof of purchase. In a culture where a man's word or handshake is his bond, it was considered offensive to demand signed agreements.

Despite all the cultural gaps between Arabs and Americans, communication was relatively good. Saudis and Americans got along well. Both sides showed respect, exercised patience and went to great lengths to avoid friction that might have otherwise burdened the coalition. The months of Desert Shield proved to be an important transition period in which the two peoples learned each other's cultures and became used to each other's sensitivities and idiosyncrasies. By the time they had to start fighting together, they were already compatible.

In the hands of Allah

A month before the Iraqi invasion of Kuwait, during the annual pilgrimage to Mecca, a tunnel connecting Mecca and the nearby plain of Mina collapsed. More than 1400 pilgrims were crushed to death in the panic, 680 of them Indonesians. There was no investigation, nor was there any acknowledgement of responsibility. It was simply, according to Saudi officials, an act of God. In a statement to security officials, King Fahd said: "No one can blame this country for this accident because its authorities and people provided all facilities to the pilgrims. This was an accident and not intentional. [...] It was God's will, which is above everything. It was fate. Had they not died there, they would have died elsewhere, and at the same predestined moment."[70] This incident was indicative of some of the unique traits of Saudi culture. First, it showed a tendency to ignore problems rather than treat them in a constructive and comprehensive way. The Saudis refused to investigate the cause of the disaster, because they feared that such an investigation might reveal flaws in the way the regime handled the *Hajj*. Since any form of public or private criticism of the royal family was prohibited, no one dared seeking the truth. The inability to assume responsibility or admit mistakes created a habit of deflecting the blame to someone else or simply declaring the incident an act of God. This pattern of behavior was symptomatic of all walks of life. As a result, most Saudi institutions, including the military, lacked the ability to follow a learning curve that would improve their performance over time. The fatalistic belief that everything that happened to a person was God's will left very little desire for the believer to interfere with the work of divine powers. If everything was predestined, there was no point investing time and effort in planning, improving processes or reforming dysfunctional systems. An American pamphlet distributed to U.S. troops in the Gulf claimed that Arabs did not plan more than one week in advance "because it tempts fate and the anger of God."[71] Saudi attitude toward the future was optimistic regardless of how one prepared for it since God never failed to reward his devout subjects. But the suggestion that Saudis were averse to planning was simplistic and unjust. It did not reflect the true nature of modern Saudi society, which was involved in business, commerce and public planning. It created a false sense among the Americans that their partners were incapable of military planning.

Another lesson gleaned from the tunnel incident was that the Saudi attitude toward life was very different than that in the U.S. One could only imagine what the reaction to a disaster on such a scale would have been had it occurred in the U.S. The Saudis, for their part, received the news about the accident with what appeared to almost be indifference. In fact, the Saudi press barely covered it. The Saudi attitude toward human life was also reflected by its justice system, which allowed public beheading and stoning. Amputations of hands could be punishment for theft.[72] Although the U.S. is one of the few countries in which capital punishment is practiced, most Americans were repulsed by the cruel and inhumane punishment system applied by the Saudi justice system.[73]

Americans and Saudis also had very different attitudes toward achievement and individualism. Conformity in Saudi Arabia is the key to a secure place in society. When one deviates from the norm, whether for good or for bad, it could inflict a degree of shame and loss of prestige. American society on the other hand elevates individual success as one of the highest virtues. People are encouraged to stand out, to excel in what they do and accomplish more than their colleagues. They get rewarded with prestige, publicity and material benefits. In American society the word 'mediocre' carries negative connotations. In Saudi Arabia, being mediocre means being part of a collective, conforming. When a Saudi pilot, for example, shot down two Iraqi planes, he was celebrated in the U.S. press, but in the Arabic newspapers his achievement was hidden, his name not even mentioned.[74]

But perhaps the most difficult cultural gap to bridge was the Saudi attitude toward foreigners, especially those adhering to a belief system other than their own. Both the U.S. - where more than 95 percent of the population professes a belief in God - and Saudi societies are considered religious. But whereas religious freedom has always been the centerpiece of American democracy and an important part of its constitution, Saudi Arabian society, as mentioned earlier, is considered extremely intolerant of any non-Islamic faith. In a country where the law imposes a punishment more severe for smuggling in a Bible or Christian prayer book than for smuggling drugs, non-Muslims enjoyed no freedom to express their religious beliefs.[75] Non-Muslim rituals and ceremonies were prohibited by law; as were external symbols of other religions. In addition, secular books, pictures and popular magazines were controlled and limited. Saudis were forced to close their businesses during prayer times and observe the fast during the month of Ramadan. The country's religiosity strongly impacted the lives of non-Muslim coalition soldiers. The Saudis' hypersensitivity to any religious expression by foreigners clashed with the basic need for spiritual comfort soldiers in life threatening situations usually have. A compromise was achieved. Soldiers could practice their faith only discreetly and in closed quarters. Religious ceremonies could not be publicized or advertised and were disguised as "morale calls." There was a "morale call-C" for Catholics, a "morale Call-P" for Protestants and a "morale call-J" for Jews.[76] In addition, chaplains were renamed "morale officers" and were ordered by General Schwarzkopf to remove their religious insignia. "Let's not put the Saudis in a position that they'd feel obliged to say, 'no religious services' - that would be unacceptable to us, to our troops, and to the American people," Schwarzkopf justified his order. [77]

To placate the Saudis and prevent unnecessary cultural tension, on August 30 Schwarzkopf issued, General Order 1, which said: "Operation Desert Shield places U.S. Armed Forces into USCENTCOM AOR countries where Islamic Law and Arabic customs prohibit or restrict certain activities that are generally permissible in Western societies. There would be no alcohol, no gambling, no pornography, no body building magazines, swim suit editions of periodicals, lingerie or underwear advertisement, and catalogues...[that displayed] portions of the human torso (i.e., the area below the neck, above the knees and inside the shoulder.)"[78] Many soldiers were staggered by the intrusive restrictions on their private leisure time, viewing it as a violation of their constitutional rights. Schwarzkopf's response was: "I hope you recognize that the Constitution of the U.S. applies only on U.S. soil, and therefore, we don't have any constitutional rights in Saudi Arabia. The law of the land here happens to be Saudi law. So just as we require them to obey our laws in the U.S., they have every right to require us to obey their laws here."[79]

The holiday season which started with the Jewish holidays in September and ended with Christmas and New Year's Eve in December brought with it more restrictions and with them more resentment among the troops. Both Saudis and Americans were concerned about the ramifications of foreign troops performing religious rituals in Saudi Arabia. Henry Kissinger even warned the Senate Armed Services Committee that Saddam Hussein might use the observance of Jewish and Christian holidays as a pretext to destroy the coalition with the Saudis.[80] Consequently, Christmas in the desert was celebrated almost clandestinely. The Saudis gave the Americans advance warning that no public Christian worship would be tolerated and they prohibited any Christmas symbols such as Christmas trees and other holiday decorations.[81] Both the Americans and the British had to send religious troops from each unit to Bahrain, a more liberal Arab neighbor where there was no objection to Christian worship.[82] The Saudis also tried to enforce a ban on Christmas cards. But their censorship was not equipped to deal with the 400 tons of mail that arrived in theater every week, and they finally gave up. Many American soldiers complained that denying them the ability to practice their holiday rituals was unfair. They felt that if they were being called on to defend Saudi Arabia, the least the Kingdom could do was to make an exception for them and allow them to celebrate their holiday. They also felt somewhat betrayed by their military and political leaders for not taking a tougher stand vis-à-vis the Saudis. The time arrived for the Saudis to also make some compromises. They agreed, for example to turn a blind eye to the little aluminum trees and other decorations placed inside the tents of the American soldiers.[83] After asking the Americans to turn off the radio transmitters that aired news and entertainment to U.S. personnel, fearing they would broadcast Christmas carols, the Saudis agreed that the carols could be broadcast in the instrumental version without the words.[84] But even these compromises were conditioned on complete secrecy. They made it clear that publicizing the concessions would lead to their withdrawal. Therefore, the Pentagon forbade journalists from covering or photographing any of the religious ceremonies or the holiday activities taking place on U.S. bases. [85]

The Saudi way of life imposed limitations on Westerners' dietary habits too. U.S. Marines found themselves spending their first days in the Gulf separating pork portions from the Meals Ready to Eat (MREs), instead of training for their missions.[86] Consumption of alcoholic beverages was also banned by General Order 1 after General Khaled warned General Schwarzkopf that any American soldier caught drunk outside the perimeter of a U.S. base would be punished according to Saudi law. This could have created a clash between the U.S. and the Saudis. Dry as the climate outside was, U.S. camps inside were equally dry of alcohol.[87] Ironically, the only times American officers found alcohol was when they were invited to parties in Saudi homes. While the Saudis were remorselessly drinking alcohol surreptitiously, the Western guests had to politely decline their host's hospitality - something not to be done in the Middle East - or else face the risk of a court-martial for violating General Order 1.[88] The British Ambassador in Riyadh, Alan Munro, described how tough a pill to swallow the prohibition on alcohol was for the Western soldiers.[89] But many of the officers, accustomed to dealing with disciplinary problems resulting from drunkenness, were quite satisfied with the ban and reported fewer alcohol-related incidents of violence and misbehavior than usual in their units.[90] With the approach of Christmas, the issue of alcohol even created mild tension between the British and the Americans. The British Ministry of Defense had suggested that each soldier receive, as a special gesture, two cans of beer. This was not only inflammatory vis-à-vis the Saudis but also threatened to destroy the uniformity among the Western coalition members. Hence, both Ambassador Munro and the Commander of British Forces Lt. General Peter de la Billiere voted against the beer allowance. Their stance was highly appreciated by the Saudis.[91]

Throughout the war, Schwarzkopf showed a remarkable degree of respect for Saudi religious sensitivities. He took every avenue to avoid conflict even on issues about which the Saudis were not forceful. For example, in November 1990, when President Bush came to visit the American troops for Thanksgiving, Schwarzkopf unilaterally decided to celebrate the event aboard the USS *Nassau* which had been positioned outside Saudi waters so that religious services could be conducted without offending the Saudis.[92] The Saudis, on the other hand, did not live up to the same standards they demanded of the Americans. They made no effort to hide their missionary efforts among the thousands of young men and women who were stationed in their land. Efforts to convert U.S. soldiers to Islam were explicit and were even a source of pride among the Saudis. Saudi lecturers appeared before U.S. troops with the aim of explaining the fundamentals of Islam, the customs and the rituals. With them came missionaries who offered gifts and money to potential converts.[93] According to Khaled's account, more than 2,000 American servicemen converted to Islam during the war.[94]

"Non women" in Humvees

More so than in any other place in the male dominated Middle East, the status of women in Saudi society is particularly subordinated. To any Western observer, women in Saudi Arabia are treated as second-class citizens. They are not allowed to: walk alone unaccompanied by her husband, drive a car, check into a hotel or order in a restaurant. Saudi women are not often seen in public or in workplaces. When they are, they must be covered, head-to-toe, by a long, black cloak called an *abaaya*. They sit in the rear of public buses and are forced to enter public buildings through a back door.[95] The deployment of U.S. forces in Saudi Arabia raised ethical as well as operational questions about the status of servicewomen deployed in a gender discriminating environment. In contrast to previous U.S. conflicts, Desert Storm was the largest deployment of military women in history. More than 26,000 women served in Operations Desert Shield and Desert Storm. Women accounted for 17 percent of Army reservists in Saudi Arabia at the height of the conflict and in total more than 8.6 percent of the Army's deployed force.

At the beginning of Desert Shield, when it was still unclear how massive the deployment would be, many American units were reluctant to send their women to the Gulf until they knew what the status of servicewomen would be.[96] All women Marines were pulled out of their units and replaced by men. "This is a perfect example of how the Marine Corps is paying lip service to us," said an angry women officer.[97] As it became clear that the American deployment in the kingdom would be long and intensive, U.S. commanders insisted that women be deployed with their units and perform all of their duties, including driving military vehicles. However, strict limitations were imposed on the servicewomen's freedom of movement. Outside the bases, American servicewomen were not allowed to walk around alone and were required to cover themselves with black robes. In several cases, the *muttawwa'in* harassed American servicewomen who were not sufficiently covered. Most at risk were servicewomen with long, blond hair – a rarity in the Middle Eastern country – said to excite the Saudi males. Like men, women were required to participate in manual work such as loading and unloading supplies, but unlike the men who were allowed to work in the hot weather with T-shirts, females were not allowed to remove their long-sleeved military attire.[98] In one incident, Pagonis described, tension rose when a contingent of soldiers, both male and female, were sent to a nearby city to unload supplies. Due to the heat, some of the servicewomen rolled up their sleeves while others took off their jackets under which they wore T-shirts. The local residents took offense at what they considered excessive exposure of the female body. An official complaint was submitted to Schwarzkopf's headquarters. As a result, all soldiers in the area were forced to work with long sleeves despite the heat.[99] Most male Saudis were unaccustomed to dealing with women in their daily lives. They were embarrassed by the fact that women were guarding them and simultaneously felt threatened by their presence.[100] At the same time, American prestige in the eyes of many Saudis somewhat diminished when they saw American female officers commanding men. Maj. Deborah Gilmore recalled: "I remember the astonished looks of the Saudi military as I gave orders. They didn't understand why I was giving orders, but even more, they couldn't comprehend why the men were listening."[101] The Saudis did not know how to communicate with foreign women or how to address them. They preferred to simply ignore them. American woman who entered a store were often ignored or refused service. In more severe cases, this conduct affected military cooperation. On one occasion, for example, the woman pilot of a Galaxy plane was refused permission to land by the Riyadh airbase. The Saudi air traffic controller demanded to hear a man on the radio. But all the crew members were women. The male loadmaster had to be brought into the cockpit from the back of the plane to talk the aircraft down.[102]

In his book, Khaled played down the concessions women had to endure, claiming that American females seemed eager to respect Saudi customs and were even more compliant than some Arab women.[103] Many U.S. servicewomen who had joined the military with the intention of promoting gender equality did not feel that way at all. They felt that they were fighting to defend and perpetuate a morally corrupt social system where women were treated as a piece of property. "It's frustrating," said USAF Lt. Colonel Lois Schwartz in an interview, "We work long hours, it's hot, and we can't even have the release of going across the street to the store."[104] The most difficult issue involving women was driving since approximately a third of American vehicles were driven by women. The Saudis – who do not grant driver's licenses to women – quickly realized that preventing the American women from driving would seriously hinder the coalition effort. They agreed to a compromise. It came in the form of a remarkable decree issued by King Fahd saying that: "U.S. female military personnel in uniform are not women when driving military vehicles."[105] Unlike the men who at times drove vehicles in civilian clothes and for civilian purposes, the decree allowed "non-women" in the kingdom to drive military vehicles only on official duty and only when in uniform.[106] The spectacle of women behind steering wheels hit a raw nerve among many Saudis. For others, it was an opportunity to promote liberal reforms including what was referred to as 'the driving incident.' On November 6, 1990, in Riyadh, a group of well-connected Saudi women who had obtained driver's licenses abroad dismissed their drivers and began driving around the city on their own. The action shocked the Saudi public, as it was an open challenge to the status quo. Many Saudis perceived this act as directly related to the American presence in the country. The incident enraged the Islamic fundamentalists across the country who demanded the women be put to death. The public outrage forced the regime to adopt a heavy-handed approach toward the specific offenders as well as against women in general. Saudi women were fired from their jobs, and a *fatwa* warning against similar incidents was issued by the *ulama*.

The women drivers were imprisoned, dismissed from their jobs and were denounced as "whores."[107] The 'driving incident' was a seminal event in Saudi history. It was the first time that women stood up in an organized manner against the existing social order. Clearly, many Saudi women had their dreams of emancipation long before the Gulf War, but what the war did was present them with an alternative way of life. Though the incident could have provided a trigger for social change, the opposite occurred. Already agitated with the presence of American forces in the kingdom, the religious establishment coerced the King into taking more active measures against the liberal intelligentsia and increasing the level of morality enforcement by the *muttawwa'in.*

The domestic developments in November also had a direct effect on relations with the Americans and other Western members of the coalition. To placate the radicals, the Saudis felt obligated to step up their cultural restrictions and show the highest degree of sensitivity to any provocation that could enrage the religious establishment. The main issues that emerged around the holiday season were dancing and entertainment for the troops. The Saudis were specifically sensitive to any publicity of "immoral" behavior involving the foreign soldiers in their country. A CNN report, showing American troops from the 82nd-Division dancing with members of the opposite sex, enraged the Saudis and almost created a diplomatic incident between the two countries.[108] In addition, the Saudis denied visas to any entertainer, especially female, who was a singer or dancer, allowing in only comedians and magicians.[109] Popular American entertainers like Brooke Shields were thus denied the opportunity to lift the spirits of American men and women in uniform. The soldiers had to settle for a comedy show with male performers like Bob Hope and Jay Leno.[110]

Schwarzkopf and the other senior American commanders had no intention of challenging the Saudis over petty issues such as entertainment. They preferred to pick more important battles. The French felt differently. Shortly before Christmas a popular French singer, Eddy Mitchell, arrived in Saudi Arabia with his band to entertain the French contingent. The Saudis were outraged upon hearing about the concert that was about to take place and even more so about the fact that the Mitchell trip was about to be televised on French TV and covered in the French press. The King ordered that the officer who had issued the visas be court-martialed, and the Saudis informed the French that there was no way the concert could take place. The French were not impressed by the Saudi reaction. French Defense Minister Jean-Pierre Chevènement instructed his commander in the Gulf, Lt. General Michel Roquejeoffre that Eddy Mitchell must sing. But there was one problem. At the outset of Desert Shield, the French decided that they did not want to serve under American command and therefore submitted themselves to the Joint Forces Command under General Khaled. The Prince, therefore, had command authority over Roquejeoffre which he used to veto the concert. Caught between Khaled and Chevènement's conflicting orders, Roquejeoffre was experiencing one of the most typical dilemmas of a coalition commander: whose order to follow? The issue was later put before President François Mitterrand himself. Foreseeing a major crisis with the Saudis, the president overruled his defense minister and ordered to cancel the concert. But that was not the end of the affair. Chevènement, who was on his way to Saudi Arabia to visit the troops, was so angry by the turn of events that he decided not to attend a lunch reception planned for him by the Saudi Defense Minister.[111]

Rigid as the Saudis were on cultural issues, they were not blind to the frustration thousands of troops under the desert sun could harbor if not provided with some form of relaxation and entertainment. They had to make some concessions. One major concession was allowing the activity of the U.S. Armed Forces Radio and Television Service that broadcasted 24 hours a day of light music and news, though they closely monitored the programs to ensure that the content was appropriate. But this was not enough. The heat, the boredom, the no-prostitution and no-alcohol policy, and the tense anticipation of combat made U.S. commanders realize that it was necessary to provide an escape valve to reduce the pressure on the troops. Veterans of Korea and Vietnam remembered how soldiers were shipped from the front to places like Japan, Hawaii, Hong Kong or Bangkok for rest and recreation. In the Gulf, the U.S. had the *Cunard Princess.* This was the Middle Eastern version of the Love Boat, a cruise ship docked in Bahrain where the troops could relax for a few days, eat good food including copious pork products and enjoy real American entertainment. Between December and June, more than 50,000 soldiers were able to enjoy the amenities of the boat.[112]

Bear and prince

As mentioned before, most of the top echelon of Saudi officers were familiar enough with the Western way of life to understand the habits and attitudes of their partners. General Khaled, for example, was a graduate of Britain's prestigious Sandhurst military academy, the U.S. Army Air Defense School at Fort Bliss, Texas, the U.S. Army Command and General Staff College at Fort Leavenworth, Kansas and the Air War College at Maxwell, Alabama. He also held a graduate degree from Auburn University. One of his subordinates, Maj. General Sultan Ibn Al Mutairi, the commander of Joint Forces Command East who also commanded the ground forces fighting at Khafji, was a graduate of advanced courses at Fort Bliss, Texas, Fort Sill, Oklahoma and the Army War College in Carlisle. The Americans could communicate with people with whom they had many common experiences. On the other hand, many of the American and some of the British senior officers were equipped with rich Middle East experience. Lieutenant General John Yeosock, commander of the U.S. Third Army had worked with the Saudis in the early 1980s. He was the Program Manager for the Saudi Arabian National Guard (PMSANG).[113] Yeosock's deputy, Major General Paul Schwartz also had experience working with PMSANG. He had spent two years in Saudi Arabia and had great respect for Saudi culture.[114] Brig. General James Monroe, Yeosock's logistics officer had also served in Saudi Arabia.[115] The British commander Peter de la Billiere had served in Aden and Oman and knew the Arab culture well.

Schwarzkopf was perhaps the least familiar with the region. As a young boy he had visited the Middle East with his father who had been deployed there.[116] He also attended a course at the State Department's Foreign Service Institute - an institute that prepares

American diplomats and other professionals for their overseas missions - and took great interest in cultural issues.[117] After being appointed the commander of CENTCOM, he had spent a few days in each of the Arab countries in the region. He spoke no Arabic and was, according to Khaled's impression, "as different from the Middle East as it is possible to imagine."[118] But Schwarzkopf proved to be an extremely capable coalition commander showing a great deal of patience and sensitivity to all of his foreign subordinates, and the Arabs in particular. To those who knew the man, it was a surprise. The robust general had a reputation of impatience and a quick temper. Both in his early years and in his command of CENTCOM, he was known for fits of rage, which terrified the staff surrounding him. His deputy during the Gulf War, Lt. General Cal Waller said that the CINC's staff officers always appeared to be timid, "a little bit like walking around on eggshells, they were very reluctant to give bad news to General Schwarzkopf for fear that they would cause some minor eruption."[119] Surprisingly, none of this side of his personality appeared in any way in his relations with his coalition partners. His relations with Khaled knew more ups than downs. Considering the disparity of experience, rank and the forces commanded between the two officers, Schwarzkopf showed a remarkable degree of tolerance, patience and respect.[120] Rick Atkinson wrote that privately Schwarzkopf despised Khaled, viewing him as a pompous, arrogant and spoiled prince who was an amateur in military matters. "A Joke."[121] If true, Schwarzkopf knew how to skillfully hide his personal feelings. He treated Khaled not only as a fellow general but also as a prince. Throughout the war, as Michael Gordon and Bernard Trainor wrote, "Schwarzkopf sought to preserve the fiction that Americans and Saudis were operating as equals."[122] *The Washington Post* reporter Molly Moore argued that Schwarzkopf's efforts were generally successful: "Privately, American commanders conceded that Khaled was little more than a figurehead but thought that Schwarzkopf had done a masterful job at helping preserve the public image."[123]

Not having too much experience dealing with Arabs, Schwarzkopf showed that he was a fast learner. He was resolute not to let cultural issues dominate the relations between Arabs and

Westerners. Showing great diplomatic skills, he maneuvered himself among all the minor crises that developed with the Saudis and solved them with a mixture of goodwill and grace. In fact, some of his subordinates thought he was going too far to accommodate every Saudi peculiarity even at the expense of his own soldiers. Gordon and Trainor wrote that Americans on his staff "who were on the receiving end of the beefy general's tantrums marveled at his forbearance with the Arabs and wished that he would extend some of it their way."[124] Schwarzkopf's great achievement was not only in reducing cultural tension but also in his ability to prevent problems from occurring in the first place. He fully understood the sensitive position of the Saudi leaders vis-à-vis the fundamentalists and was determined not to put them in difficult situations likely to weaken the coalition. He took some constructive measures to prevent petty incidents from assuming large proportions. He repeatedly demanded of his subordinates to respect the host country's culture and imposed disciplinary measures to achieve this goal. "If you show respect for the cultural ways of the Arab world, your stay in the Middle East will be much more enjoyable," he wrote in a message delivered to the troops.[125]

Another way to reduce friction was to institute a community relations program in which U.S. officers in each major Saudi community were assigned to communicate with the town's civilian leadership and, hence, solve culturally-related problems arising between U.S. troops and the local population. The idea was to improve communication between the U.S. forces and the Saudis and solve small problems on the community level before they reached the press. This reduced the number of problems that made it up to the level of Khaled or the palace, problems that might have, under other circumstances, created diplomatic incidents.[126] Schwarzkopf was much more of a Wedemeyer than a Stilwell. He did not try in any way to Westernize or reform the Saudis. He accepted and respected them just the way they were even though their way of life was anathema to him and to most Americans. At the same time, one needs to recognize that the military situation Schwarzkopf confronted was far less problematic than Stilwell's. Resources were limitless, victory came fast and there was not much opportunity for conflict. Regardless, it is widely accepted that Schwarzkopf deserved the credit for keeping the coalition forces glued together. Peter de la Billiere saw his cultural suavity and understanding of the Arab world as one of the main contributors to the coalition's success:

> He knew that you don't do things in Arabia the American way if you want to get 'em done. And he was able to adjust his pace of doing things and the way in which he did things, to meet the Arab style, which was very important. You must remember we were guests out there. [...] He was a great diplomat when dealing with other nations. And because of this diplomacy, he was able to keep the coalition together.[127]

Respectful distance

FDR's meeting in 1945 with Ibn Saud symbolized the nature of future Saudi-American relations. FDR, a dying man and a chain smoker, decided to respect the customs of the King and refrain from smoking in his presence throughout the conference. When he could not hold out any longer, he excused himself and went to the ship's elevator to smoke a cigarette. Three days later, when Winston Churchill met with the King and the issue of abstention from tobacco and alcohol, again, came up, he had a very different attitude from Roosevelt's: "My religion prescribed as an absolute sacred rite smoking cigars and drinking alcohol before, after, and if needed be during all meals and the intervals between them."[128] Unlike the British, who even during the Gulf War tried to challenge some of the Saudi restrictions, debating sending beer to their soldiers for Christmas is only one example, when it came to culture, American presidents, senior officials and soldiers have always treated Saudi monarchs with considerable deference. They firmly believed that the only way to preserve good working relations with the world's largest oil supplier was by being attuned to the sensitivities of its unique cultural system and showing the utmost respect for it. This was perhaps what helped the Saudis make the difficult decision to invite them into the kingdom in the first place.

Between August 1990 and March 1991, a total of 697,000 Americans served in the Persian Gulf. They camped and fought in a country that represented many of the values they abhorred. Some of their freedoms were curtailed or taken away from them, and their values were derided by the same people they came to defend. Some were verbally, at times even physically, attacked. And, yet, they managed to put the cultural differences aside, focus on the more important strategic issues and win the war. The Gulf War - at 47 days the shortest in American history - was an easy victory. Casualties were relatively low - 148 Americans were killed - and, by and large, there were no major crises in the relations with the Saudis, at least not ones that could endanger the coalition in any way. Those Saudis who talked about winning the war and losing the country were surprised by the exemplary forbearance, discipline and sensitivity the Americans demonstrated. The Americans, for their part, were no less surprised that they were able to overcome the cultural gaps.

The operational success of the Gulf War coalition stemmed from the fact that the Saudis and the Americans were united in their war objectives; they provided their forces with ample logistical support, coordinated their forces in a superb manner, integrated their command and control systems and successfully shared technology and intelligence. From a cultural point of view, considering the tremendous difficulties involved in introducing so many foreigners to a culturally-intolerant country, the Gulf War coalition was a success story. Its success should be seen not only based on the crises that occurred, but also by those that did not occur by virtue of the sides' ability and determination to forestall them. Why was the coalition such a success? First, as specified earlier, Saudi and American societies had not been exposed to each other. Americans knew close to nothing about the Saudis and the Middle East, and the Saudis, with few exceptions, knew even less about Americans and the West. But the Gulf War coalition showed that lack of national exposure to foreign cultures could be offset by increased exposure of the people who really matter in coalition operations, the field commanders. Both American and Saudi senior commanders, in light of their diverse careers, were much more culturally seasoned than the societies from which they came. This could be attributed to the tradition of the U.S. military to open its academies and training installations to foreign nationals, a tradition that gave many Saudis and others the chance to learn about Western military culture well before the coalition was formed. Over the years, thousands of officers from different countries have received their military education in these bases and have established professional as well as social relations with American colleagues. These officers have returned to their countries to assume senior command posts and instill some of the knowledge of American military culture and doctrine in their organizations. This tradition proved to yield good returns in the contingencies that the U.S. was called to participate in combined operations with these countries. The Gulf War case also showed that capable military leadership and highly disciplined soldiers could adapt to foreign norms of behavior, even if those norms deviated from the way of life in the country from which the soldiers came. The war also proved that in the modern world the problem of lack of exposure could be treated quickly and effectively. A cultural infrastructure of Foreign Area Officers, language and cultural experts, interpreters, and language schools were important assets that could in a short time assemble cultural acclimatization programs for all troops sent to an unfamiliar theater of operations and provide them with all the knowledge they needed for dealing with the indigenous population. The Saudi fear of cultural contamination posed limitations on the interaction between the host population and the guests. Their policy was simply to keep the two sides physically apart from each other. Gordon and Trainor described it as a successful policy of keeping a "respectful distance" even at the expense of "lockstep teamwork."[129] At the beginning of Desert Shield, the Saudis underestimated the scope of the American deployment in their country. When the nature of the deployment became apparent to them, they did all they could to reduce the profile of the foreign presence. Foreign forces were positioned in bases remote from civilian population centers and advised not to spend time in the cities unless they were on official business and only while in uniform.[130] They also tried to supply the guests with all their needs on their bases so they did not have too many reasons to seek the outside world. To discourage Americans from leaving their compounds, the Saudis requested that an escort accompany any military vehicle that came into their cities. That probably occurred for a couple of weeks. But once forces began to arrive en masse and the Saudis realized the volume of traffic they were really proposing to control, it clearly overwhelmed them and they gave up.[131]

Second, the implicit U.S. policy of cultural obedience can be explained by the changes in racial and social attitudes of American society during the last decade of the 20th century. American society in 1990 was egalitarian and culturally tolerant. Racially biased sentiments about enemies and allies expressed regularly by prominent Americans until the early 1970s became socially objectionable to the majority of Americans. American society developed high cultural sensitivity and a socially binding regime of political correctness making people more aware of cultural, ethnic and racial diversity. Even though most Americans could not agree with the Saudi way of life, their attitude was: "how can we work best with these people to achieve common objectives" rather than "how can we change these people and make them behave like us."

The third factor contributing to the cultural stability in the Gulf War was the strategic parity of the U.S. and Saudi Arabia and the host-guest balance they formed. The U.S. was by far militarily superior and by far the bigger force contributor. But at the same time the U.S. was completely dependent on the host country. The Saudis supplied the stage, the logistics and the political legitimacy in the Muslim world, all crucial components to the success of the war. This dependency forced the American guests to be on their best behavior and to go to great lengths to avoid insulting their hosts.

The fourth component of success was the sides' willingness to compromise and concede their cultural sovereignty on issues that were at the core of their culture. The Saudis compromised on fundamental parts of their lifestyle. They allowed women to drive, Western music to be aired in their land and inquisitive Western journalists to wander freely in their cities. These concessions should not be taken lightly, for they invited domestic unrest, strengthened the Islamic opposition and were a catalyst for changes in the internal and external policies of Saudi Arabia.[132] The Americans made no smaller concessions. For the first time in American military history, constitutional freedoms of U.S. servicemen, such as the freedom of worship, speech, press, assembly and association, were curtailed. For the sake of the survival of the coalition it was perhaps the right thing to do, but the price paid in terms of the morale of the forces was significant, though it has never been sufficiently addressed. Saudi Arabia may have been, as Khaled boasted, "the biggest health farm in the world," no alcohol, no prostitution, no distractions. But the soldiers in this health farm were not happy. (As it turned out, thousands of them contracted a mysterious disease, the Gulf War Syndrome, and many other thousands were exposed to various toxic agents.) They felt betrayed by the policies that they viewed as complete deference to the host nation. Many served under the impression that any unintended cultural transgression they might commit could turn into an international incident. In other words, they felt the burden of the responsibility for the future of the coalition.[133] An American military columnist William M. Arkin wrote: "American commanders and politicians bent over backward to assuage Saudi "sensitivities." But in doing so, geopolitical interests outweighed American values. It is a scandalous compromise that continues to this day."[134]

And indeed in 2001 the Air Force's highest-ranking female fighter pilot, Lt. Colonel Martha McSally sued the Department of Defense to try to overturn the policy requiring servicewomen to leave their base only if accompanied by a man and only if wearing the *abaaya* when off-base in Saudi Arabia.[135] McSally claimed that the policy was unconstitutional because it discriminated against women and violated their religious freedom.[136] She also claimed that most American servicewomen in Saudi Arabia found the policy offensive, "but they are reluctant to tell the brass."[137] In June 2002, the U.S. Senate voted 93-0 in favor of an amendment to prohibit the Department of Defense from requiring or even formally urging servicewomen stationed in Saudi Arabia to wear the *abaaya*.

The role played by culture in the Gulf War cannot be ignored. Ambassador Munro described the cultural issue in the Gulf War as "a real obstacle to the close working relationship which was a prerequisite for effective political and military cooperation between Saudi Arabia and the Western countries."[138] Schwarzkopf also concluded that culture carried significant weight in the coalition, writing that the Saudis cared much more about the cultural consequences of inviting the Americans onto their domain than about the management of the war.[139] Admirable as the military achievement of the Gulf War coalition was, one should not forget that it was, in the words of Saudi Brig. General Abdul-rahman Marshad, "a war without battles."[140] In light of the sparse Iraqi resistance, some even saw it as a war without an enemy. Had the war turned out differently, the operational effect of culture could have been much greater. Arab sensitivities concerning one Arab nation attacking another were a major influence on the conduct of the coalition and, indeed, when time came for the coalition forces to enter Iraqi soil, the only ground forces prepared to do so were the British, the French and the Americans. Furthermore, Schwarzkopf was convinced that if the war had continued and the coalition had to move toward Baghdad, it would have disintegrated due to lack of Arab support.[141] One can only speculate on the implications had the war dragged on to Ramadan and the possible effect on the kingdom's ability to host the pilgrimage.

Operation Desert Storm ended, but Saddam Hussein's regime remained intact for another twelve years and with it, his ability to threaten his neighbors. For this reason Operation Desert Farewell, the U.S. redeployment from the Gulf, did not remove all the foreigners from Saudi soil. The thousands of Americans left behind, with Saudi permission, remained a red flag waving in the face of the self-appointed guardians of the Islamic faith, the thousands of fundamentalists who vowed to fight until the last American left Islam's holy soil. The name of one of them was Osama bin Laden.

6

SABRAS AMONG THE CEDARS: ISRAEL AND THE SOUTH LEBANON ARMY, 1985-2000

⌘ ⌘ ⌘

This is not Norway here, and it is not Denmark
Bashir Gemayel, shortly before he was assassinated

They were Arabs, but not exactly, they were
more sophisticated, more cultured
Senior Israeli commander in Lebanon

On February 28, 1999, Brig. General Erez Gerstein, Commander of the Israel Defense Forces (IDF) in southern Lebanon was killed in a roadside bomb explosion planted by the Lebanese resistance movement, Hizballah. Gerstein was en route to pay a condolence call to the family of one South Lebanon Army (SLA) officer who was killed in action a few days earlier. The death of Israel's highest-ranking officer in Lebanon shocked the country, at the time in the midst of an election campaign. Then prime ministerial candidate Ehud Barak declared that, if elected, he would withdraw all IDF soldiers from Lebanon within one year of his election. Fourteen months later, with Barak as prime minister, Israel ended its 18-year occupation of southern Lebanon, the SLA was disbanded and thousands of its soldiers and families became refugees in Israel. Thus ended the first, and probably the last, Jewish-Arab coalition in history.

Relations between Israel and the SLA - a militia trained, financed and coordinated by Israel to defend the south Lebanese community along the Israel-Lebanon border - differed from all of the other cases presented thus far. First, the relationship was long, stretching over a period of more than 15 years, in which the two parties grew to know each other well and developed mechanisms to overcome cultural and strategic gaps between them. Second, the SLA was not a cultural monolith as were the other militaries in this book. It was an amalgamation of ethnic groups including Maronite Christians, Shiite Muslims, Sunni Muslims, Druze and Bedouins all living in southern Lebanon for centuries. All of these groups defined themselves as Arabs, but each had a different interpretation of what being Arab really means. Third, it was a case of an alliance between a state actor and a non-state actor fighting together against enemies: Hizballah and other state-sponsored guerrilla groups, themselves also non-state actors. Both the SLA and its enemy, Hizballah, were proxy militias working in the service of strong patrons. Hizballah, "The Party of God," was established by the Iranians in Lebanon at the close of 1982, as a Shiite political group with a military wing. Since then, the organization began to enjoy the sponsorship of Syria, the dominant power broker in Lebanon, which used it as a tool to fight and weaken Israel on the Lebanese front. Israel, for its part, became the patron of the SLA, using it as a tool to counter the threats to its northern border and to prevent south Lebanon from becoming a Syrian-Iranian sphere of influence. Both patrons provided materiel and moral support to their proxies. Both proxies over time developed an independent agenda that, at times, stood in contrast to their patron's wishes.

The strategic alliance between Israel and the south Lebanese goes back to the early days of the Lebanese Civil War, which, from the mid-1970s to the mid-1980s, destroyed the country through sectarian violence and episodes of armed invasion. Fearing a massacre by the Muslims, Maronite Christians in Beirut, under the leadership of the influential Gemayel family, asked Israel for help in their war. In mid-1976, Israel began sending the Christians food and weapons and established in the Galilee the first training base for Christian soldiers. Israel also helped the Christians in northern Lebanon by sending them tanks and artillery.[1] However, the war in the southern part of Lebanon had more to do with the

Israeli-Palestinian conflict than with Lebanese domestic rivalries. In the decade following Jordan's September 1970 expulsion of the Palestine Liberation Organization (PLO) south Lebanon served as the battleground for fighters of Fatah, the PLO's military branch, in their war against Israel. The otherwise peaceful community of the south - sixty percent Shiite Muslims, thirty percent Christians and the rest Druze, Sunni Muslims and Bedouin - found itself caught in the midst of a war in which it had no stake. Palestinian attacks on Israel invited Israeli retaliation and the southerners were the prime casualties. After the collapse of the Lebanese Army, Israel developed close relations with the local Christian militia under the command of Major Saad Haddad, a Greek Catholic Lebanese Army officer who, in 1979, broke off from his central government and founded the "Free Lebanese Army," which, in time, came to be known as the SLA.[2] The connection with the Christian community of Lebanon had both political and cultural grounds. Politically, Israel and the Christians were united in their animosity toward the Palestinians. Israel found the enemy of the enemy to be a useful tool in its war against the PLO. The Maronites, for their part, needed Israel's support to win the civil war and to dominate all of Lebanon without sharing their power with the Muslims. "Give us the arms and we'll slaughter the Palestinians," promised Danny Chamoun, a Maronite warlord, to then IDF Colonel Binyamin Ben-Eliezer.[3]

Despite the brutality of such remarks, the Israelis had always viewed the Christians as "more civilized" than the Muslims and as a people with whom they were, more or less, culturally compatible. They toyed with the idea of turning Lebanon into a friendly Western island in the midst of an ocean of Arab hostility. Israelis also believed that the Christians would, in time, recognize the state of Israel and would be an easy partner with whom to reach peace. Israeli Mossad and IDF members who dealt with the Maronite Phalangist militia under the leadership of Bashir Gemayel misinterpreted the Christians' Middle Eastern hospitality, expressed in feasts of food, wine and presents, as a sign of genuine affection. "They bought us with food," recalled one Israeli intelligence officer.[4] "It was like drugs. It was an addiction," commented another Mossad agent about the relations with the Christians.[5] Additionally,

Israeli Prime Minister Menachem Begin was very sensitive to the suffering of the Christians in Lebanon. He saw them as a persecuted sect similar to the Jews and was puzzled by the indifference of the Christian world to their plight. He thought that due to the Holocaust, Israel had a moral responsibility to prevent genocide from occurring in Lebanon.[6] The Christian Phalangists, as it turned out, were, in the words of New York Times columnist Thomas Friedman, "Christians like the Godfather was Christian."[7] They were corrupt and consumed with deep hatred toward the Muslims, hatred that brought them to commit horrendous acts of violence against the Palestinians and the Druze. Israel displayed no aversion to the Maronites' conduct. It preferred to turn a blind eye and entertain the idea of a Christian Lebanon. This mirage led Begin's government, spearheaded by Defense Minister Ariel Sharon, into the June 1982 Operation Peace for Galilee, the IDF invasion of Lebanon.

The campaign began as a great military success. Within days the IDF was on the outskirts of Lebanon's capital. But within weeks it became apparent that the campaign was a disaster in the making. Avenging the September 14, 1982 assassination of the newly elected president, Bashir Gemayel, Phalange militiamen entered the Palestinian refugee camps Sabra and Shatila in Beirut and between September 16 and 18 massacred hundreds of Palestinians, including scores of women and children. The massacre not only tarnished Israel's image in the world - the Phalangists after all were being funded by Israel - but also shocked and disgusted the Israeli public which no longer saw the war as legitimate. From the events in Sabra and Shatila and the collapse of a subsequent May 1983 peace deal with Lebanon, the unruly confessional groups of Lebanon showed no ability to coexist and the country was soon taken over by a corrupt central government, a puppet in the hands of the Syrian regime. With no functional central authority in Beirut to protect them, the 150,000 residents of south Lebanon were determined to maintain their autonomy, and for this they were willing to ally themselves with none other than Israel - the foremost enemy in the view of the Arab people.

Israel was desperately seeking an honorable way to withdraw from Lebanon. But disengaging from the Lebanese quagmire was

Israeli and Lebanese Phalangists in south Lebanon during the 1982 invasion

not easy. For two more years, it tried to withdraw as part of some agreement that would guarantee the safety of its northern border. When it became apparent that such an agreement was impossible to achieve, the Israeli government under Prime Minister Shimon Peres decided in January 1985 to unilaterally withdraw to the international border while retaining a security zone in south Lebanon where the SLA backed by the IDF would operate. The so-called Security Zone was a 480 square mile area in south Lebanon adjacent to the border with Israel. It extended about 56 miles in length from the slopes of Mount Hermon in the east to the shores of the Mediterranean. It wound for some 78 miles along the curves of the mountainous border. At its narrowest point, it was two miles wide and at its widest, it extended for about 15 miles from Metulla northwards to the border checkpoint at Kfar Huneh. IDF Chief of Staff, Lt. General Moshe Levi, defined the purpose of the security zone as follows: "…to serve as a buffer zone, to prevent the firing of weapons directly at our territory, to prevent the movement of terrorists into our territory, and to serve as a base for activating the troops and artillery fire of the IDF."[8]

Thus, for fifteen years, centered in the small Lebanese town of Marjayoun, opposite Metulla in Israel, under the command of

Haddad's successor General Antoine Lahad, the SLA shouldered a major burden of Israel's operational activity along its northern border. The Israeli patron and its Arab proxy militia faced an array of enemies. In addition to Hizballah, there was the Shiite movement, Amal, as well as a handful of Palestinian dissident groups that continued their struggle against Israel despite the peace process with the PLO. Their goals were to liberate Lebanon from the presence of the approximately 2,000 IDF troops regularly stationed there, to dismember the SLA and to punish its members for treason. Against them, the SLA deployed some 2,500 fighters who manned 37 out of 45 outposts in the security zone, the remainder staffed by the IDF.[9]

The Security Zone was divided into an eastern sector and a western sector. Each sector had its own brigade headquarters, armored, artillery and training units, support groups, local security action-groups, and a Civil Administration unit taking care of the daily needs of the population. In total, the SLA had six infantry battalions and an artillery battalion each representing the ethnic make-up of its region. One Druze battalion was deployed in the eastern sector of the Security Zone in the Druze enclave of Hasbaya. A predominantly Shiite battalion and four Christian battalions were spread from there all the way to the Mediterranean.[10] The Christian battalions were not exactly Christian. Over the years, the number of Shiites in them rose to almost 70 percent, leaving the Christians to staff mainly the command echelon.

Operationally, the SLA was almost completely dependent on the IDF. The idea was to turn the SLA into an effective fighting force. SLA soldiers and officers underwent basic training, platoon and company training according to IDF doctrine, and were equipped with armored personnel carriers, tanks and artillery pieces. Coordination of activities between the IDF and the SLA was carried out by the Lebanon Liaison Unit (LLU), established in 1985. The LLU directed a system of mentors, *chonchim*, at the battalion and company level whose responsibility was to train, coordinate, pay salaries and provide liaison for the Lebanese. It was an effective system allowing the Israelis to be on top of things and always monitor the morale and performance of SLA units.

Throughout the years of collaboration with the Lebanese, Israel held to the view that its control of the region could be achieved only by maintaining the SLA's dependence on Israel. A Senior IDF officer in Lebanon explained: "The great success of south Lebanon is the creation of a situation of dependency. That dependency leads to a freedom of operation and movement by the IDF. Our operations and presence in built-up areas in south Lebanon can only work as long as we can control the population."[11] To achieve such dependence Israel committed itself to improving the lives of the south's residents by funding civilian projects and providing psychological aid to the people. It invested tens-of-millions-of-dollars in roads, schools, hospitals and other services. The economic benefits, important to ensure continuous allegiance to Israel, were coordinated by the LLU. The Civil Affairs Administration of the LLU funneled money for these projects and controlled the border crossings from the south into northern Lebanon through the so-called Red Line, as well as the border crossings southwards into Israel through the so-called Purple Line. The latter crossings were those that enabled families of SLA personnel to enter Israel and work there, creating more economic incentive for the alliance.[12] The two sides also developed interdependence in the field of intelligence. South Lebanon was a goldmine for the Israeli intelligence services. It was a place where they could operate freely in the territory of an Arab country and collect valuable information.[13] But they could do so only with the support of the local population. The SLA had strong human intelligence resources but lacked surveillance equipment and other signal intelligence components that the IDF had. In 1989, a decision was made to set up an intelligence service within the SLA called Mabat (an abbreviation of *manganon habitachon,* or "security apparatus") to allow Israel and the SLA to supplement each other's intelligence needs. Mabat was a prolific intelligence apparatus that worked directly under the supervision of the Israeli General Security Service, *Shin Bet.*[14] South Lebanese agents provided the IDF with information which it used to strike at Hizballah targets and remove threats to the SLA.

Following the 1985 withdrawal of its troops, Israel abandoned hopes of installing a friendly regime in Lebanon. Instead, it focused on the protection of its border and on maintaining south Lebanon as a zone free of hostile elements. The presence of the IDF in the Security Zone was limited to goals such as intelligence gathering, observation, patrols and artillery assistance. SLA and IDF soldiers worked side by side trying to seal the Security Zone from Hizballah squads advancing toward the border to attack Israel or launch rockets at Israel's northern communities. Hizballah's guerrilla operations against Israel's north and south Lebanese forces were directed mainly at outposts and logistic supply convoys running in the south's mountainous terrain.[15] Both parties were interested in keeping the south clear of Hizballah influence, but they had differences of opinion as to how to achieve this goal effectively. Though their disagreements seldom reached the level of public debate, there was divergence of interests and, at times, deep tension.

The main interest and allegiance for the Lebanese, naturally, was to their immediate communities and villages - not to Israel. They viewed themselves as local patriots whose purpose was to protect their economic interests and maintain their autonomy.

Survival in Lebanon's anarchy precluded sole allegiance to one party; rather, one cut deals with different players at odds with each other. One SLA member asked if he was afraid to collaborate with Israel explained: "One of my brothers collaborates with the Syrians, another brother works with the Iranians, my cousin is linked to the French intelligence and I work with the Israelis. As long as it helps us to safeguard our families and our villages, we have no problem with this."[16] The Israelis were much more conservative in their views. To them, one could either be an enemy or a friend, and the friend of the enemy was essentially a potential enemy. They could not reconcile with the cynical Lebanese view of fidelity. "The Israelis thought they had a friend," recalled a veteran Israeli officer, "but the Lebanese only looked out for their self-interest."[17] The IDF viewed the SLA and the Security Zone as a shield whose purpose was to protect northern Israel and serve as a cushion to absorb Hizballah's attacks. "They are our flack jacket," said former Israeli Deputy Defense Minister Efraim Sneh.[18] SLA members did not like the role Israel assigned them. Despite their divorce from the rest of Lebanon, they were very sensitive to any questioning of their Lebanese patriotism. In their eyes, their raison d'etre was resistance to Syrian and Iranian influences on Lebanon, not to play the role of Israel's lackeys. They insisted on presenting their undertaking as something they did for themselves and not as an act serving any foreign power, assuredly not Israel.

Israel always perceived the fighting in Lebanon in the wider context of the Arab-Israeli conflict. Escalation in Lebanon had various political, strategic and economic implications. The economy of the Galilee, Israel's northern region, was economically dependent on tourism, which suffered serious setbacks whenever fighting in south Lebanon escalated.[19] Escalation in the north also meant potentially luring a clash with Syria, Hizballah's patron, and possibly with other Arab countries. This was a scenario that Israel clearly wanted to avoid and, as a result, was reluctant to further challenge the status quo in Lebanon. SLA members, on the other hand, believed that defending the villages inside the Security Zone should be carried out north of the zone itself and tried to encourage Israel to operate in Lebanon beyond the Security Zone. But the Israelis preferred to limit their ground operations to the Security Zone and to attack targets north of the zone only on rare occasions.

SLA soldiers who worked closely with the IDF learned to appreciate its operational capabilities and technological edge. They were, however, critical of the disparity between the equipment the IDF used and the weapons the IDF supplied them. Most of the weapons and ammunition they received were low-grade and obsolete. While IDF soldiers were operating the highly sophisticated Merkava tanks, SLA troops operated old Soviet T-55 tanks lacking protection against Hizballah's anti-tank weapons. IDF officers were also equipped with armored vehicles, while SLA officers drove regular cars. This was a constant source of resentment in the SLA. Its members felt they were treated as cannon fodder, that their blood was somewhat cheaper than that of the Israelis.[20]

From 1990-92, the situation in Lebanon began to once again deteriorate. Hizballah improved its tactical sophistication, and the number of SLA and IDF casualties mounted from a ratio of one IDF/SLA death to 5.2 for Hizballah in 1990 to a ratio of 1:1.7 in 1992.[21] After a series of Hizballah rocket attacks on civilian communities in the Galilee, Israel launched "Operation Accountability" in the summer of 1993 aiming to destroy Hizballah's military infrastructure and deny it the capability to threaten the Galilee. A similar operation, "Grapes of Wrath," was carried out in April 1996, ending tragically when a stray Israeli shell hit a United Nations' compound killing 103 Lebanese civilians from the village of Kana. Both operations eroded Hizballah's power but failed to deny it its military capabilities. By 1997, Israelis began to grow impatient with the situation in southern Lebanon. This sentiment strengthened after the mid-air collision of two Israeli transport helicopters in February 1997 ended in the death of 73 soldiers. More and more Israelis viewed Lebanon as "Israel's Vietnam" and joined the protest movements calling on the government to bring the boys home.[22]

The question of Israel's continued presence in Lebanon stood at the center of the 1999 elections. Ehud Barak's pledge for unilateral withdrawal within one year of his election was one of the main factors contributing to his landslide victory. The Israeli change of heart toward the occupation of south Lebanon dramatically changed relations with the SLA. A unilateral Israeli withdrawal without an agreement with the Lebanese government implied the demise of the SLA and the subjection of its members and their families to the severe punishments to which they had been sentenced in abstentia.[23] While Israel tried to make every arrangement possible to ensure the safety of SLA members after its withdrawal, including asking some Western countries to absorb them and facilitating relocating others to Israel, SLA soldiers dreaded the idea of Israel leaving them at the mercy of Hizballah and the Lebanese government. Increasing their anxiety, Hizballah launched a massive psychological warfare campaign against the SLA using its 24-hour satellite television station, *Al-Manar*, internet web sites, radio and newspapers.[24] They called on SLA soldiers to lay down their arms and desert their units, promising them clemency if they did so voluntarily prior to an Israeli pullout. Hizballah's propaganda intended to exploit the cultural dissimilarity between Israel and the Lebanese just as the Japanese and the Iraqis had tried to separate the U.S. from its allies during World War II and the Gulf War. SLA soldiers were scolded for collaborating with the Zionist enemy and were reminded of the religious implications of such a sin. To establish its image as an organization fighting for pan-Lebanese objectives, Hizballah also showed news clips of Christian soldiers taking part in its own organization's training.

In June 1999, under enemy pressure, the SLA started to withdraw from the northernmost part of the Security Zone, the Jezzine area. Later on, in January 2000, the SLA's second highest-ranking officer, Colonel Akel Hashem, was killed by Hizballah. These setbacks caused a significant decline in morale and combat motivation in the SLA; this, as voices in Israel calling for withdrawal grew stronger. SLA soldiers became preoccupied with post-withdrawal plans and searched for ways to save their lives and property.[25] At the same time, they tried to dissuade Israel from pulling out by increasing IDF involvement, beyond what was required only to back up and support the SLA. SLA officers also sent the IDF warnings that soldiers may stop obeying orders and start worrying about themselves. "Israel is abandoning us," they said.[26] Their commander, General

Antoine Lahad, went even further alluding to the fact that SLA soldiers might turn against Israel and join Hizballah if abandoned by Israel.[27] The crisis in relations between the allies was characterized by a high degree of distrust and hampered their cooperation. By 1999, approximately 70 percent of the Shiites in the SLA had first-degree relatives who were members of Hizballah.[28] IDF officers suspected that SLA troops were becoming untrustworthy and that many of them were collaborating with the enemy.[29] In some cases, SLA soldiers suspected of treason were arrested by Israel. "We share no more information with them," said a senior IDF officer.[30] SLA soldiers were also accused of not carrying out orders to attack certain Hizballah targets or of deliberately firing inaccurately at them. The Israeli alliance with the SLA ended abruptly in May 2000 when SLA outposts collapsed one after the other – not on any timetable in sync with Israel's withdrawal – and their fighters surrendered their weapons to Lebanese authorities. The occupation of south Lebanon ended in this humiliating manner for many with thousands of SLA refugees seeking asylum in Israel.

Despite the messy and bitter end, judging by standards of military cooperation, overall, the alliance was a success and the SLA proved to be an effective ally for Israel. Contrary to popular belief in Israel, the Security Zone concept was not as strategically misguided as many now say. For 15 years, it prevented terrorists from reaching Israel's northern border to attack civilians and kept Hizballah rocket fire far enough from the border to deem it ineffective.[31] Over the years, the SLA successfully resisted most of Hizballah's assaults and inflicted considerable numbers of enemy casualties. The price was high, though. Throughout the life of the SLA, Lahad's men suffered 450 killed in action and more than 1,400 wounded. For the small population of the south, this was a very high number. Were the U.S. to suffer battle deaths at the same rate, it would lose 50,000 soldiers per year. Many had to deal with the psychological implications of fighting and killing relatives fighting in opposing militia. But with few exceptions, SLA members fought valiantly and showed loyalty to their cause. Weeks before his death, Colonel Hashem explained in an interview some of the dilemmas SLA soldiers faced:

Not every Muslim or every Shiite is Hizballah and Amal. Sometimes, the line passes down the middle of one family. I was once present at an encounter in Kfar 'Aytaroun. Deputy unit commander Abdel Karim Mansur was leading the force. We killed three terrorists. After we got to the bodies of the terrorists, [...] Mansur saw that he had mowed down his cousin. I asked Mansur if he would have pulled the trigger had he known whom he was shooting at. He answered in the affirmative - without any hesitation.[32]

Israeli views of their allies

By the time Israel invaded Lebanon, some 40,000 Israelis had been killed or wounded in wars between Israel and its Arab neighbors. In a population of 3.3 million Jews, there were very few families unhurt by the conflict. Although the country had signed a peace treaty with Egypt, it was still at war with the rest of the Arab world, and most Israelis still felt the conflict was far from over. They continued to view the Arabs as enemies. As a result Israeli Jews harbored very negative feelings toward their neighbors. Attitudinal surveys among the Jewish population in the 1970s showed a high level of hostility, disdain, fear and suspicion toward the Arabs.[33] American journalist David Shipler who reported from Israel for five years observed:

For many Israeli Jews, the Arab dwells at the heart of darkness, deep in the recesses of fear and fantasy. He appears almost as another species, marching to the beat of some primordial drum whose resonance stirs an ancient fear and fascination. He is backward, uncivilized, a man of animal vengeance and crude desires, of violent creed and wily action. [...] The image of the Arab as primitive evokes both contempt and romance among Israeli Jews. Many are disgusted, others patronizing, a few infatuated. And some indulge themselves in all of those contrasting emotions simultaneously, always yielding to the invincible stereotype.[34]

Israelis saw themselves as an enlightened nation besieged by a human mass of backward Arabs committed to destroy them. They saw their vibrant democracy and fast economic progress as a testimony to their intellectual and cultural superiority over their neighbors. More than 80 percent of those surveyed agreed to the proposition that the Arabs will never reach the level of progress of Jews.[35] Arabs were viewed as irrational, inflexible and lacking the ability to practice intellectual discourse. Close to 90 percent of Israelis endorsed the proposition that Arabs understood only force.[36] Israeli anti-Arab prejudice spread through its education system. Textbooks published by the Israeli Ministry of Education and Culture depicted the Arabs in one sided and shallow ways, showing them as camel riding tent dwellers, robe wearing peasants and old men in *kaffiyahs* puffing on water pipes and sipping coffee.[37] One reason that during the time of the Lebanon invasion attitude toward the Arabs was solidified was that there were already several decades of uneasy relations between Israeli Jews and the 700,000 Arabs that lived in Israel. These Israeli Arabs formally enjoyed equal civil rights but their situation, de facto, was unfavorable. Over the years, Israeli governments neglected their communities and failed to bring them to par with the rest of the Jewish population.[38] Specifically complicated were relations between the Arabs and the Sephardic Jews, those who had fled to Israel from Muslim countries of North Africa and the Middle East and comprised approximately 40 percent of Israeli Jews in the beginning of the 1980.[39] Many of those Jews had been expelled, robbed or mistreated by Arab regimes and carried bad memories of their birthplaces. As a result, they harbored greater antipathy toward Arabs than Ashkenazi Jews, those with origins in Europe and North America.[40] At the same time, Sephardic Jews were more culturally similar to the Arabs. They ate Arabic food, listened to Middle Eastern music and adhered to norms of behavior akin to the Arab culture. Many of them thought that they could deal with the Arabs more successfully than the Ashkenazis.[41]

All of this was a difficult starting point for favorable relations with the Lebanese. Before 1982, Lebanon was to most Israelis a neighbor about which they knew very little. Scholarship on Lebanon was scarce, and unlike countries like Morocco, Egypt or Iraq from where many Jews fled, few Lebanese Jews had settled in Israel, able to educate Israelis about the country that was geographically so close to them.[42] The little that was known about Lebanon was limited to myths and headlines. Israelis knew that Lebanon was inhabited by a large French-speaking, Christian population. They thought of Lebanon as the "Switzerland of the Middle East" and the "world's biggest duty-free shop."[43] However, very few Israelis were truly familiar with the ethnic makeup, the history of the various groups and the different rivalries between them. The idea of turning Lebanon into a Christian country was Israeli wishful thinking stemming from ignorance. It overlooked the hard reality that the Christians made up no more than 35 percent of Lebanon's population. Israeli lack of knowledge of Lebanon expressed itself best in its dismissive attitude toward the Lebanese Shiites, the largest ethnic minority. Thomas Friedman wrote that an IDF education corps' pamphlet given to every soldier upon entering Lebanon widely covered the Christian community and hardly mentioned the fact that the largest religious minority was the Shiites.[44] The Shiite community in the south felt no particular friendship or animosity toward the Israeli invaders. Like the Druze and the Christians, they were pragmatic enough to maintain good relations with the dominant power broker of the moment.[45] Israel, for its part, treated them with inherent distrust since it viewed people of Muslim faith as less reliable than Christians. This approach ended in calamity for which Israel has paid a heavy price.

In one of the most culturally insensitive incidents of the war, the Israelis destroyed their relations with this important group and turned it from potential ally to a tough enemy. It took place on October 16, 1983, in the Shiite dominated town of Nabatiya. Some 60,000 Shiites had gathered to celebrate the Ashura, the commemoration of the martyrdom of the Imam Hussein at the battle of Kerbala in 680 A.D. and the most important holiday in their calendar. It is a day of great emotion in which the Shiites identify with the suffering of all those oppressed by evil powers by self-flagellating to the point of drawing their own blood. In the middle of the ceremony, an IDF convoy tried to force its way through the crowded streets of Nabatiya. The Israelis blew their horns and showed little respect for the holiness of the day. Angry Shiites began hurling stones and attacking the Israeli vehicles. The Israelis panicked and began firing at the crowd, killing two and wounding 15 people. The incident incensed the Shiites and almost overnight created a big wave of resentment toward Israel. The next day, the Shiite religious leader issued a *fatwa* calling on all Shiites to conduct active resistance against the Israeli forces.[46] The emergence of Amal and Hizballah as Israel's staunchest enemies followed in short order. Lebanon expert Augustus Richard Norton proclaimed the Israeli mishandling of the Shiite population of south Lebanon its biggest blunder in Lebanon and the most far ranging in effect.[47] This blunder reflected most of all Israel's cultural ignorance and lack of sensitivity toward the population of the south.

As mentioned earlier, the Israelis had difficulty classifying the Lebanese Christians as purely Arab despite the fact that the Christians viewed themselves as such. To them, they were sort of quasi-Arabs who, if only helped, could be westernized. Israelis were also overwhelmed by the animosity Christian Lebanese showed toward the Palestinians. For this reason alone, the south Lebanese were natural allies, so it was thought. SLA family members who enjoyed privileges of working in Israel were well received by the Israeli public that saw them as "our Arab friends." They were hard working and were very appreciative of their wages, which by Lebanese standards were very high. IDF officers working with the SLA were less enthusiastic. On its face, the IDF showed great respect toward the SLA. Their holidays and rituals were respected. Except during periods of emergency, operational activities that fell on religious holidays were in most cases postponed. Israeli generals did not forget to send greeting cards to SLA soldiers and their families on their religious holidays. It was even customary for IDF officers to travel to remote SLA outposts to greet them personally. These tours, deep into the remotest parts of the Security Zone, were dangerous. One IDF veteran interviewed for this book was severely wounded and lost both of his legs on one of these trips. Despite the risk, it was an IDF policy to maintain good and friendly relations with the SLA, host them and be attuned to their problems. But under the veneer of warm relations, Israeli officers looked down on their SLA colleagues and viewed them as culturally inferior. They saw in them many of the traits they detested and which they believed characterized their Arab enemies. "I had an aversion to the SLA because I associated them with the Arab mentality," said one Israeli lieutenant colonel.[48] IDF officers serving with the SLA kept a certain distance from their allies and failed to reciprocate the social advances the Lebanese made. They wanted to do their job in the best manner and had no interest in further engaging or developing personal friendships with their allies.

Lebanese attitude toward the Israelis

Unlike the Israelis' unfamiliarity with Lebanon, the residents of south Lebanon were more familiar and immersed in the Israeli way of life than one would expect. Their social and commercial relations with the Israelis were made possible thanks to what was referred to as the "Good Fence policy," which allowed them from 1976 to cross into Israel at Metullah to receive medical care.[49] Considering the fact that Lebanon and Israel remained in an official state of war, this humane policy was unprecedented. What started as a humanitarian gesture slowly developed into a flow of job seekers from the war-torn south who began receiving permits to work in northern Israel. Thousands of Lebanese came every day to work in Israel earning salaries that were two or threefold higher than what they could have earned in Lebanon. The opening of the fence warmed the relations considerably between citizens of the two countries. Lebanese who had relatives among the Christian community in Israel were allowed to visit them. Children whose parents served in the SLA visited tourism sites in Israel and attended vacation camps organized for them by the IDF. Strong commercial ties between Israel and south Lebanon were established. The Lebanese provided various products and services, and Israel responded by granting agricultural, veterinary and medical aid. In 1981 alone, one out of three south Lebanese visited Israel, and in the first four years after the opening of the fence, Israeli doctors treated some 200,000 patients.[50] The Lebanese could move freely in Israel, shop there, enjoy the amenities a modern country offered and become exposed to its culture.

Relations were good. The Lebanese were treated respectfully and reciprocated accordingly.[51] One Maronite SLA soldier summarized his experience with the Israelis: "Over the years, each one of us received, at least once, a blood transfusion in an Israeli hospital. Our blood is Jewish."[52]

Druzeland

Despite being a very active modern military, the IDF has had more experience fighting *against* coalitions than being part of one. In fact, the only time in its history the IDF cooperated with foreign militaries in combat was during the 1956 Sinai Campaign when Israel, France and England joined forces against Egypt. But even then, there was hardly any tactical cooperation to expose the IDF to the art of coalition warfare. Without a previously established doctrine for combined operations, communication with the SLA was an ongoing learning experience, which began during the period of cooperation with Sa'ad Haddad's Free Lebanon Army in the late 1970s.

The first problem the IDF faced in its work with the Lebanese was a lack of Arabic speakers. By law, both Hebrew and Arabic are official languages in Israel. However, most Israeli Jews do not speak Arabic. A 1983 survey showed that only 11.5 percent of Jews spoke Arabic as a second language, most of them immigrants from Arab countries.[53] The percentage of Arabic speakers among the population of IDF conscripts was even smaller. A main reason for lack of Arabic speakers was the failure of Israel's education system to standardize an Arabic studies curriculum in Jewish schools. To this day, Israeli schools teach literary Arabic as a mandatory subject but not spoken Arabic, necessary for verbal communication with Arabic speakers. Most of the students never reach proficiency. Out of 150,000 students who start studying Arabic every year, only 1,500 finish the program.[54] The Israeli Army that entered Lebanon in June 1982 relied on a small cadre of specialized Arabic speakers and interpreters for liaison with the local population. Some Lebanese in the south, especially those whose families worked in Israel as part of the Good Fence policy, spoke some Hebrew, but most were civilians who could not be utilized by the IDF. From the outset of the establishment of the Security Zone, the language gap emerged as a problem, preventing easy communication between IDF soldiers operating in south Lebanon and the indigenous population . They could not collect human intelligence effectively and experienced miscommunication problems with their allies in the already complex environment of Lebanon. Additionally, the language barrier burdened the mutual military support system of IDF and SLA forces in the field. When an SLA outpost was under attack, for example, the unit under attack could not ask directly for Israeli fire support. It had to communicate with its person on duty in the LLU who would, in turn, address the request to an IDF officer who could alert Israeli artillery batteries and direct the fire. This process took precious time in which the attacked forces on the front could suffer a heavy toll. Alternatively, when Israeli officers gave orders in Hebrew appealing to SLA units, these orders had to first be translated into Arabic and transmitted by radio to the units. This, again, took time and often involved the usual translation problems.[55]

To mitigate problems related to language and mentality gaps, the IDF found a convenient solution. It mobilized one of its greatest assets, Druze soldiers, as a cultural bridge between Jewish and Arab soldiers. It was not a formal policy but an arbitrary solution that soon institutionalized itself. Shortly after the establishment of the LLU, most officers working as *chonchim* were Israeli Druze. They also served as members of the Civil Administration, responsible for liaison with the local population.[56] The Druze in Israel are a small minority that in 1982 numbered approximately 70,000.[57] They live in small communities in the northern part of Israel and regard themselves as distinct from both Muslims and Christians. They maintain their own carefully guarded cultural autonomy. They marry within the community, maintain their ancient traditions and practice a religion they keep secret from outsiders. The sect's beliefs include a loyalty to the countries in which they reside. Therefore, Syrian Druze serve in the Syrian army, Lebanese Druze serve in the Lebanese army, and Israeli Druze serve in the IDF.[58] Their integration into the IDF has been, by and large, a success story.[59] Many young Druze have taken part in the daily defense burden along Israel's borders, most of them serving in combat units. Over the years, several Druze officers have climbed to high ranks and have commanded over units with a Jewish majority successfully. The Druze are considered by Israeli Jews to be brave, professional and motivated soldiers. They view their service in the IDF as a sacred duty and means for social mobility. Consequently, the community has lost many in the battlefield. The casualty toll paid by the Druze over the years has been larger than its proportional share in the Israeli-Jewish population. South Lebanon was an attractive place for the Druze to serve. They enjoyed a language advantage over the Jewish soldiers, which allowed them to communicate freely with the local population and the SLA. Service in the LLU also offered them a fast promotion track in comparison with other IDF units as well as geographical closeness to their homes in the north of Israel. In addition, the Druze found their service in Lebanon to be an opportunity for social interaction with fellow Druze communities in Lebanon with which there was very little contact before the Israeli invasion in 1982. As a result, the LLU became a unit dominated by the Druze. "We called it Druzeland," recalled one Jewish LLU officer.[60]

The Druze prevalence among the ranks of the IDF in Lebanon created some tension with the Jews who served there and held senior positions. In fact, not one LLU commander was ever a Druze. The many senior officers in the LLU were Jewish and had undergone no cultural preparation to work with the Lebanese, nor could they speak the language. Many of these officers viewed the Druze relations with the SLA with ambiguity and even with suspicion. They understood the benefits of using a cultural bridge, but they often noticed that the cultural affinity between the Druze and the SLA tainted the IDF with undesirable practices. For some of the Jewish officers, the Druze were behaving too much "like Arabs," and their mentality resembled that of the Lebanese. During their service in Israel, the Druze were conditioned to behave like Jews, in other words, to speak only Hebrew and to adapt to Jewish norms of behavior. In Lebanon, on the other hand, the Druze felt free to live by the culture and customs of the region, to talk to each other in Arabic even in the presence of Jews, and to develop personal relations with the SLA, unlike the Jewish Israelis who were more aloof. The Druze, for their part, professed they simply better understood the Lebanese mentality. "We knew the sensitivities of the Lebanese and knew how to manipulate them," explained a Druze officer.[61] Some Jewish officers also complained about the alleged double loyalty of the Druze. They were aware of the social relations that were forming between Israeli and Lebanese Druze and were concerned that they might leak information to their kinsmen in the Druze battalion of the SLA. The same officers also alluded to uneasy relations between the Druze and the Christians, a remnant of the long-lasting hostility between the two communities going back to their 19th century feud.[62] Some Israelis claimed that Israel failed to recognize the depth of hatred the two communities felt for each other.[63] They alleged it was a mistake to allow the Druze in the IDF to have an authoritative position over the Maronites and that Druze prejudice made them behave in a patronizing way toward the Christians. Another negative attitudinal issue: the Druze who enjoyed a high standard of living in Israel and were economically better off than the Lebanese felt superior to their allies and often failed to hide their feelings.[64]

Four teeth for a tooth

Nothing influenced Israel's fate in Lebanon more than its inability to comprehend the norms and codes of conduct by which relations between the confessional groups there were defined. The Lebanese way of solving problems and the cruelty involved were notoriously unique even in the violence-ridden Middle East. It was a place in which no ethnic group was spared some form of ill-treatment by another. To the outsider, it seemed a war of all against all. Throughout the history of modern Lebanon, tit for tat massacres among its 17 ethnic and religious groups were a sad part of life. In 1975 and 1976, Christians and Muslims massacred each other in a chain reaction of atrocities. In December 1975, some 600 Muslims were slaughtered and 20,000 were driven from their homes at the Qarantina refugee camp in Beirut in what was known as 'Black Saturday.'[65] Three months later, their death was avenged when 500

Christians from Damur were massacred by the Palestinians.[66] The Christians, in turn, took their revenge, killing 2,000 Muslims at the Tel Za'atar refugee camp near Beirut. The Lebanese did not seem to view these killings as out of the ordinary. Nobody established committees of investigation. Nobody was indicted or held accountable for the atrocities. These massacres were just bricks in the road that ultimately led to Sabra and Shatila.[67] In the absence of a strong, centralized regime, Lebanon was governed by the culture of bloodshed and warlordism. Assassinations and mass killings between Christians and Muslims were not unique. A long history of animosity and bloodshed going back to the 19th century defined the relations of the Maronites and the Druze who fought over control of the Shouf Mountains southeast of Beirut. This rivalry culminated in the 1925-27 Druze Revolt against the French.

Israelis on the other side of the border were hardly moved by their neighbor's bloody history. They neither understood the internal rivalries of Lebanon, nor did they see a reason to intervene when Arabs killed Arabs. Israelis always disassociated themselves from their Arab neighbors and regarded themselves as more noble and civilized. Purity of arms was one of the most abiding principles of Israel's military culture. It was a kind of elitism, a unique ability to rise above what they perceived as the barbaric instinct of revenge that was part of Arab culture.[68] Israel professed that it tolerated the use of weapons only for self-defense purposes, pledged decent treatment of POWs, and granted immunity to the defenseless civilian population of the enemy. Over the years, as Israeli historiography developed, Israelis learned that their military was less pure than they thought but, by and large, most Israelis still cherished the principle of purity of arms and expected their military to adhere to higher moral and ethical standards than those of the Arabs. This explains the disgust and disappointment in the Israeli public regarding the IDF's failure to anticipate and prevent the massacres at the Sabra and Shatila camps and the rage of hundreds of thousands of Israelis who demonstrated in the streets of Tel Aviv against what they viewed the moral degradation of the IDF in Lebanon.

On the other side, Israel's reluctance to abide by the norms of the region was not appreciated by the Lebanese factions. Many interpreted it as softness. Walid Jumblatt, the head of the Druze community in the Shouf Mountains, told Israeli agents who came to recruit his support that he was not interested in doing business with the Israelis because they were not as ruthless as the Syrians.[69] Once in control of a large part of Lebanon, Israelis soon learned the rules of the land. They knew about Lebanon's history of bloodshed, but there was a naïve belief that such horrors could not occur under Israeli supervision. Sabra and Shatila disproved their assumption.[70] But even after Sabra and Shatila, Israeli commanders were surprised again and again each time they were faced with the brutality of the Lebanese conduct. The following personal experience as told by Amnon Shahak, a division commander stationed in the Shouf Mountains in 1983 who later became the IDF Chief of Staff, was typical among the many IDF commanders in Lebanon. While the Druze and the Phalangists were embroiled in a war for the control of the mountains, a group of Druze elders came to Shahak's head-quarters and pleaded he come with them to a local hospital where he saw a horrifying sight. There were three crates. In the first, he saw human heads, in the second torsos, and in the third limbs. Shahak recalled:

> I was really shocked. I had never seen anything like this in all my years as a soldier. I decided that no matter what time it was I was going to go down to the Phalangist head-quarters in Beirut and get an explanation. So I got in a jeep and went down to Beirut. Fuad Abu Nadar, one of the Phalangist commanders, was waiting for me with some of his men. [...] I demanded an explanation. [Abu Nadar] said to me, "Oh, I know this trick." He said there had been a fight this day between some of his men and some Druze, and that some Druze were killed [...] and the dead were left in the battlefield. He said the Druze took their dead away and then carved them up to make it look like the Maronites did it and then the Druze brought the chopped-up bodies to Aley to stir up their own people. I just shook my head. I realized at that moment that I was in the middle of a game I did not understand.[71]

To understand the Lebanese 'game,' one must understand the history, the geography, the social structure and the culture of the land. The Lebanese defined themselves according to their ethnicity. Their allegiance was first and foremost to the extended family and the community in which they lived. "The sense of family honor [...] is of paramount importance," wrote David Jordan. "and the values of the village, where kinship ties are strong and identity is communal, continue to form the basis for the socialization of most Lebanese."[72] There was also a great deal of pragmatism and a businesslike approach among the communities, allowing them to coexist while maintaining a delicate balance of power. However, changes in the fragile status quo sent out tremors that could quickly turn the communities against each other.

It was a country in which the weakling stood no chance, and in which blood could only be avenged by more blood. "The Lebanese operated under a different rule: the rule of the strong," explained a veteran IDF intelligence officer.[73] "Avenging one's blood fed the cycle of violence but failure to take revenge was perceived as weakness and invited harder repercussions," explained a Lebanese officer.[74] One Druze officer of the IDF observed: "The Lebanese mentality has great appreciation for force, overwhelming use of force regardless of political and strategic consequences. They did not believe in the biblical principle of a tooth for a tooth but in the principle of four teeth for a tooth."[75] Lebanese conduct has been tied to the important role that the notions of honor and pride play in their culture. Like in many other Arab communities and as seen in the aforementioned China case study, the shame associated with losing one's face is a dominant consideration. A threat to one's honor could precipitate aggressiveness.[76] Raphael Patai, in his book *The Arab Mind*, explained the "honor syndrome" as prompt revenge for past injuries of honor in order to avoid loss of face.[77] In Lebanon, blood revenge was not only a personal duty, it characterized relations between the various communities. In other words, when the honor of one in the community was injured, the community as a whole felt obligated to undo the damage by taking revenge. The important role of blood revenge in Lebanese culture had a strong influence on the relations with the Israelis. Israeli military doctrine has never accepted the idea of turning the other cheek. In fact, retaliation, *tagmul,* has been one of the fundamental principals of Israel's national defense strategy. But the logic, the means and the ferocity in which Israelis executed the *tagmul* were different. The Israeli doctrine of retaliation emphasized the principle of proportionality and was directed against military, rather than civilian, targets. SLA troops expected an overwhelming IDF response for every enemy provocation and were disappointed when the response was measured. They held to the philosophy that every attack should be answered with harsh measures and that failure to respond appropriately was perceived as weakness and invited more attacks by the enemy. "Israel does not know how to avenge and does not understand the Middle East," an SLA officer complained.[78] Although, in principle, the SLA submitted to Israeli authority, some of its commanders who were not satisfied with the Israeli military response took 'private initiatives' that fanned the flames in Lebanon and caused regional escalation, something Israel wanted to avoid.

Many SLA soldiers were under the impression that Israel responded more severely to attacks against Israeli soldiers than to those on their soldiers.[79] They were frustrated when Israel tried to rein them in and prevent them from using their weapons. In some cases when SLA soldiers lost family members or comrades in Hizballah attacks, they took liberty to use their weapons in an unauthorized manner and launch retaliatory revenge attacks showing little patience or sensitivity for the diplomatic, strategic or economic repercussions of such unmeasured responses. Because uncoordinated attacks could lead to additional escalation, this behavior was resented by the Israelis.[80] IDF commanders often had to visit their SLA colleagues, calm them down and plead with them to restrain themselves and avoid taking any independent action. In several cases, they failed to prevent SLA vigilantes from firing artillery at villages from where they believed those responsible for a particular provocation came.[81] Some cases resulted in civilian deaths and, in turn, brought counter-retaliation and regional escalation.[82] Such discipline problems actually emerged during the very first days of the SLA. Rephael Eitan, IDF Chief of Staff during the war in Lebanon, recalled how the pride and patriotism of Haddad's SLA were a source of constant difficulties and disagreements with the Israelis.[83] In some cases, for example, when the Lebanese government cut off electricity to the south, Haddad fired artillery, against Israeli wishes, at the city of Zidon. Israeli commanders of the IDF northern command were furious.[84]

SLA commander Major Saad Haddad (center) and IDF Chief of Staff
Lt. General Rephael Eitan (siting on the right)

In comparison with their Jewish Israeli colleagues, Druze *chonchim* understood the motivation behind the SLA's desire for retaliation, another case where Druze cultural affinity with the Lebanese was apparent. "We understood the Oriental honor and the Oriental pain. The need for revenge when somebody injures you. With the Jews, honor was not that important," reflected a Druze IDF colonel.[85] The Druze also understood better the culture of manliness and pride among the Lebanese and the need to always be perceived as courageous and resilient. They knew how demeaning it was for the Lebanese to have to buy protection from a more powerful group and understood their need to overcompensate for their inability to defend themselves. This sensitivity facilitated unique working relations between the *chonchim* and the SLA, relations that were based on consent more than on discipline.

Formally, the *chonchim* had no means to enforce their will on SLA troops. The SLA was not a unit subordinate to the IDF but an independent militia. In practice, however, the SLA was dependent on the IDF on every level from payload to paycheck. Due to the pride of SLA officers, Israelis made every effort to treat them as equals. They understood that if bossed around, the Lebanese would respond with antagonism. "We knew that their job was to protect their homes and how sensitive they were not to be seen as servants in the eyes of their families. Therefore, we did not order them but *asked* them to do things," revealed one Israeli, adding, "in most cases it worked." [86]

When clashes of interest emerged, good Middle Eastern bargaining skills were required, and the Druze knew those well. One of them explained: "With the SLA, the most important thing was not to bring yourself to a situation in which you have to give an order to an SLA person. The issue of face was extremely important. If you brought an SLA person to lose face, he would never forgive you. We have the same mentality and we knew how to manipulate their feelings and make them do exactly what we wanted without insulting them."[87] The Jewish officers were not nearly as savvy. They were more remote and more impatient. They had a business-like approach and less desire to spend precious time on long sessions of small talk. Unlike American officers who received cultural training before deploying in Saudi Arabia, Israeli soldiers and officers received no cultural preparation. They were expected to learn from their own mistakes and rely on the collective experience of their predecessors. But there were gaps in information flow that, at times, caused unpleasant incidents.

Ethical gaps

Like most Arabs, SLA soldiers and officers were gracious hosts. When IDF commanders came for a visit in their village, SLA commanders went to great lengths to impress them with lavish hospitality that included food and drink for which they paid from their own pockets. Jewish officers felt uncomfortable by the expenses incurred considering the fact that their hosts had spent their meager salaries on what would otherwise have been routine working meetings.[88] Reciprocal visits of SLA soldiers to IDF bases were free of pleasantries and collations. The Israelis felt no need to impress or grant their partners any special treatment and saw no point in cultivating social relations with their allies.

Corruption was also a bone of contention. With loose government control and perpetual disunity among its communities, Lebanon experienced over the years a severe decline of public morality. Corruption pervaded every part of life, and one could not go far without encountering graft and bribery. The situation in the south was no different, and it did not take long before the Israelis faced problems similar to those of the Germans and the Americans in Turkey and China: how to deal with norms anathema to their own. Culturally averse to corruption, IDF troops and officers made it clear from the beginning of the relations that public norms of bribing and smuggling would not be acceptable. Nevertheless, Israeli officers were bothered by the high level of corruption they found among their Lebanese allies.[89] "We knew that the Lebanese were good traders and that SLA troops were mainly motivated by money," recalled one Israeli, "but it was hard for us to turn a blind eye to their corrupt practices. [...] SLA salaries were 500-1,000 dollars per month, which was way above the average income in Lebanon. We did not understand the need for such behavior."[90] Israeli officers were concerned that soldiers who came in contact with the SLA would be tempted by bribes or become involved in smuggling of weapons, narcotics and merchandise. In fact, there were a few cases of individuals in the SLA and IDF working together on drug deals.[91] Many IDF commanders were concerned by the operational ramifications of corruption. They believed SLA soldiers were susceptible to bribery by the enemy and, therefore, could not be trusted. In addition, IDF commanders were unhappy to discover instances in which SLA soldiers sold weapons and ammunition supplied by the IDF to local arms dealers and even directly to Hizballah.

Gidon Ezra, former deputy head of the Shin Bet and later a member of the Israeli parliament, assembled and publicized information about SLA corruption. SLA members extorted Lebanese civilians, received bribes, and collected customs on cigarettes, gas and other merchandise. Controlling the checkpoints and passages in and out of the Security Zone, SLA soldiers allegedly collected transit fees from the local population and were involved in drug trafficking and smuggling.[92] Many Israelis were appalled by the revelations, which surfaced simultaneously with reports in the media and by international human rights groups about human rights violations carried out by the SLA, and called for a reassessment of the relations with the SLA.[93] They claimed Israel had associated itself with a dubious ally and that its presence in Lebanon was corrupting.

Trinity of force

Despite its appearance as a region characterized by cultural dogmatism, the Middle East has had a long history of producing the strangest of partnerships between Arabs and non-Arabs. Crusaders, British, French, Germans, Russians and Americans all collaborated with the Arabs with varying levels of success. But the story of Jews and Arabs, two sworn enemies, collaborating for almost two decades in Lebanon, fighting together against a common enemy, sounds almost surreal. The fact that 70 percent of the SLA's members were Shiites who fought against their kinsmen from Hizballah makes the survival of the alliance for so long an even more striking achievement. Israel's encounter with Lebanon had been from its start a cultural journey. Its two low points, the Sabra and Shatila massacre and the rift with the Shiites in October 1983, both stemmed from a lack of cultural awareness rather than from ill intention. For Israelis, Sabra and Shatila was an earthshaking experience that brought with it the IDF's withdrawal from Beirut and popular opposition to the presence in Lebanon, which, in turn, brought about the resignation of Prime Minister Begin and ultimately the unilateral withdrawal from Lebanon in May 2000. The massacre also triggered the birth of Israel's peace movement, Peace Now, giving rise to a new Israeli approach toward the Arab-Israeli conflict. In the past two decades, the massacre has been politicized, personalized and debated in at least three judicial systems and in the media. Many questions are still unanswered. Who knew what? What was the understanding achieved between IDF commanders and the Phalange leaders? Why didn't the Israelis stop the massacre? Could they have? What seems to be clear is that Sabra and Shatila was among other things a cultural blunder caused by the inability of Israeli commanders to comprehend the ferocious nature of the Lebanese blood revenge culture. Even the few Israelis who suspected some sort of Phalangists' revenge did not anticipate their partners would indiscriminately kill women and children and behave as savagely as they did.[94]

The 'Nabatiya incident' was another example of a lack of cultural awareness for which Israel paid a heavy price. It unleashed a religious rage against Israel that gave birth to Hizballah, and brought about decades of bloody guerrilla warfare in south Lebanon. Sabra and Shatila and the 'Nabatiya incident' affected the IDF in a way similar to the way the Indian Mutiny affected the British Army in the years prior to World War I. Cultural blunders serving as catalysts to events of strategic magnitude. But at the same time they were also learning experiences that generated stronger cultural awareness and facilitated future relations with culturally dissimilar allies. Israel entered Lebanon with a remarkably low level of familiarity with the country and its people. This changed over time. The Israelis learned the local culture, smoothed cultural incompatibilities with their allies and established strong relations with them. By the time Israel pulled out to the Security Zone, the two sides were sufficiently exposed to each other and this was the key facilitator for easy relations. Despite some of the problems mentioned earlier, SLA and IDF soldiers visited each other frequently, trained together and felt comfortable in each other's company. But what contributed most to their effective cooperation was the cultural bridge mechanism embodied by Israeli Druze.

Most militaries have refrained from utilizing ethnic groups as cultural bridges seeing such a practice as risky and self-defeating. In World War II, for example, Japanese Americans of the 442nd Regimental Combat Team, the most decorated unit in U.S. military history, were deliberately sent to fight on the European front rather than in the Pacific, where they could have been utilized in the China-Burma-India Theater. There are three main reasons militaries have refrained from using minority units as cultural bridges. First, exposing minorities to their original cultural environment could pose a test of loyalty they might not be able to pass. Such was the risk in allowing Israeli Druze to work with their kinsmen in Lebanon. There was concern among some that the Israeli Druze would be prone to prefer their ethnic group over their military. Second, the use of minority groups as cultural bridges can hinder the cohesiveness of the patron's military, create divisions, double standards, misunderstandings and discipline problems. It allows the proxy to find cracks and weaknesses in the patron's military to exploit for personal benefit. Third, using people of similar ethnic and cultural backgrounds as a bridge to the indigenous population may compromise their security. If perceived as collaborators and traitors, their lives could be at risk. The sad story of the "harkis," the Muslim Algerians who fought on the French side during the Algerian war of independence with the objective of "taming" the Muslim population, is one example of the potential outcome of the use of cultural bridges. It is estimated that about 100,000 harkis were killed by fellow Algerians in savage reprisals after the war. Thousands of others were condemned to a life of poverty, mostly in southern French ghettoes. Nevertheless, the Israeli-Lebanese experience with the cultural bridge mechanism was positive.

Apart from facilitating communication with the coalition partner by displaying an understanding of its language and mentality, there are also side benefits for the minority group serving as the cultural bridge. Their role allows them to distinguish themselves and to fulfill a mission in which they have an advantage in comparison with their colleagues. It allows them a special promotion track in a niche where there is very little threat of competition. So successful and rewarding was the service of the Israeli Druze in Lebanon that the IDF allowed a similar process to happen again when military relations began to develop with the Palestinian Authority following the signing of the Oslo Agreement in 1993. According to the agreement, the IDF and the Palestinian security services were to coordinate activities in the West Bank and Gaza Strip via eight liaison units called District Coordinating Offices (DCO). Here again, Israeli Druze officers emerged as a valuable asset. They soon staffed most of the positions in the Israeli-Palestinian liaison mechanism and proved to be irreplaceable in their communication skills and their understanding of both Palestinian and Israeli mentalities.

Like in other patron-proxy relations, IDF-SLA relations were characterized by a great disparity in military power between the two partners. The Israelis knew the SLA was completely dependent on them and worked hard to perpetuate this dependence. The Israelis' sense of control over the Lebanese population spared them the feeling of being guests operating in a host environment and some of the hazards implied by the traditional model of host-guest relations as we have seen in the U.S. experience in China and Saudi Arabia. The Israelis did not feel compelled to accommodate their partners' needs when interests diverged. Furthermore, Israeli commanders were not deterred from confronting their partners and even censure them when deserved. They also prohibited them from conducting themselves in a manner objectionable to Israeli society and the Western world. The Lebanese, dependent on the Israelis, often felt compelled to behave in a way contrary to their upbringing in order to save the friendship. They were forced to act in moderation and refrain from satisfying their urge to avenge their losses in the Lebanese fashion to which they were accustomed. They were also forced to forego their long-lasting feuds with fellow confessional groups also serving in the SLA and cooperate with them in order to fulfill common strategic objectives. Israel was the glue that held them together.

With IDF soldiers positioned south of the border and south Lebanon turning into the land of Hizballah, Lebanon may be sliding back into chaos. The south, once a place where Israelis felt almost at home, is sprinkled today with thousands of Hizballah rockets and missiles aimed at Israel's population centers. Renewed skirmishes along the border and Hizballah's kidnapping of two Israeli soldiers led Israel to reinvade south Lebanon in the summer of 2006 as part of a 34-day war that devastated Lebanon. This time it faced a very different reception by angry, betrayed southerners. This hostile reception was one of the main reasons that Israel had no desire to remain in the south a day longer than necessary. The Jewish-Muslim-Christian military coalition was an anomaly not seen in the world since the days of St. Ferdinand III, king of Castile, in the 13th century, who called himself 'king of the three religions.' Such an alliance is not likely to happen again any time soon. But in a region that has yielded some of the strangest bedfellows, nothing should be considered inconceivable.

7
CULTURE WARRIORS

⌘　⌘　⌘

Cross-cultural cooperation, even in times of peace, has always been a daunting task. When communicating with partners possessing different belief systems, attitudes, values and habits, there is always a danger that the collaborative endeavor will suffer setbacks as a result of cultural misunderstandings or insensitivities. This, in turn, could tear the delicate fabric of trust and understanding that the cooperating parties invest so much in creating and, thus, hinder the operational effectiveness of their combined effort.

When collaboration takes place in the midst of war, a time troops are already operating under immense physical and emotional hardship, the danger to the collaborative effort is infinitely greater. This book has attempted to draw on the experiences of past coalitions and present some of the problems that characterized the relations between coalition partners in various settings. It also tried to shed light on some of the solutions adopted by the parties. We have seen troops from nine military forces, coming from nine different cultures. These militaries were forced by circumstances to cooperate with men and women very different from themselves. Some coalitions won their war, others lost. Most had to accommodate themselves in one way or another to their partner's values and often compromise their own way of life for the sake of maintaining healthy coalition relations. Less clear from the outset was whether culture is a force strong enough to truly be successfully hinder a coalitions' operational effectiveness. In other words, can culture create such a rift between collaborating forces and harm their relations to such an extent that the outcome of their collaborative endeavor be significantly impaired?

Many examples in this book showed how this could, indeed, happen. Language gaps led to misunderstandings, confusion and badly executed military operations (Germany in Turkey). Lack of attention to religious sensitivities bred resentment that turned a friend into a foe (Israel in Lebanon). Differing attitudes toward the future and the need for planning created conflict, at times even hatred, between force commanders (U.S. in China). Troops appalled by their partner's attitude toward human life, treatment of women or corrupt practices found themselves demoralized and disassociated from their mission (U.S. in Saudi Arabia).

Interestingly enough, culture emerged as an element that had an impact far beyond the tactical or operational levels. In some cases it generated strategic changes and influenced the outcome of entire wars. It was the cultural insensitivity and callousness of the British Army in India that triggered the outbreak of the Indian Mutiny in 1857, an event that rocked the foundations of the British Empire and changed the history of the Indian subcontinent. The manipulation of Kaiser Wilhelm II's manipulation that pushed the Ottomans to declare *jihad* against the Entente powers in World War I was a cynical misuse of religion as a tool to promote strategic interests. This gambit not only sealed the fate of non-Muslim communities in the Ottoman Empire but also compromised relations with fellow coalition members, like Austria-Hungary, as well as neutral states, like Italy, which ruled over significant Muslim minorities. The relations between the U.S. and Chinese forces in World War II were uneasy and often hostile due to, among other things, their cultural incompatibility. The Americans' attempt to impose new norms and military culture on the Chinese and to purge deeply rooted corruption and inefficiency bred antagonism and inhibited cooperation. Lack of awareness by American commanders of the importance of face in the Chinese mind and how much Chinese commanders were willing to sacrifice for the sake of saving face, also created incidents that could have changed the outcome of the war in the CBI front. The Gulf War, a modern case of coalition war, exemplified how culture in the era of globalization could still be a central theme in relations among coalition counterparts. Though on its face the coalition was a success, cultural tension between Western militaries and their Saudi hosts was always in the background threatening to break it apart. The Saudi fear of loss of legitimacy and cultural pollution of their society skewed their military judgment and led them to pressure the U.S. to begin its campaign before it was ready to do so. It also promoted a militarily senseless idea - launching the ground campaign from Turkey - in order to avoid being seen as a facilitator of war against a fellow Arab nation. One should not interpret the fact that the coalition performed so well as a sign of culture's triviality. It was the deference to Saudi sensitivities and the extraordinary patience that American commanders demonstrated - in addition to the Iraqis being less of a challenge than thought - that allowed the coalition to succeed as it did. The Israelis also learned the hard way the perils of not being culturally aware. Their failure to comprehend the complexity of Lebanon's culture and heritage and their condescending treatment of the Shiite population, as expressed by the Nabatiya incident, had far-reaching consequences, many of which are felt to this day.

Culture *does* matter. But the extent of its influence on coalition relations varies from one case to another. Each cross-cultural combination produces a unique set of problems and challenges based on the specific sensitivities, personalities, prevailing attitudes and degree of openness of each partner. As we have seen, each case of military cooperation was affected by a different set of cultural traits. In some cases it was religion that generated most of the tension, in others, there were gaps in mentality, communication, code of behavior, norms or ethics. But if each case is unique, can we reach some general conclusions or establish some guidelines or principles for overcoming the cultural challenge? Furthermore, can we conclude that certain cultures are more adept at working with others? If so, what are the characteristics that make these cultures more open and cooperative? Can we expect certain cultural problems to be more prevalent in coalitions that consist of certain combinations of cultures?

Can gods cooperate?

A nation's belief system is one major determinant of the set of attitudes and perceptions that characterize its people. It determines the attitudes toward life, the future and uncertainty, the role of the individual as part of the collective and his or her relationship with God. We have seen that the coalitions between Western and Muslim forces, such as the Turko-German alliance and the U.S.-Saudi coalition were characterized by strong religious tension between the parties. Both the Ottoman Empire and Saudi Arabia, each in its time, were the center of the Islamic world and their people did not enthusiastically support the association of their armies with non-Muslim partners. Both leaderships felt uneasy about their military dependency on the infidel and went to great lengths to show themselves and their followers that they were not controlled by people whom they perceived to be culturally inferior. As a result, relations with their partners were susceptible to mutual suspicion, superstition, misperception, and jealousy. Both the Ottomans and the Saudis refused to submit their forces, receive orders or appear to be controlled by those perceived as non-believers. Even good-intentioned instructors, who had left the comfort of their homes and went to the Near East to modernize the local militaries, often found their trainees obstinate and unwilling to take good advice from an infidel.

Working with Asian nations such as the Chinese, the Vietnamese, the Koreans or the Japanese presented similar challenges. The Asian partners were very sensitive to the issue of face and often viewed the subordination to Westerners as a humiliating experience. They were also sensitive about rank and often refused to cooperate with Western officers junior to them. But unlike the Muslims, their behavior was not rooted in religious prejudice. Religion played almost no role in both the Anglo-Japanese coalition and the Sino-American coalition. There is little evidence that religion was an inhibiting factor in the American experience in either Korea or Vietnam. By and large, East Asian cultures are known to be more religiously tolerant than those in the Muslim world, and their peoples do not feel as religiously threatened by the presence of a people adhering to other belief systems. However, observing early 21st century geopolitics, it appears that Western-Muslim coalitions will continue to play a key role on the world stage. This is likely to make Islam a central issue in future coalitions, which requires Western militaries to familiarize themselves with the unique sensitivities of this fast growing religion. Religious holidays, for example, should always be taken into consideration in the planning and execution of coalition campaigns. In the case of a coalition involving a Muslim partner they should be treated with extra care. Recent coalition campaigns involving Muslim counterparts, such as the Gulf War, the war in Afghanistan and the Iraq War, raised the issue of the month of Ramadan, holy to Muslims, as a determining element in the planning and execution of military campaigns. During the Gulf War, the Saudis, anxious about the possibility of hosting the pilgrimage while foreign troops were still in their country, made it clear that they wanted the war to be as short as possible. U.S. commanders and planners were mindful of the approaching Ramadan and were committed to end the war before it started. Later, in December 1998, during Operation Desert Fox - designed to degrade Iraq's capability to produce weapons of mass destruction - the U.S. began its bombing campaign a few days before Ramadan, inviting pressure from Muslim states to end the bombing by Ramadan's beginning. President Bill Clinton assured them: "For us to initiate military action during Ramadan would be profoundly offensive to the Muslim world, and therefore, would damage our relations with Arab countries and the progress we have made in the Middle East. That is something we wanted very much to avoid."[1] The war in Afghanistan presented a similar dilemma. The success of the war against terrorism depended to a large extent on the cooperation of Pakistan, a predominantly Muslim state. Fearing the loss of his people's support for the war against the Taliban, Pakistani President Pervez Musharraf demanded of CENTCOM commander General Tommy Franks that the bombing be suspended during Ramadan. He claimed that failure to do so would aggravate the Islamic world and harm its support for the coalition.[2] This time, the U.S. was not accommodating and the bombing continued according to plan. To the surprise of many, the Muslim world responded less vehemently to U.S. resolve than thought. But it took great effort to achieve this result. A "Ramadan public relations offensive" was launched by the White House spearheaded by the Coalition Information Center - a body formed during the war to solidify the relations with coalition partners to demonstrate America's feelings of respect toward the Muslim religion.[3] Both President George W. Bush and Secretary of State Colin Powell held *Iftar* dinners, the meal held at sundown when the fast is broken, with representatives from more than 50 Muslim states. To warm the hearts of Muslims even further, the State Department launched a program portraying Muslim life in America focusing on the religious freedom afforded in this country. It also printed and distributed a series of posters with pictures of mosques in the U.S.[4] Throughout the war in Afghanistan, the U.S. struggled to fight the image propagated by many in the Muslim world, that the war was, in fact, a precursor of a Huntingtonian "clash of civilizations" or some sort of modern crusade. The effort to 'secularize' the war was a component of the buildup of the coalition, the definition of the strategy and the operations. The U.S.' main challenge was to create a public image that the war was exclusively against "terrorism," not against Arabs and Muslims. On the eve of military action in Afghanistan, the White House summoned top Muslim officials to address the Muslim world, to try to persuade them of the legitimacy of the war. But whereas Muslim leaders in the U.S. were easy to convince, clergy in key Muslim allies were far less responsive to the American pledge. Egypt's Grand Sheik of Al-Azhar, Muhammed Sayed Tantawi, considered by many to be the highest religious authority in the Sunni Muslim world, issued an authoritative statement saying that religion prohibits any Muslim country from joining an alliance with non-Muslims.[5] Other Islamic leaders tried to weaken the U.S. military using the same methods used by the Germans and the Turks in 1914, namely by instilling doubts among Muslim troops serving in Western militaries about the legitimacy of participating in a war against fellow Muslims. Muslim leaders in the U.S. had to issue an opposing religious ruling that such action was in accordance with Islamic law saying that "all Muslims ought to be united against those who terrorize the innocents," and that it was in fact a "duty" of every Muslim to take part in the war.[6] Religion had symbolic significance on more trivial issues like choosing a name for the operation. The name first selected by the Pentagon,

"Infinite Justice," had to be changed, because Muslim partners found it offensive, as, according to them, only Allah was capable of administering infinite justice.[7]

Despite all that, Islam is too broad a religion to conclude that relations between westerners and Muslims are always likely to produce religious tension. Some historical cases show otherwise. For example, British officers trained the Jordanian army and fought in its ranks with great success until the 1950s; the U.S. enjoyed tension-free military relations with Turkey both during the Korean War and in the framework of NATO. The Israeli relationship with the SLA, 70 percent of which was Muslim, is another good example of successful cross-religious cooperation with a predominantly Muslim partner. Three factors could predict the degree of religious tension that is likely to occur in a coalition. First is the level of religiosity and religious tolerance of the society in general. Both Islamic oppositions in Saudi Arabia and in Pakistan are extremely intolerant groups with an uncompromising worldview and a deeply embedded hostility toward the West. Their views are not reflective of the entire Muslim world. But it is very likely that the U.S. and its allies will continue to participate in coalitions shadowed by Islamic fundamentalism and will have to cooperate with countries where there is strong anti-West sentiment. Second, the level of religiosity in the ranks of the armed forces is a predictor of the nature of relations that might evolve between coalition counterparts. The more pious the soldiers, the higher the risk of religion-driven tension. Third, the location of the coalition's activity is a predictor of how dominant the religion factor is likely to be. Multinational operations may take place on neutral ground or on a host nation's territory. In the latter case, as U.S. presence in Saudi Arabia showed, there was frequent tension due to the potential for contact with the host's population. Guest militaries are often confronted with antagonism due to their hosts fear of cultural contamination and due to a strong sense of shame by the host for being unable to defend itself and being dependent on foreign forces. Without such contact with the locals there is less ground for friction.

Religion dictates other issues in relations between militaries. Armies march on their stomachs, said Napoleon, but since armies pray to different gods, their stomachs respond to different tastes. Working with coalition partners entails satisfying their unique dietary needs. Certain religious groups, like Muslims, refrain from consuming pork and alcohol; others, like Hindus, do not touch beef; Gurkhas ate meat but only that of male animals, and others are vegetarian altogether. These religious requirements should be addressed by a coalition's logistics team and are likely to add to the burden of its work. Satisfying dietary requirements of small coalition contingents could be such a demanding task that it may place their overall value in doubt. The 840-strong Royal Hellenic Battalion that fought in the Korean War under the U.S. First Cavalry Division was one of the smallest contingents of the coalition. Yet, the infantrymen's dietary needs were complex. They required live lambs to perform their religious rituals, and the U.S. Quartermaster had to go to great lengths to satisfy their request. Even so, they failed to accommodate the Greeks' requirement that all lambs be female. Both the Greeks and the Americans were unhappy. The Greeks felt the Americans were not sensitive enough, and the Americans felt that the Greeks did not appreciate their great efforts to obtain live lambs in a country where such a commodity was scarce.[8]

Hosts and guests

A recurring characteristic of coalition operations is the encounter between the culture of the host nation and the guest military coming to fight on its territory. Host-guest relations are complex and rich in opportunities for tension. The host nation is usually militarily weak - otherwise, to begin with, it would not need the assistance of the guest - and is humiliated by the fact that it has had to invite foreign forces to its rescue. The guest is militarily strong but must behave politely and refrain from overstaying its welcome. In some cases, the guest may have to compromise its operational agenda to save the coalition from breaking apart. Long deployments on foreign territory may not only create tension with the civilian population, as the case of U.S. presence in China and Saudi Arabia clearly demonstrated, but can also cause moral degradation or adoption of foreign, at times objectionable, habits in the ranks of the guest. German officers in Turkey went native and became *'verturkt'*; American GI's in China lost their sense of time and respect for life; and Israelis lost their purity of arms in Lebanon. The encounter with foreign norms and work ethics could also be detrimental. Soldiers deployed in countries where corruption is prevalent face the risk of becoming corrupt. Many might stretch the meaning of the maxim "when in Rome, do as the Romans do" to allow themselves to accept bribes, mistreat the local population, adopt gender and class distinctions, engage in unorthodox sexual practices or change their physical appearance to blend in with the local people. The war in Afghanistan again demonstrated the phenomenon of soldiers going native when deployed far from home. Pictures of U.S. Special Forces soldiers growing beards and wearing untidy local costumes infuriated many Pentagon officials. The scruffy looking soldiers were ordered to immediately shave their beards and wear standard uniforms. "In this culture, men respect men who have the ability to grow facial hair, and the longer the better. I don't know how they are going to receive us in the villages when we come back looking like this," complained one soldier.[9]

U.S. Special Forces becoming 'vertuked' in Afghanistan
(U.S. Department of Defense)

Some militaries have come up with creative solutions to address these problems. Realizing that an extended stay in a foreign land can be achieved only through good relations with the local population, guest countries have provided their host communities more than just a military presence. The Israelis, for instance, invested a great deal of money in infrastructure and civilian projects designed to improve the life of the host population. So did the Germans in Turkey. Others placed more attention on cultural exchange programs to strengthen the familiarity between the host and the guest. The program initiated by Schwartzkopf in Saudi Arabia in which American commanders worked with local community leaders to resolve disputes between U.S. servicemen and Saudi civilians was particularly effective. It emphasized yet again how much power to mitigate cultural tension is in the hands of senior coalition commanders. In Afghanistan and Iraq, the U.S. Army embedded Human Terrain Teams, groups of anthropologists, linguists and culture experts with a mission to advise commanders at the brigade level on the cultural landscape, mapping the relationships of the power players and the local people in the theater of operation. While many anthropologists rail against the militarization of their discipline, the commanders on the ground have found the Human Terrain Teams to be extremely helpful, and in 2007 the Pentagon announced an expansion of the program.

Attitude toward life

The cases presented earlier showed how variations between coalition partners in attitude toward life affected their cooperation. The Ottomans, the Japanese, the Chinese, the Saudis and the Lebanese were less sensitive to individual casualties than their German, English, American and Israeli partners. Their willingness to suffer casualties in battle was a product of their cultural heritage, though in each case different traits were behind it. The Ottomans were fascinated with the prospects of martyrdom; the Japanese with the values of personal sacrifice and devotion to the Emperor; the Chinese lacked a sense of collective responsibility and compassion toward fellow humans with whom they had no familial ties; Saudi fatalism and deep piousness made them attribute loss of life to God's will which they saw no sense in questioning or intervening in. Lebanese violence was driven by the culture of honor killing and blood revenge that pervaded every one of Lebanon's cultural groups. In all of these cases, the Westerners were disheartened and appalled by what they perceived as cruel and inhuman behavior. By and large, Westerners were much more calculated, reserved and economical in their application of force. They invested in careful planning and relied on technology and firepower rather than on costly frontal assaults. Western coalition commanders Liman von Sanders, Stilwell and Schwarzkopf resented their partners' uneconomical, reckless, and capricious use of their human resources. They tried to dissuade them from wasting their forces in hopeless campaigns and believed their behavior was damaging to the overall war effort. They were aggravated by their partners' contempt of detailed military planning and refused to let fate or other divine powers decide the outcome of their battles. The problems described above become even more pressing as Western societies and their militaries show decreasing tolerance for casualties. The American public, its representatives and policymakers, have become increasingly aware that casualty aversion is often not appreciated in certain cultures. It is perceived as a sign of weakness and half-heartedness evoking similar emotions to those the Japanese had toward the British or the Lebanese toward the Israelis. Countries operating in a coalition setting with the U.S. or European allies may not understand and share the Western attitude toward casualties and might want to pursue, perhaps even impose, operational plans that are too costly by Western standards.

Communication across cultures

Smooth communication between coalition partners has proven to be a crucial element for successful military cooperation. Almost every coalition case reveals a struggle by the participating forces to overcome verbal and non-verbal communication problems. Despite the fact that most communication between human beings is non-verbal, militaries tend to invest much more effort in improving verbal communication skills. This is understandable. No cooperation is possible if the counterparts cannot understand each other. Different methods were used by coalition partners to bridge their language gaps. The Ottomans and the Germans could not communicate with each other in either Turkish or German and therefore resorted to the use of a neutral language, French, which was a second language in both countries. The British and the Japanese relied entirely on language officers who studied each other's tongue during peacetime and served as interpreters during the campaign. The Chinese recruited thousands of young interpreters, mainly from China's middle class, and deployed them in U.S. training bases as well as among U.S. liaison teams. The Americans, for their part, greatly benefited from the graduates of the Chinese Language Officer Program of the U.S. Army, a program that operated for more than twenty years prior to the war. In the Gulf War, the U.S. military enjoyed a coalition partner whose senior officers were conversant in English as well as a large cadre of Arabic speaking American Foreign Area Officers. Kuwaiti students who volunteered to serve as interpreters for the coalition forces were also a great help. The Israelis offered an interesting mechanism to overcome the language problem both with the SLA and the Palestinian Security Forces. They utilized the Israeli Druze in the ranks of the IDF as a cultural bridge. Despite being the senior member of the alliance, the Israelis agreed to relinquish the use of Hebrew as the official language of communication and conducted most of their business with their allies in Arabic. This prevented misunderstandings. The Saudis in the Gulf War were extremely sensitive to their pride and status but at the same time they were pragmatic enough to accept English as the official language of the coalition. These cases show us that there is not necessarily a correlation between the level of seniority or the level of force contribution and the choice of the coalition language. The emergence of English as the world's most commonly used language has created a perception in military circles that language is a diminishing problem in coalition warfare, with every coalition contingent arriving at the theater with ample English speakers. But one should not assume that all future coalitions will be conducted in English. In some potential flashpoints English is not a widely used language, and the emergence of conflict in these regions could foster non-English-speaking coalitions. For example, coalition operations in East Europe or Central Asia, where most senior officers understand Russian, could require that language to become the official language of any coalition. In some African countries, French is more widely spoken than English, and a coalition in this region could therefore be conducted in French. Similarly, coalitions in central or Latin America could be conducted in Spanish or Portuguese, and coalitions in the Middle East, unlike the Gulf War, could be conducted in Arabic. To a large degree 21st century technology can help bridge the language barrier. U.S. troops in Afghanistan and Iraq have been able to communicate with local citizens by using a hand-held device called the Phraselator. This device uses computer chips to translate English phrases into as many as 30 foreign language equivalents. Users either speak into the device, which translates the English into the foreign-equivalent phrase or they can punch a button to call up the desired phrase. Another device, the Voice Response Translator stores 125 languages and 125,000 phrases in each language.

A U.S. soldier in Iraq using the Phraselator

Problems related to non-verbal communication are also likely to continue to burden the joint work of coalition partners, but can be mitigated with sufficient preparation and attention. As mentioned in previous chapters, certain types of rhetoric, body signals and mannerisms perfectly acceptable in one culture can be perceived as offensive to another. Each culture has its own set of gestures and different degree of physical contact between people. Understanding the way people of different cultures communicate their feelings and preferences is a prerequisite for successful relations. Sufficient preparation in the form of do's and don'ts manuals or cultural acclimatization programs, similar to the program used by the U.S. military during the Gulf War, and later in Somalia, Iraq and Afghanistan can reduce tension with allies. Failure to address these issues may lead to difficult relations between the forces on the ground. The IDF provides an example of how lack of sensitivity to body language and gestures could harm relations. Between 1994 and 2000, Israeli soldiers participated in joint patrols with Palestinian policemen in the West Bank and Gaza Strip. The purpose of the patrols was to show joint Israeli-Palestinian presence along the main roads in the areas where sovereignty was shared between the two nations. Joint patrol units consisted of two vehicles, one Israeli and the other Palestinian. Rules of engagement determined that in Palestinian controlled areas the Palestinian vehicle would lead the force and in Israeli controlled areas the IDF vehicle would assume the leading role. A study conducted in Israel on the joint patrols revealed that the atmosphere and the relations between Israelis and Palestinians were more tense on shifts in which the Israelis led. It so happened that the Palestinian soldiers were offended seeing Israeli soldiers sitting in the rear of the vehicle ahead such that the soles of their shoes were exposed toward the Palestinians, something Arabs find to be insulting. The Palestinians saw such behavior as disrespectful and were, therefore, unenthusiastic to work with their colleagues. Furthermore, the study showed that the Palestinians saw great symbolism in a friendly handshake at the beginning of each patrol shift. If the Israelis failed to extend their hand for whatever reason, working relations on that day were severely damaged.[10]

Insensitivity to customs is usually a result of ignorance rather than ill intentions. One fine example of how good intention unaccompanied by cultural knowledge may cause the opposite effect is the famous meeting between Winston Churchill and King Ibn Saud toward the end of World War II. In accordance with Middle Eastern tradition, the two leaders exchanged presents. The King gave his English guests lavish presents, jeweled swords, perfumes and diamonds worth thousands of pounds. To his embarrassment Churchill in return gave Ibn Saud £100 worth of perfume. But he promised that this was just a token present and the real gift was due to follow in the shape of the finest car in the world. And indeed, shortly after, a Rolls-Royce especially designed and built to fit the special needs of the ailing king arrived at the palace. The King expressed his admiration for the precious vehicle. But before he left, the British emissary who delivered it overheard the king saying to his brother that he could have the car. The King noticed that the steering wheel was on the right-hand side of the car. Since the custom in Saudi Arabia was that the King sat in the front of his car, it meant that he would have to sit to the left of his driver, and this was not appropriate since the place of honor was on the right. "The finest motor car in the world was unusable," lamented the British emissary.[11] In the case of military cooperation, a small mistake like this, caused by lack of understanding of the peculiarities of a friendly culture, could be a real relationship spoiler. Another example: A U.S. Army officer who served in Korea told a story about a crisis between the soldiers of a U.S. battlion and its Korean augmentation force. For morale purposes, the Americans decided to design a new battalion sign, and the one chosen included a human skull taken from a human skeleton. Seeing the new sign, the Korean soldiers immediately deserted. When found and asked why they deserted, they said they could not serve in a unit where the men had no respect for human beings. They insisted the skull receive a decent burial before they returned to the unit.[12] Here too, one partner trivialized something that the other side cared a great deal about.

Aside from issues of language and non-verbal signals, another communication problem stems from the different ways military forces communicate orders along their chains of command. Some militaries are more formalistic and bureaucratic than others and tend to put greater emphasis on the written word than on oral communication. Officers of non-Western militaries, such as the Japanese, the Chinese and the Saudi militaries, showed a tendency to communicate their orders orally and use very little documentation. Conversely, British and American military culture relied heavily on documentation. In these militaries, orders and directives issued orally carried less authority than the written word.

Cultural exposure

Prior exposure of military organizations to other cultures clearly provides members of these organizations with a better understanding of their partners' sensitivities and reduces the risk of culture shock when dealing with them. None of the coalition partners presented earlier were completely foreign to each other by the time they fought together. The Germans had more than 70 years of military missions in Constantinople prior to World War I; the British spent about 40 years working with the Japanese before Tsingtau; a similar period of time had the Americans in China and Saudi Arabia before they were called to fight alongside the local armies; the Israelis had almost a decade of experience working with Lebanese players before 1985. By and large, cooperation in these preparation periods was low in its intensity, the number of Western troops in the host countries was relatively small, and their involvement in their hosts' cultural life was minimal. Nonetheless, the period of interaction prior to the war was important. The presence of Western troops on the ground provided them an opportunity to study their partners' culture and way of life and establish a kernel of experience that served the greater bulk of forces that followed. Naturally, without the prior period of mutual exposure, the culture shock for both sides would have been much greater.

Not all militaries enjoyed the same level of cultural exposure to their allies. In fact, there is no correlation between the length of peacetime cooperation and the quality of the relations. The Germans in general were not well exposed to the Turks despite the fact that they had the longest period of peacetime cooperation with them. They had no linguistic infrastructure, no joint training and hardly any experience fighting with non-European allies. Their army was culturally homogeneous as was German society at the time. Many German soldiers had never interacted with non-Europeans. The British, by virtue of their colonial experience, were different. They were highly exposed to foreign cultures. They trained with foreign armies and navies, and their enlisted personnel were culturally and racially diverse. Most British soldiers had some experience working with people different from themselves. The Japanese had no colonial assets or garrison forces abroad, but they showed a remarkable degree of openness to the West and great inclination to learn about it and adopt its ways. Just like the Ottomans, they hosted French, British and German military missions. But whereas the Ottomans were guarded and averse to change, the Japanese were committed to reform and were undeterred by interaction with the Occidentals. As a result, military cooperation between Japanese and Westerners both during the Boxer Rebellion and World War I was fruitful, operationally as well as culturally.

The U.S. military's sufficient experience of joint work with both the Chinese and Saudis supplied it with cadres of men who had served in these countries and spoke the vernacular. Most of the troops and the officers were experienced in some sort of overseas missions. Furthermore, the enlisted corps itself was culturally diverse, employing African-Americans, Hispanics, Asian-Americans and other minorities. The Israelis were completely unexposed to the Arab world, and the Lebanese in specific, prior to 1982, but they improved their familiarity and exposure as time went by. Their cross-cultural cooperation with the SLA showed progress as the relations solidified.

Not surprisingly, the quality of cross-cultural cooperation is likely to be better between coalition partners who have been exposed to each other than between militaries completely foreign to each other. Alas, one may not enjoy the benefit of prior exposure to all potential coalition partners. A country with world wide strategic interests such as the U.S. should, therefore, develop tools to engage with potential future coalition partners to whom it has little cultural exposure. The main peacetime mechanism to increase such exposure and strengthen military relationships is joint training. This could take place through routine field and naval exercises involving regional countries and orchestrated by the relevant Commander in Chief (CINC). One example of such a venture is an annual multinational exercise called *Bright Star*, which, since

1980, has brought together militaries from countries located in the realm of CENTCOM to improve their interoperability. In 1999, *Bright Star* involved eleven NATO and Arab countries and over 73,000 military personnel. An additional 32 nations sent observers to the exercise.[13] Participants in these exercises are able to meet their partners in peacetime and interact with them both socially and professionally. Joint exercises enable U.S. military personnel to learn more about the potential cultural problems that could arise in case of combined military action. Early detection of these problems enables military planners to address them as part of their training programs and hence, improve their readiness for coalition operations. The role of military attachés in providing useful information about the host country has always been crucial. But military attachés are not always mindful of the potential implications of culture on military relations. In addition to the conventional intelligence passed on by diplomats and attachés, there should be sufficient thinking about the contingency of engagement between their armed forces and the local military. Such thinking can predict potential problems in future cooperation, identify sensitivities and assist in selecting the right commanders to carry out the job.

Important as it is to introduce Americans to foreign cultures, it is no less crucial to teach officers of foreign militaries about the West and its military culture. To give foreign officers a taste of American culture, the U.S. has opened a series of military bases, academic military institutions and regional study centers with a mission to enhance cooperation and build relationships between Americans and foreign militaries. The Marshall Center in Germany, for example, is dedicated to educating officers from Europe and Eurasia in the American way of war; the Asia-Pacific Center for Security Studies (APCSS) in Honolulu, Hawaii, has hosted hundreds of officers from over 40 countries in Asia and the Pacific providing them an opportunity to sit with American colleagues and understand them better. The National Defense University in Fort McNair, Washington D.C., offers fellowships every year to select senior officers from about 40 nations, all personally invited by the Chairman of the Joint Chiefs of Staff. The program includes extensive travel within the United States to military, industrial, and cultural locations. In addition, the university is the host of several regional centers such as the Center for Hemispheric Defense Studies, which brings together officers from Latin and Central America, the Near East South Asia Center for Strategic Studies and the Africa Center for Strategic Studies. Each of these centers brings top-ranking military officers, civilian national security officials, and defense attachés from embassies in Washington to participate in different educational programs that familiarize them with the U.S. military. The benefit of these familiarization programs is immense. Besides the personal acquaintances formed between American and foreign officers, these officers, as the Gulf War case showed, could become goodwill ambassadors in their countries and serve as a cultural bridge in the case of a combined operation involving their country.

No less important than the level of exposure of the military organization as a whole is the individual degree of exposure of the officers selected to lead the coalition forces. As we have seen, coalition command requires a unique set of diplomatic and personal qualities not commonly found among senior officers. The commander must be sensitive, inquisitive, savvy, patient and at times theatrical. To create harmonious relations with his counterparts, he must be able to gather sufficient knowledge of the partner's sensitivities and act upon this knowledge. A coalition commander operating on the territory of a host nation faces a specifically challenging task. He should always maintain a delicate balance between the military and diplomatic objectives of the coalition and the cultural constraints imposed by the host. Common wisdom says that officers with prior experience in working with the partner and a command of the indigenous tongue stand a greater chance of success in their mission. This may be true in many cases. There is no doubt that Generals Kamio Mitsuomi's and Khaled bin Sultan's command of English smoothed their communication with Bernardiston and Schwarzkopf respectively. Schwarzkopf's successor at CENTCOM, General Anthony Zinni, used his command of the Italian language to overcome tension with the Italian contingent of the UN forces in Somalia in a similar way that Lord Beresford, a Field Marshal under the Duke of Wellington, used his command of Portuguese to reconcile differences between British and Portuguese units in the Spanish Peninsula wars. But language skills do not necessarily predict harmony. Enver Pasha spoke German, lived in Germany and knew its culture, and, yet, his relations with the Germans were troubled. Similarly, General Stilwell's familiarity with China and the Mandarin language did not spare him tension with Chiang Kai-shek and his generals. Successful coalition commanders, as the above cases show, are not necessarily the officers with the highest exposure to the partner's culture but rather those equipped with excellent social, diplomatic and communicative skills which enable them to build a strong team with their allies. Furthermore, coalition commanders who try to impose change on their coalition partners in order to make them more compatible with Western military culture are likely to fair poorly. Those who accepted their partners as they were, even if some of their customs were objectionable to Western taste, showed better results.

A cadet at the U.S. Air Force Academy works through a blackboard exercise in Chinese. All three U.S. military academies are putting new emphasis on language and regional studies coursework to help their graduates as they deploy around the world.

(U.S. Air Force)

Core society influence

Are conscripts and officers influenced by their own society's prevailing attitudes toward the coalition partner's society? All cases examined in this book indicate that indeed they are. All case studies

presented here showed a strong correlation between the home society's general attitude toward the coalition partner's culture and the
degree of cross-cultural tension during the joint work. The Germans
and the Turks were both affected by the strong ethnocentric sentiments that prevailed in their respective societies. Both felt culturally superior and looked down on their partner. This bred resentment
and antagonism. The Americans and the Chinese suffered a similar
problem. However, we have seen that a change of heart in American
society since World War II, with growing cultural tolerance and
social equality between races and cultures, brought the U.S. to the
Gulf War with a completely different attitude toward non-Western
players. Whereas Americans in China were rude, arrogant, rowdy,
impatient and culturally insensitive, in Saudi Arabia they were the
exact opposite. In fact, they have been criticized for moving to the
opposite extreme by treating the Saudis with excessive deference,
often at the expense of the most fundamental values of American
society. Both the British and the Japanese had great respect for each
other's cultures and achievements even before heading for battle.
Their mutual respect was a facilitator for fruitful and cooperative
coalition relations. The Israelis were overly burdened by a long history of antipathy toward Arabs. With such a collective sentiment,
it was hard for them to treat their Lebanese allies as equals. They
made a clear distinction between Christians and Muslims and were
biased in favor of the former even though nothing in the behavior
of the Christians in Lebanon indicated that they were more progres-
sive than the Muslims. All of us are products of our upbringing,
experiences and the explicit and implicit signals and attitudes that
our society embeds in our collective consciousness. When people
are raised to believe in a hierarchy where one culture or race is
superior to another, their prejudiced attitudes are likely to affect
their behavior toward members of the allegedly inferior culture if
and when they are called to work together with them. Soldiers, as
this book showed, are not immune to this danger. Modern military
personnel, whether conscript or professional forces, are products
of the cultural and intellectual lives of their home societies. They
absorb the same hidden signals and reflect the same sentiments,
biases, prejudices and stereotypes held by the population in their
countries. They cannot leave those feelings behind when sent to

remote theaters to cooperate with people from cultures they view as inferior. Even if they are consciously aware of the need to treat their partners with utmost respect, deeply embedded sentiments are likely to express themselves in various ways and affect the quality of cooperation.

There is no simple solution to this problem, which reflects a fundamental part of human nature. However, egalitarian and democratic societies with advanced education systems are likely to be more protected from it. Genuine integration of a wide array of cultural and racial groups in the armed forces' officer corps helps remove some of the cultural barriers and make the military an effective multi-cultural organization. Here again, the selection of suitable coalition commanders is important. The effective coalition commander, like the effective manager of a multinational firm, can do a lot to improve cultural tolerance and inhibit social biases among his troops. He should be aware that the mere fact that he occupies a superior position over the foreign group could be a problem in itself. Some non-Western societies still carry collective recollections of abuse and exploitation by the white man and might react negatively to the idea of their people obeying his orders. Black troops from African militaries might feel subconscious, antagonistic feelings if put in a subordinate position to a white officer, especially those coming from countries with a recent history of racial discrimination or colonialism. This is not to say that race considerations should dictate appointments of coalition commanders. It does mean that such sensitivities should be taken into account when the chosen coalition commander prepares for his challenge. He should realize that such sensitivities may have an effect on his command and may require some modifications. In order to avoid the tension that could stem from an allies' inferiority or superiority complex, he should command by consent and compromise rather than by power and hierarchy. Similar logic applies to the incorporation of women in command positions in some Western militaries. The number of female officers in the U.S. military's command echelon is growing and, yet, the U.S. military is increasingly required to collaborate with countries in which women are not viewed as equal to men. The wish to remove existing gender barriers and provide equal opportunities for women in the armed forces may not necessarily be in sync with the need to maintain tension-free coalition relations.

The Crusade Effect

One theme that recurred throughout this book was the attempt by a coalition enemy to exploit weak cultural relations to drive a wedge between the allies. Many coalitions involving members of dissimilar cultures, especially those occurring along civilizational fault lines, were exposed to systematic destabilization efforts by means of culturally or racially charged propaganda. The idea was to exploit cultural links between the enemy and the culturally similar coalition partner and at the same time emphasize the cultural dissimilarity and differences between the coalition partners. Such propaganda aimed to deflect the attention of the allied populations from the war effort and to create a new cultural agenda that would de-legitimize the relations. I call this phenomenon the "Crusade effect." It suggests triangular relations among three actors: the "collaborator," the "contaminator" and the "instigator." The collaborator and the instigator are enemies, but share a similar cultural background, language, religion or heritage. The collaborator's invitation of the contaminator, a guest military that is culturally or racially foreign, is denounced by the instigator as cultural treason or religious heresy. Coalitions involving Western militaries fighting with Muslim partners have always stood in the shadow of a broader inter-civilizational tension between the Muslim and the non-Muslim worlds. During the Gulf War, Iraq assumed the role of the instigator. Its propaganda aimed to break the U.S.-led coalition during the Gulf War and called on the Saudi collaborators not to abandon their faith by allying themselves with the American contaminator. Hizballah used similar propaganda calling Muslim soldiers of the SLA to rejoin their co-religionists and fight together against the non-believer. This theme was strongly manipulated during the war in Afghanistan against Al-Qaida. Osama bin Laden and his followers exploited Islam repeatedly, alleging that the war was part of a struggle between the Muslim world and the

"Crusaders," evoking the religious wars of medieval times in which the Muslims finally prevailed over the Christian invaders. Here again, the Americans were presented as a contaminating agent and the government of Pakistan, the main U.S. ally, was presented as a collaborator. The Islamists' instigation was designed to put a wedge in the coalition by evoking cultural themes.

The Crusade effect expressed itself not only in relations with the Muslims but also in the Western fight against the Japanese in World War II. Japanese propaganda focused on the cultural similarities between China and Japan to create a sense among the Chinese that the enemy was the West rather than Japan. They invoked religious and racial themes to hint at an imminent clash between the White and Asian civilizations. Interestingly enough, all of the attempts to destroy coalitions utilizing the Crusade effect failed. However, the military and political leaderships of Western nations should be well aware of this method and be cautious not to make unhelpful statements that might play into the hands of the enemy. Lord Halifax's repeated use of the term "Crusade" during World War II as well as President George W. Bush's unfortunate use of the same term to describe the war against terrorism, a statement for which he had to profusely apologize, offended the non-Western coalition partners and did not help strengthen the coalition at all.[14] To avoid falling into the crusade trap, Western leaders went to great lengths to ensure cultural diversity of the coalitions they managed. They specifically insisted on the incorporation of as many nations as possible similar in culture to the collaborator. Such action derails any attempt by the instigator to give the war a racial or cultural connotation. During the Korean War, for example, General Douglas MacArthur advocated getting as many Asian nations to assist in the war as possible so that the Chinese and the North Koreans could not turn it into a racial war. Against the wish of the Truman Administration, he even recommended admitting into the coalition a contingent of Nationalist Chinese, a decision that was likely to deepen the tension with Communist China. Both during the Gulf War and during the war on terrorism, the U.S. deemed it necessary to recruit, often at a high price, Muslim countries into the coalition. Many of the these members contributed very little to the war effort in terms of their military capabilities, but their political contribution, by virtue of their siding with the West against a fellow Muslim country, was invaluable.

Just as cultural elements could be used to break coalitions, they could also be manipulated as a device to build or strengthen them. Coalition partners sometimes search for common cultural points in order to strengthen their bond. These commonalities are often artificial, but are invoked with the hope of strengthening the sides' commitment to each other. To bridge the religion gap between the Turks and the Germans, the Germans helped create a myth that the Hohenzolerns were in fact of Muslim origin. This helped them legitimize themselves in the eyes of the Ottomans and alienate themselves from their enemies. The Israelis equated the situation of the Christians in Lebanon to that of the European Jews prior to the establishment of the state of Israel. Both were in their eyes persecuted minorities that suffered ill treatment in face of the world's indifference. Soldiers of the SLA, for their part, often used rhetoric - "our blood is Jewish" for example - and themes that implied a bond of blood with the Israelis. They used images from Jewish history and culture as analogies to their situation as a besieged, persecuted group. To dissuade Israel from withdrawing from Lebanon, General Lahad promised: "just like the Jews in Masada, we will fight for our land."[15] The use of the image of Masada was not coincidental. By comparing the situation in south Lebanon to the struggle of the Jews against the Romans in the first century, which ended in a mass suicide of Jewish rebels who refused to surrender, Lahad manipulated an important Jewish theme. He was well aware of the strong feelings Masada story provokes and decided to appeal to the Israeli consciousness through a cultural metaphor.

EPILOGUE

It has been claimed by some that the refusal to accept the notion that culture determines international behavior is a typical American cultural trait. One of those critics, himself an American, wrote: "Only Americans could assume that all men and women are purely rational beings upon whom societal values have only minor influence."[1] Yet, the intricacies of the international system and the growing need to cooperate with fellow nations have brought many Americans to adopt a less simplistic view of the world. Hence, the role and the importance of culture are slowly gaining their well-deserved recognition both in academic and military circles. Consequently, the U.S. military has been able to improve coalition relations with partners around the world and to carry out one successful coalition endeavor after another. The same is true for other militaries. The chronicle of culture's influence on military collaboration through the past century therefore leaves us with great sense of optimism. While still an important factor, culture is today a well managed element in the complex web of multinational operations. This can be mainly attributed to our enhanced tolerance of cultural dissimilarity, our religious pluralism, and our collective efforts to repair race relations, which reached a new climax in January 2009, when the first African-American president moved into the White House. But with all the progress made in the West, in many parts of the world likely to become our future battlefields such progress is far from sight and cultural rifts among nations and ethnic groups are deeper than ever. In the complex and tumultuous international environment of the beginning of the 21st century, it is hard for military planners to predict who will be their next coalition partners, in which setting the coalition will take place, and toward which objectives it will fight. As these lines are being written, new military relations are being formed. American and European forces are deployed around the world as part of the war against terrorism and in other peacekeeping missions. Whether in Africa, Asia, or the Middle East, each one of these engagements between Western and non-Western militaries will have an interesting cultural component. It is likely that just like in the past it will be the earthy issues like who will command the force and what will be the rules of engagement that will draw most of the public attention. But if history is our guide, it is safe to assume that the cultural dimension is likely to continue to play an important role. Only a deeper look into the cultural background of our prospective allies can make us able to better forecast the problems that might emerge in the course of our common work with them. Hopefully they will do the same.

NOTES

INTRODUCTION

[1] William C. Westmoreland, *A Soldier Reports* (NY: Dell, 1976), 340.

[2] Khaled bin Sultan, *Desert Warrior* (NY: Harper Perennial, 1995), 258.

[3] E. V. Badolato, "A Clash of Cultures: The Expulsion of Soviet Military Advisors from Egypt," *Naval War College Review* (March 1984): 69-81.

[4] *The Christian Science Monitor,* 17 October 1972.

[5] David S. Landes, *The Wealth and Poverty of Nations: Why Some Are So Rich and Some So Poor* (NY, London: W.W. Norton & Company, 1998), 516.

[6] Jongsuk Chay, ed., *Culture and International Relations* (NY, Westport and London: Praeger, 1990); Yosef Lapid and Friedrich Kratochwil, eds., *The Return of Culture and Identity in IR Theory* (Boulder and London: Lynne Rienner Publishers, 1996); Lawrence E. Harrison and Samuel P. Huntington, eds., *Culture Matters* (NY: Basic Books, 2000); Francis Fukuyama, *Trust: The Social Virtue and the Creation of Prosperity* (NY: Free Press, 1995); Lucian Pye and Sidney Verba, eds., *Political Culture and Political Development* (Princeton, N.J.: Princeton University Press, 1963); Gabriel Almond and Sidney Verba, *The Civic Culture* (Boston: Little, Brown, 1966); David J. Elkins and Richard E. B. Simeon, "A Cause in Search of Its Effect, or What Does Political Culture Explain?" *Comparative Politics* 11 (January 1979): 127-145; Landes, *Wealth and Poverty of Nations*; Lawrence E. Harrison, *Who Prospers? How Cultural Values Shape Economic and Political Success* (NY: Basic Books 1992).

[7] Samuel P. Huntington, *The Clash of Civilizations and the Remaking of World Order* (NY: Simon & Schuster, 1996).

[8] David Irving, *The War Between the Generals: Inside the Allied High Command* (NY: Congdon & Lattes 1981), 81.

CHAPTER 1: CULTURE AND WAR

[1] For a review of definitions of culture see A. L Kroeber, and C. Kluckhohn, *Culture: A Critical Review of Concepts and Definitions*, Peabody Museum Papers, vol. 47, no. 1 (Cambridge, Mass.: Harvard university, 1952).

[2] Ziya Gökalp, *Turkish Nationalism and Western Civilization* (London: Allen and Unwin, 1959); Edward B. Talor, *Primitive Culture: Research into the Development of Mythology, Philosophy, Religion, Art, and Customs* (NY: Henry Holt & Co., 1877), vol. I, 1; Clark Wissler, *Man and Culture* (NY: Crowell, 1923); Ralph L. Beals and Harry Hoijer, *An Introduction to Anthropology* (NY: Macmillan Co., 1961), 229; E.A. Hoebel, "The Nature of Culture," in Harry L. Shapiro ed., *Man, Culture and Society* (NY: Oxford University Press, 1956), 176.

[3] Fukuyama, 34.

[4] Ruth Benedict, *Patterns of Culture* (London: Routledge & Kegan Paul 1935), 33; Kroeber and Kluckhohn, *Culture,* 181; Ralph Linton, *The Cultural Background of Personality* (NY: Appleton Century Co., 1945), 32; Clifford Geertz, *Interpretation of Culture* (NY: Basic, 1973); Richard Porter in Larry A. Samovar and Richard E. Porter, *Intercultural Communication: A Reader* (Belmont, California: Wadsworth Publishing Company, Inc. 1972), 3; T.S. Eliot, *Notes toward the Definition of Culture* (NY: Harcourt Brace, 1949), Victor Barnouw, *Culture and Personality* (Homewood, Illinois: The Dorsey Press, 1973), 6.

[5] Samuel Taylor Coleridge, *Essays on his own Times* vol. 2 (London: William Pickering, 1850), 668; Alex Inkeles, *National Character: A Psycho-Social Perspective* (New Brunswick and London: Transaction Publishers, 1997), 12.

[6] Margaret Mead, "National Character," in A. L. Kroeber ed., *Anthropology Today* (Chicago: Chicago University Press, 1953), 642-667; David McClelland, *The Achieving Society* (Princeton: Van Nostrand, 1961), 7-42; F.L.K. Hsu, *Americans and Chinese: Two Ways of Life* (NY: Abelard-Schuman, 1953); G. Gorer,

Exploring English Character (London: Cresset Press, 1955); Sellin Thorsten, *National Character in the Perspective of the Social Sciences* (Philadelphia: The Annals of the American Academy of Political and Social Science, 1967); Alex Inkeles, *National Character: A Psycho-Social Perspective* (New Brunswick and London: Transaction Publishers, 1997).

[7] George Peter Murdock, *Outline of World Cultures* (New Haven: Human Relations Area Files, 1963).

[8] Thucydides, *The Peloponnesian War* (Baltimore, MD: Penguin Books 1954), 51.

[9] Carl von Clausewitz, *Historical and Political Writing* ed. Peter Paret and Daniel Moran, (Princeton: Princeton University Press, 1992), 252-259.

[10] Quoted in Len Deighton, *Blood, Tears and Folly* (London: Pimlico, 1993), 113.

[11] Friedrich von Bernhardi, *Germany and the Next War* (NY: Longmans, Green, 1914).

[12] Alexis de Tocqueville, *The Old Regime and the French Revolution* (NY: Doubleday Anchor Books, 1955), 211.

[13] Ardant du Picq, "Battle Studies," in *Roots of Strategy,* book 2 (Harrisburg, Pennsylvania: Stackpole Books, 1987), 66.

[14] Winston S. Churchill, *A History of the English-speaking People: The Birth of Britain* (NY: Dodd, Mead, 1956), 92-103.

[15] Alfred Thayer Mahan, *The Influence of Seapower upon History* (NY: Hill and Wang 1957), 46.

[16] Ruth Benedict, *The Chrysanthemum and The Sword* (Cambridge, MA: Riverside Press, 1946).

[17] Hans J. Morgenthau, *Politics among Nations: The Struggle for Power and Peace* (NY: Alfred A. Knopf, 1948).

[18] Raymond Aron, *Peace and War: Theory of International Relations* (NY: Frederick A. Praeger, 1967), 288-291.

[19] Rudolph J. Rummel, *Understanding Conflict and War,* vol. 1: *The Dynamic Psychological Field* (NY: John Wiley and Sons, 1975).

[20] Jack Snyder, *The Soviet Strategic Culture: Implications for Nuclear Options* (Santa Monica, California: RAND R-2154-AF, 1977).

[21] Ken Booth, "The Concept of Strategic Culture Affirmed," in Carl G. Jacobsen ed., *Strategic Power: U.S.A/USSR* (London: The

Macmillan Press 1990), 121-130; see also Yitzhak Klein, "A Theory of Strategic Culture," *Comparative Strategy* vol. 10, (1991): 5.

[22] Alastair Iain Johnston, *Cultural Realism: Strategic Culture and Grand Strategy in Chinese History* (Princeton NJ: Princeton University Press 1995), 1.

[23] Colin S. Gray, *Nuclear Strategy and National Style* (Lanham, MD: Hamilton Press 1986).

[24] On the debate about China's strategic culture see Alastair Iain Johnston, *Cultural Realism: Strategic Culture and Grand Strategy in Chinese History* (Princeton NJ: Princeton University Press 1995); Alastair Iain Johnston, "Cultural Realism and Strategy in Maoist China," in *The Culture of National Security: Norms and Identity in World Politics,* Peter J. Katzenstein ed., (NY: Columbia University Press, 1996), 217-268; Frank A. Kierman and John K. Fairbank eds., *Chinese Ways in Warfare*, (Cambridge, Massachusetts: Harvard University Press, 1974); Edward Boylan, "The Chinese Cultural Style of Warfare," *Comparative Strategy* 4 (1982): 341-46.

[25] Shimon Naveh, "The Cult of Offensive Preemption and Future Challenges for Israeli Operational Thought" *Israel Affairs* 1 (Autumn 1995): 168-187.

[26] Uri Ben-Eliezer, *The Emergence of Israeli Militarism 1936-1956* (Tel Aviv: Dvir, 1995); Anita Shapira, *Land and Power: The Zionist Resort to Force*, 1881-1948 (NY: Oxford University Press, 1992); Yoram Hazony, *The Jewish State: The Struggle for Israel's Soul* (NY: Basic Books, 2000); Avi Shlaim, *The Iron Wall: Israel and the Arab World* (NY: W.W. Norton, 2000).

[27] Stephen Peter Rosen, *Societies and Military Power: India and its Armies* (Ithaca and London: Cornell University Press, 1996).

[28] J. Stewart Black and Mark Mendenhall, "Cross-Cultural Training Effectiveness: A Review and a Theoretical Framework for Future Research," *Academy of Management Review* vol. 15 no. 1 (1990): 113-136.

[29] Geert Hofstede, *Culture's Consequences: International Differences in Work Related Values* (Beverly Hills, CA: Sage, 1980).

[30] T.S. Eliot, *Notes toward the Definition of Culture,* 124.

[31] Muriel Saville-Troike, "The Ethnography of Communication," in *Sociolinguistics and Language Teaching,* Sandra Lee McKay and Nancy

H. Hornberger eds., (NY: Cambridge University Press, 1996), 351-382.

[32] For a detailed review of the handicaps of translation see: Christiane F. Gonzalez, "Translation," in *Handbook of International and Intercultural Communication,* Molefi Kete Asante and William B. Gudykunst eds. , (London and New Delhi: Sage 1989), 484-501.

[33] Roy E. Appleman, *United States Army in the Korean War, South to Naktong, North to the Yalu* (Washington DC: Center of Military History U.S. Army, 1986), 388.

[34] *The Science Christian Monitor,* 20 July 1972.

[35] Clyde Kluckhohn, "The Gift of Tongues," in *Intercultural Communication: A Reader*, Larry A. Samovar, and Richard E. Porter eds., (Belmont, California: Wadsworth Publishing Company, 1972), 104.

[36] On language problems in the Habsburg Army see: Norman Stone, "The Austro-German Alliance," in *Coalition Warfare: An Uneasy Accord,* Keith Neilson and Roy A. Prete eds., (Waterloo, Canada: Wilfrid Laurier University Press, 1983), 19-28.

[37] For reports on significant operational implications on military cooperation due to language barriers see Erik Durschmied, *The Hinge Factor* (London: Hodder and Stoughton, 1999), 49-59; Paul Fregosi, *Dreams of Empire: Napoleon and the First World War 1792-1815* (London: Cardinal, 1989), 431; Jehuda L. Wallach, *Uneasy Coalition: The Entente Experience in World War I* (Westport, Connecticut: Greenwood Press, 1993), 45-46; Matthew B. Ridgway, *Soldier: The Memoirs of Matthew Ridgway* (NY: Harper and Brothers, 1956), 210.

[38] Fons Trompenaars, *Riding the Waves of Culture* (London: Nicholas Brealey, 1994), 68-69

[39] Edward T. Hall, *The Silent Language* (Garden City, N.Y: Doubleday, 1959).

[40] Ibid., 69.

[41] Helen Deresky, *International Management Managing Across Borders and Cultures* (NJ: Prentice Hall, 2000), 145-146; Hall, *The Silent Language*, 187.

[42] Westmoreland, *A Soldier Reports,* 329; David H. Hackworth and Julie Sherman, *About Face* (NY: Simon and Schuster 1989), 718.

[43] Edward Hall and Mildred Reed Hall, *Understanding Cultural Differences* (Yarmouth, Maine: Intercultural Press, Inc. 1990), 172.

[44] Hall, *The Silent Language,* 13-15.

[45] Hall, *Understanding Cultural Differences*, 184.

[46] Ibid., 6-9.

[47] C. Roetter, *Psychological Warfare* (London: Bastford, 1974),136-137 see also Edward T. Hall, *The Silent Language,* 77-78.

[48] Alex Inkeles, *National Character: A Psycho-Social Perspective* (New Brunswick and London: Transaction Publishers 1997), 170-171, see also Richard Mead, *International Management: Cross Cultural Dimensions* (Malden, Massachusetts: Blackwell Business 1998), 289.

[49] Hofstede, *Culture's Consequences,* 110-138.

[50] Ibid., 67-77.

[51] John H. Cushman, *Command and Control of Theater Forces: The Korea Command and Other Cases* (Cambridge: Harvard University, Center for Information Policy Research, Program on Information Resources Policy, 1985), 3-5.

[52] P. Collett and G. Oshea, "Pointing the Way to a Fictional Place: A Study in Direction Giving in Iran and England," *European Journal of Social Psychology* (1976): 447-458.

[53] David C. McClelland, *The Achieving Society* (Princeton, NJ: D. Van Nostrand, 1961), David Landes, *The Wealth and poverty of Nations.*

[54] Hofstede, *Culture's Consequences,* 148-166.

[55] David Reynolds, *Rich Relations: The American Occupation of Britain, 1942-1945* (NY: Random House, 1995).

[56] Carol Morris Petillo," Leaders and Followers: A Half Century of the U.S. Military in the Philippine Islands." In James C. Bradford ed., *The Military and Conflict Between Cultures* (Texas: Texas University Press 1997), 198-222.

[57] Lawrence James, *Raj: The Making of British India* (NY: St. Martin Press, 1998), 218; Alan R. Skelley, *The Victorian Army at Home* (Montreal: McGill-Queen's University Press, 1977), 53-58; John Ellis, *The Sharp End of War: The Fighting Man in World War II* (NY: Scribner's Sons, 1980).

CHAPTER 2: PASHAS AND PRUSSIANS: OTTOMAN TURKEY AND GERMANY DURING WORLD WAR I

[1] On the reforms of the Ottoman Army since 1750 see David B. Ralston, *Importing the European Army: The Introduction of European Military Techniques and Institutions into the Extra-European World, 1600-1914* (Chicago and London: University of Chicago Press, 1990), 43-78.

[2] For a good general treatment of the history of Ottoman-German military relations see Carl Mühlmann, *Das deutsch-türkische Waffenbündnis im Weltkriege* (Leipzig: Koehler & Amelang, 1940); Ulrich Trumpener, *Germany and the Ottoman Empire, 1914-1918* (Princeton: Princeton University Press, 1968); Frank G. Weber, *Eagles on the Crescent: Germany, Austria and the Diplomacy of the Turkish Alliance 1914-1918* (Ithaca: Cornell University Press, 1970); Jehuda L. Wallach, *Anatomy of Military Assistance: The German Military Mission in Turkey 1835-1919* (Tel Aviv: Maariv, 1981) [Hebrew].

[3] Wallach, 25.

[4] Ibid., 61-82.

[5] Among the key officers that received training in Germany and later assumed key positions in the Turkish army were Ahmet Izzet Pasha, deputy commander in chief and later war minister, Ali Riza Pasha, navy minister, Mahmet Sevket Pasha, War Minister, Hasan Riza Pasha, Commandant Military Staff College, Djevad Pasha, Commander in Chief at the Dardanelles, Ali Ihsan (Sabis) Pasha, commander 6th Army, Asim Gündüz, Division Commander in Palestine, Enver Pasha himself served in the years 1909-11 as military attaché in Berlin.

[6] For a detailed review of Enver's relations with Germany see: Charles D. Haley, "The Desperate Ottoman: Enver Pasha and the German Empire," *Middle Eastern Studies* vol. 30 no. 1 (January 1994): 1-51 and part II vol. 30 no. 2 (April 1994): 224-251.

[7] Kural Shaw, *History of the Ottoman Empire and Modern Turkey*, vol 2: *Reform, Revolution and Republic: The Rise of Modern Turkey, 1808-1975* (Cambridge: Cambridge University Press, 1977), 311.

[8] On the background to the conspiracy that led to Turkey's alliance with Germany see Carl Mühlmann, *Deutschland und die Türkei 1913-1914* (Berlin-Grunewald: Walther Rothschild, 1929); David Fromkin, *A Peace to End all Peace: The Fall of the Ottoman Empire and the Creation of the Modern Middle East* (NY: Avon Books, 1989), 62-76.

[9] Ahmed Emin, *Turkey in the World War* (New Haven: Yale University Press, 1930), 67.

[10] Wallach, 126.

[11] For the Russian reaction see: Fritz Fischer, *War of Illusion: German Policies from 1911 to 1914* (NY: Norton, 1969), 338-340.

[12] Wallach, 143-144.

[13] On the extent of German supplies to the Turkey see: Ulrich Trumpener, "German Military Aid to Turkey in 1914: A Historical Re-evaluation," *Journal of Modern History* 32 (1960): 145-149.

[14] Henry Morgenthau, *Ambassador Morgenthau's Story* (NY: Doubleday, Page & Company 1918), 210.

[15] Ulrich Trumpener, "Turkey's Entry into World War I: An Assessment of Responsibilities," *Journal of Modern History* 34 (1962): 369-380; Gerard E., *The Troubled Alliance: German Austrian Relations 1914-1917* (Lexington, Kentucky: The University Press of Kentucky, 1970), 82.

[16] Fromkin, 120-121; Trumpener, *Germany and the Ottoman Empire,* 79-80; Winston S. Churchill, *The Unknown War: The Eastern Front* (NY: Charles Scribner's Sons, 1931), 269-270.

[17] Trumpener, *Germany and the Ottoman Empire,* 80.

[18] For Djemal's account of the operation see: Djemal Pasha, *Memories of a Turkish Statesman-1913-1919* (NY: George H. Doran, 1922), 142-159.

[19] Kress von Kressenstein, Friedrich freiherr, *Mit den türken zum Suezkanal* (Berlin, Vorhut-verlag Otto Schlegel, 1938), Weber, 98.

[20] Alexander Aaronsohn, *With the Turks in Palestine* (Boston and NY: Houghton Mifflin Company, 1916), 45-46.

[21] See the report of a German war correspondent in Turkey, Harry Stuermer, *Two War Years in Constantinople* (NY: George H. Doran Company 1917), 40.

[22] Morgenthau, 275.

[23] Ulrich Trumpener, "Suez, Baku, Gallipoli: The Military Dimensions of the German-Ottoman Coalition, 1914-1918," in Keith Neilson and Roy A. Prete eds., *Coalition Warfare: An Uneasy Accord* (Ont. Canada: Wilfrid Laurier University Press, 1983).

[24] Mühlmann, *deutsch-türkische Waffenbündnis*, 106-108.

[25] Ibid., 276.

[26] Ibid., 207.

[27] Trumpener, *Germany and the Ottoman Empire*, 21.

[28] See for example, E.F. Benson, *Crescent and Iron Cross* (London and NY: Hodder & Stoughton, 1918).

[29] Trumpener, *Germany and the Ottoman Empire*, 70-72; Trumpener, "Liman von Sanders and the German-Ottoman Alliance," *Journal of Contemporary History* vol. 1 no. 4, (1966): 179-192.

[30] Liman's version of the relations with Enver appears in his memoirs see Otto Liman von Sanders, *Five Years in Turkey*. For a more balanced version see: Wallach, 137-139 and Trumpener, *Germany and the Ottoman Empire*, 80-81, 89-97.

[31] Wallach, 132.

[32] Haley, 36.

[33] Ibid, 7.

[34] Ibid, 11, 25, 45.

[35] Wallach, 139, Fischer, 336.

[36] On influence of French, British and German culture on Turkey see: Henry Elisha Allen, *The Turkish Transformation* (NY: Vail-Ballau, 1935), 10-27.

[37] Ibid., 14-15.

[38] Emin, 230.

[39] A. J. Toynbee, *Turkey: A Past and a Future* (NY: George H. Doran Company, 1917), 53.

[40] Ziya Gökalp, *The Principles of Turkism* (Leiden, Netherlands: E.J. Brill 1968), 75.

[41] Ibid., 102.

[42] Morgenthau, 276.

[43] The Germans experienced severe discipline problems in the late 19th Century with Moroccan NCOs who refused, for the above reason, to obey orders of their Prussian officers while serving in Prussian units.

[44] Wallach, 84.

[45] Otto Liman von Sanders, *Five Years in Turkey* (Annapolis: The Unites States Naval Institute, 1927), 11.

[46] Ibid, 49-51.

[47] Andrew Mango, *Ataturk: The Biography of the Founder of Modern Turkey* (NY: The Overlook Press, 2000), 148.

[48] This sentiment was conveyed, among others, by the Turkish ambassador in Paris, Rifat Pasha on September 4. See Emin, 74.

[49] Morgenthau, 206.

[50] Wallach, 23.

[51] Quoted in Robert Rhodes James, *Gallipoli* (NY: Macmillan, 1965), 4.

[52] Heinrich von Treitschke, *Germany, France, Russia, and Islam* (NY and London: G.P. Putnam, 1915), 20-24.

[53] Andre Servier, *Islam and the Psychology of the Musulman* (NY: Scribner's 1924), 252.

[54] "Instructions to Officers Deployed as Advisors to the Turkish Army," in Wallach, 244-246.

[55] Sanders, 95.

[56] Trumpener, *Germany and the Ottoman Empire*, 94.

[57] Wallach, 129-130.

[58] Ibid, 220.

[59] Daniel J. Hughes, *The King's Finest: A Social and Bureaucratic Profile of Prussia's General Officers, 1871-1914* (NY and London: Praeger, 1987).

[60] Mark Twain, "The Awful German Language," *A Trump Abroad* (NY: 1879).

[61] Andrew Mango described how rare was Mustafa Kemal's knowledge of French among Turkish cadets in the military academy. This was a rare distinction among the 750 first year students. See Mango, 45.

[62] Trumpener, *Germany and the Ottoman Empire,* 92.

[63] Sanders, 19.

[64] Sanders, 176; James, 150.

[65] Wallach, 183-184.

[66] Trumpener, *Germany and the Ottoman Empire*, 377.

[67] Wallach, 186. This point was also raised among other critics of Germany who saw the German tone as offensive and patronizing. See for example: Sir Charles Waldstein quoted in Charles Altschul,

German Militarism and its German Critics (Washington, DC: The Committee of Public Information, 1918), 19.

[68] Stuermer, 154-156; Morgenthau, 285.

[69] Sanders, 176.

[70] Lucy M. Garnett, *Turkey of the Ottomans* (NY: Charles Scribner's 1914), 169. See also Emin, 171.

[71] Emin, 171.

[72] Sanders, 10.

[73] Ibid., 11-12.

[74] Sanders, 11, 30, 49; Emin, 252.

[75] Sanders, 176.

[76] Mühlmann, 326.

[77] The indictment of Germany's responsibility for the misuse and the manipulation of Islam was Christian Snouck Hurgronje, *The Holy War-"Made in Germany"* (NY and London: G.P. Putnam, 1915). A new attempt to shed light on the German-Turkish conspiracy to unleash a Holy War against the British and Russians was described in Peter Hopkirk, *Like Hidden Fire: The Plot to Bring Down the British Empire* (NY: Kodansha, 1994).

[78] Trumpener, *Germany and the Ottoman Empire*, 113.

[79] For German attempts to promote pan-Islam in the Ottoman Empire see Emin, 181; Jacob M. Landau, *Pan-Turkism: From Irredentism to Cooperation* (London: Hurst & Company, 1981), 53; Charles Warren Hostler, *The Turks of Central Asia* (Westport, Connenticut and London: Praeger 1993), 96.

[80] Hopkirk, 4, 105-106.

[81] Aaronsohn, 21-22.

[82] Ibid, 22.

[83] Gökalp, 8, Landau, 51.

[84] Hurgronje, 34.

[85] Morgenthau, 161.

[86] Wallach, 151.

[87] Emin, 181.

[88] Trumpener, *Germany and the Ottoman Empire*, 114; Stuermer, 133.

[89] Hopkirk, 186.

[90] Morgenthau, 162.

[91] Emin, 175-6.

[92] Morgenthau, 164.

[93] Silberstein, 99.

[94] Ibid, Ibid.

[95] Trumpener, *Germany and the Ottoman Empire*, 115-116; Silberstein, 99-100.

[96] Lawrence James, *The Rise and Fall of the British Empire* (London: Little Brown, 1994), 359.

[97] Ibid., 360.

[98] Hopkirk, 181.

[99] Trumpener, Germany and the Ottoman Empire, 118.

[100] Stuermer, 148-9.

[101] Aaronsohn, 24.

[102] One can look in vain for a conclusive answer to the question which side sparked the violence and who had greater part of the blame. Many historians attributed the events of April 1915 to the rebelliousness of the Armenian population.

[103] See for example Emil Lengyel, *Turkey* (New York: 1940), 195-206; Sarkis Atamian, *The Armenian Community* (NY: 1955), 180-81; Wilhelm W. Gottlieb, *Studies in Secret Diplomacy during the First World War* (London: Allen and Unwin, 1957), 109-110; Lothar Rathmann, *Stossrichtung Nahost 1914-1918. Zur Expansionspolitik des deutschen Imperialismus im ersten Weltkrieg* (Berlin , 1963), 138-140.

[104] Toynbee, 53.

[105] Morgenthau, 281-283.

[106] Trumpener, *Germany and the Ottoman Empire*, 204

[107] Toynbee, 57.

[108] Wallach, 187.

[109] Ibid, 209.

[110] See W.E.D. Allen and Paul Muratoff, *Caucasian Battlefields: A History of the Wars on the Turco-Caucasian Border, 1828-1921* (Cambridge: Cambridge University Press, 1953).

[111] See for example the impressions of Sir Edwin Pears, *Forty Years in Constantinople* (NY: D. Appleton & Co. 1915), 5-6.

[112] Benson, 154.

[113] Fischer, 335.

[114] Emin, 177.

[115] Mango, 150.

[116] Sanders, 266.

[117] Emin, 255-256.

[118] Stuermer, 95-96.

[119] Quoted in Haley, 29.

[120] Sanders, 326.

[121] Wallach, 132.

[122] Diana Preston, *The Boxer Rebellion* (NY: Walker, 1999), 209.

[123] Gary W. Shanafelt, *The Secret Enemy: Austria-Hungary and the German Alliance, 1914-1918* (NY: Columbia University Press, 1985); Silberstein, *The Troubled Alliance*; Norman Stone, "The Austro-German Alliance, 1914-18" in *Coalition Warfare: An Uneasy Accord*.

CHAPTER 3: TOMMY DRINKS SAKI: THE ANGLO-JAPANESE WORLD WAR I ALLIANCE

[1] Basil Hall Chamberlain, *Things Japanese* (London: Kegan Paul, Trench, Trubner, 1927), 43.

[2] The title should go to the First Afghan War which began in 1839 ending in a spectacular British defeat by the Afghans.

[3] Ian H. Nish, *Alliance in Decline: A Study in Anglo-Japanese Relations 1908-23* (London: Athlone Press 1972), 135.

[4] Remarkably, mainly due to little exposure to the campaign, the British military failed to draw the important lessons from the battle and was, therefore, doomed to repeat the same mistakes in 1915.

[5] For an account of the creation of the alliance see: Ian H. Nish, *The Anglo-Japanese Alliance: The Diplomacy of Two Island Empires, 1894-1907* (London: Dover, 1985); R.P. Dua, *Anglo-Japanese Relations During the First World War* (New Delhi: S. Chand 1972).

[6] Alfred L. P. Dennis, *The Anglo-Japanese Alliance* (University of California Publications, 1923), 33. On the revision and renewal of the alliance see Peter Lowe, *Great Britain and Japan 1911-1915* (NY: St. Martin Press, 1969).

[7] *The Times,* (London), 18 August 1914.

[8] A. Morgan Young, *Japan in Recent Times, 1912-1926* (Westport, Conn.: Greenwood Press, 1973), 71-2.

[9] Charles B. Burdick, *The Japanese Siege of Tsingtau* (Hamden, Connecticut 1976), 46-47; F.P. Noseworthy, "The Capture of

Tsingtau, 1914," *The Journal of the Royal United Service Institution* vol. 81 no. 523 (August 1936): 519.

[10] Timothy D. Saxon, "Anglo-Japanese Naval Cooperation 1914-1918," *Naval War College Review* vol. 53 no. 1 (Winter 2000): 68.

[11] Nish, *Alliance in Decline,* 134.

[12] C. T. Atkinson, *The South Wales Borderers 24th Foot* (Cambridge: Cambridge University Press, 1937), 423-426.

[13] Burdick, 107.

[14] A telegram to Bernardiston from the Secretary of State for War, 20 August 1914, PRO, WO 106/663.

[15] Mr. Eckford, vice consul report, PRO, FO 371.

[16] Lecture given in 1921 by Colonel Watari, the Japanese Military Attaché in Washington, box 726, Naval Records Collection of the Office of Naval Records and Library, Record Group 45, National Archives; Burdick, *Japanese Siege of Tsingtau,* 229ff.

[17] Dispatch from Brigadier Bernardiston to the War Office, 9 October 1914, Supplement to the London Gazette, box 726, Record Group 45, National Archives; Burdick,111.

[18] Burdick, 194.

[19] John Fisher, "Backing the Wrong Horse: Japan in British Middle Eastern Policy 1914-1918," *The Journal of Strategic Studies* vol. 21 no. 2 (June 1998): 69.

[20] Document no. 163972, PRO, FO 371/2381.

[21] V.H. Rothwell, "The British Government and Japanese Military Assistance 1914-1918," *History* vol. 56 no. 186 (February 1971): 43.

[22] PRO, CAB 24/27, CAB 28/3.

[23] Saxon, 70-74.

[24] Rothwell, 35-45.

[25] Bob Tadashi Wakabayashi, *Anti-Foreignism and Western Learning in Early-Modern Japan* (Cambridge, MA: Harvard University Press, 1986); W.G. Beasley, *Japan Encounters the Barbarian* (New Haven and London: Yale University Press, 1995).

[26] Beasley, 13.

[27] David B. Ralston, *Importing the European Army: The Introduction of European Military Techniques and Institutions into the Extra-European World, 1600-1914* (Chicago and London: University of Chicago Press, 1990), 142-172.

[28] Ernst L. Presseisen, *Before Aggression; Europeans Prepare the Japanese Army* (Tucson: University of Arizona Press, 1965), 5.

[29] Ibid., 22.

[30] Ibid., 38.

[31] Ibid., 45, 59.

[32] Meirion and Susie Harries, *Soldiers of the Sun: The Rise and Fall of the Imperial Japanese Army* (NY: Random House, 1991), 48-50.

[33] Presseisen, 69.

[34] Ibid., 3.

[35] Report on the state of the Japanese army by Colonel Churchill, PRO, WO 106/48.

[36] Arthur J. Marder, *Old Friends, New Enemies: The Royal Navy and the Imperial Japanese Navy* (Oxford: Clarendon Press, 1981), 3-4.

[37] Piggott, 68-69.

[38] H.F. Walters, "International Maneuvers at Tientsin, North China, November 12th, 1913," *The Army Review* vol. 6 (April 1914): 506-507.

[39] Cecil Rhodes's remark in David Cannadine, *Ornamentalism: How the British Saw their Empire* (NY: Oxford University Press, 2001), 5.

[40] Among the best works on British supremacy are V.G. Kiernan, *The Lord of Human Kind: European Attitudes Toward the Outside World in the Imperial Age* (London: Weidenfeld and Nicolson, 1969); Thomas R. Metcalf, *Ideologies of the Raj* (Cambridge & NY: Cambridge University Press, 1994); Christine Bolt, *Victorian Attitude to Race* (London: Routledge & Kegan, 1971); Kenan Malik, *The Meaning of Race: Race, History and Culture in Western Society* (Basingstoke: Macmillan, 1996); P.J. Marshall & Glyndwr Williams, *The Great Map of Mankind: Perceptions of New Worlds in the Age of Enlightenment* (Cambridge: Harvard University Press, 1982); Ronald Hyam, *Britain's Imperial Century, 1815-1914: A Study of Empire and Expansion* (MD: Barnes & Noble, 1993).

[41] General Osborne Wilkinson quoted in Byron Farwell, *Mr. Kipling's Army* (London and NY: Norton, 1981), 109.

[42] Lawrence James, *The Rise and Fall of the British Empire* (London: Little Brown and Co. 1994), 221.

[43] For description of English prejudice against the Indians see the comments of Brigadier General John Jacob in Christopher Hibbert, *The Great Mutiny: India 1857* (NY: The Viking Press, 1978), 37-39.

[44] Surendra Nath Sen, *Eighteen Fifty-seven* (Calcutta: Government of India Press, 1958), 23.

[45] Ibid., 2-3.

[46] Ibid., 4.

[47] Gautam Sharma, *Indian Army through the Ages* (Bombay, London and NY: Allied Publishers 1966), 238.

[48] Hibbert, 53-54.

[49] Sen, 13.

[50] Sharma, 235.

[51] Sen, 42.

[52] Thomas R. Metcalf, *The Aftermath of Revolt, India, 1857-1870* (Princeton: Princeton University Press, 1964), 290.

[53] Metcalf, 292-293; Sharma, 243.

[54] George Younghusband, *A Soldier's Memories in Peace and War* (London: Herbert Jenkins, 1917), 276.

[55] Hamilton, vi.

[56] On the revival of the Yellow Peril idea in Europe see William L. Schwartz , *The Imaginative Interpretation of the Far East in Modern French Literature, 1800-1925*, (Paris: H. Champion, 1927), 153 ff.

[57] Mathew P. Shiel, *The Yellow Danger* (NY: R. F. Fenno; London: G. Richards, 1899).

[58] C.A. Spring Rice, a British diplomat in the British Embassy in Russia, 29 October 1904, in Thomas, W. L. Newton, *Lord Lansdowne: A Biography* (London: Macmillan 1929), 274.

[59] Robert Seager II, *Alfred Thayer Mahan: The Man and His Letters* (Annapolis, MD: Naval institute Press, 1977), 454, 465.

[60] Ibid, 464.

[61] Hearn's most famous work is a collection of lectures entitled *Japan: An Attempt at Interpretation,* (NY: Macmillan, 1904) but there are dozens of other works covering Japanese art, religion, family, literature and politics.

[62] Chamberlain, 64-69.

[63] Ian C. Ruxton, ed., *The Diaries and Letters of Sir Ernest Mason Satow: A Scholar Diplomat in East Asia* (NY: Edwin Mellen Press, 1998).

[64] Some of the more popular works on Japan prior to World War I were: **John Morris,** *Advance Japan: A Nation Thoroughly in Earnest* (London: W. H. Allen, 1895); **Arthur C. MacLay,** *A Budget of Letters from Japan: Reminiscences of Work and Travel in Japan* (NY: A. C. Armstrong & son, 1889); Arthur Lloyd, *Every-day Japan: Written after Twenty-Five Years' Residence and Work in the Country* (London, New York: Cassell and co., 1909); Reginald J.Farrer, *The Garden of Asia: Impressions from Japan* (London: Methuen, 1905); Walter Tyndale, *Japan & the Japanese* (NY: The Macmillan company, 1910); James Scherer, *Japan Today* (Philadelphia and London: J. B. Lippincott company, 1904); E. Bruce Mitford, *Japan's Inheritance: The Country, its People, and their Destiny* (NY: Dodd, Mead and Company, 1914); George Trumbull Ladd, *Rare Days in Japan* (NY; Dodd, Mead, 1910); Hugh Cortazzi, *Victorians in Japan: In and Around the Treaty Ports* (London: Atlantic Highlands, NJ: Athlone Press, 1987); William Elliot Griffis, *The Mikado's Empire* (New York and London, Harper & brothers, 1899); **Sidney L. Gulick,** *Evolution of the Japanese* (NY: F. H. Revell company 1905).

[65] Rudyard Kipling, *Kipling's Japan: Collected Writings*, edited by Hugh Cortazzi and George Webb (London: Athlone Press, 1988).

[66] Ibid., 168.

[67] Ibid., 165.

[68] Alan Ramsay Skelley, *The Victorian Army at Home: The Recruitment and Terms and Conditions of the British Regular, 1859-1899* (London: Croom Helm, 1977), 283.

[69] Younghusband, 225.

[70] Ian Hamilton, *A Staff Officer's Scrapbook during the Russo-Japanese War* (NY: Longmans, Green, 1912), 7-8.

[71] Colin Holmes and A. H. Ion, "Bushido and the Samurai: Images in British Public Opinion, 1894-1914," *Modern Asian Studies* vol. 14 no. 2 (1980): 315.

[72] Hamilton, 13.

[73] Ibid, 35.

[74] Report by Mr. Eckford, Vice Consul, PRO, FO 371.

[75] Report to the British Embassy in Tokyo from November 1914 by Lt. Colonel Calthorp, PRO, WO 106/661.

[76] Eckford, Vice Consul, PRO, FO 371.

[77] Ibid.

[78] Burdick, 107.

[79] Ibid., 230.

[80] Notes on the Japanese 18th Division, August 17, 1914, PRO, WO 106/663.

[81] Burdick, 78-79.

[82] Ibid, 242ff.

[83] Report of the Naval attaché in the British Embassy in Tokyo. "Siege of Tsingtau: Report on Anglo-Japanese Naval Operations August-November 1914," PRO, ADM 137/35.

[84] F.S.G Piggott, *Broken Thread*, (NY: British Book Center, 1950).

[85] Ibid., 90.

[86] Burdick, 106; 224; 232.

[87] Eckford report, PRO, FO 371.

[88] Nish, *Alliance in Decline,* 136; Burdick, 141.

[89] Dispatch from Brigadier Bernardiston to the War Office, 9 October 1914, Supplement to the London Gazette, box 726, Record Group 45, National Archives.

[90] Burdick, 111.

[91] Ibid., Ibid.

[92] Ibid., 110, 232.

[93] *The Japan Daily Mail,* 29 September 1884.

[94] Hamilton, 124.

[95] Farwell, 217.

[96] Quoted in Farwell, 94, 217.

[97] PRO, WO 106/48.

[98] Box 726, Naval Records Collection of the Office of Naval Records and Library, Record Group 45, National Archives.

[99] Nish, *Alliance in Decline,* 137.

[100] Report by J.T. Pratt, consul in Peking on how Japanese military officers stationed in Tsinan took no pains to conceal their contempt for the British army as exemplified by the force under General Bernardiston's command. They freely expressed their opinions to Chinese officials

who, in turn, passed these reflections to British diplomats, PRO, FO 371.

[101] Calthorp's letters, PRO, FO 371.

[102] Benedict, *Chrysanthemum and the Sword*, 36.

[103] Calthorp's letters, PRO, FO 371.

[104] Nish, *Alliance in Decline,* 139.

[105] Report of G. Moss, Senior District Officer at Weihaiwei, PRO, ADM 137/35.

[106] PRO, ADM 137/35.

[107] "Siege of Tsingtau: Report on Anglo-Japanese Naval Operations August-November 1914," PRO, ADM 137/35.

[108] PRO, FO 371

[109] Diary of George Gipps, HMS Triumph, 1914-1915 at the Siege of Tsingtau, Library of the Greenwich Maritime Museum, JOD/117.

[110] Ibid.

[111] Quoted in Philip Towle, "The British Armed Forces and Japan before 1914," *RUSI Journal* vol. 119 no. 2 (June 1974): 69.

[112] PRO, WO 106/660.

[113] Quoted in James, *Rise and Fall,* 354.

[114] Box 726, Naval Records Collection of the Office of Naval Records and Library, Record Group 45, National Archives.

CHAPTER 4: GI's IN THE LAND OF THE MANDARIN: U.S. MILITARY MISSION IN CHINA 1941-45

[1] John P. Davies, *Dragon by the Tail: American, British, Japanese, and Russian Encounters with China and One Another* (NY: W.W. Norton, 1972), 262.

[2] Robert L. Scott, *God is My Co-pilot* (NY: Charles Scribner's, 1943), 185.

[3] Hadley Cantril, ed. *Public Opinion, 1935-1942* (Princeton: Princeton University Press, 1951), 265.

[4] Harold R. Isaacs, *Scratches on our Minds: American Images of China and India* (NY: John Day, 1958).

[5] Barbara W. Tuchman, *Stilwell and the American Experience in China 1911-45* (NY: Macmillan, 1971); Chin-tung Liang, *General Stilwell in China 1942-1944: The Full Story* (Jamaica, NY: St. John's University Press, 1972); Fred Eldridge, *Wrath in Burma: The Uncensored Story of General Stilwell and International Maneuvers in the Far East* (NY: Doubleday, 1946); Theodore H. White and Annalee Jacoby, *Thunder out of China* (NY: William Sloane, 1946).

[6] White and Jacoby, 152.

[7] On the political and strategic wartime relations see Michael Schaller, *The U.S. Crusade in China, 1938-1945* (NY: Columbia University Press, 1979); Herbert Feis, *The China Tangle: The American Effort in China from Pearl Harbor to the Marshall Mission* (Princeton: Princeton University Press, 1953).

[8] Charles F. Romanus and Riley Sunderland, *Stilwell's Mission to China* (Washington, DC: Office of the Chief of Military History, 1953), 43; Davies, 216.

[9] Evans F. Carlson, *The Chinese Army: Its Organization and Military Efficiency* (NY: Institute of Pacific Relations, 1940), 79, see also John Magruder, "The Chinese as a Fighting Man," *Foreign Affairs* (April 1931).

[10] Joseph W. Stilwell, *The Stilwell Papers* (NY: Schocken, 1972), 26.

[11] On the Chinese Army before 1941 see Carlson and Magruder, "The Chinese as a Fighting Man."

[12] Romanus, *Stilwell's Mission to China,* 36.

[13] Ibid., 153.

[14] White and Jacoby, 133.

[15] Charles F. Romanus and Riley Sunderland, *Time Runs Out in the CBI* (Washington, DC: Office of the Chief of Military History, 1959), 65.

[16] Ibid., 34; Tuchman, 419.

[17] White and Jacoby, 164.

[18] Box 1128, Intelligence Reports 1941-45, RG 226, OSS, National Archives.

[19] Chin-tung Liang, 60.

[20] Charles F. Romanus and Riley Sunderland, *Stilwell's Command Problems* (Washington, DC: Office of the Chief of Military History, 1956), 310.

[21] Ibid, 298; Davies, 296-300.

[22] Davies, 299; Romanus, *Stilwell Command Problems*, 302.

[23] Romanus, *Time Runs Out in CBI*, 52.

[24] Frank Dorn, *Walkout with Stilwell in Burma* (NY: Thomas Y. Crowell, 1971), 75-79.

[25] PRO, PREMIER 4/42/9/1008; also Patrick French, *Liberty or Death: India's Journey to Independence and Division* (London: HarperCollins, 1997), 138-139.

[26] John W. Dower, *War Without Mercy: Race & Power in the Pacific War* (NY: Pantheon Books, 1986).

[27] "Across the Plains," in *The Travels and Essays of Robert Lewis Stevenson* (NY: Scribner's 1924), 139-143.

[28] Arthur H. Smith, *Chinese Characteristics* (NY: Fleming H. Revell, 1894); Rodney Gilbert, *What's Wrong with China* (NY: Frederick A. Stokes, 1926).

[29] On American attitude toward the Chinese see Isaacs, *Scratches*; Jerome Ch'en, *China and the West* (Bloomington and London: Indiana University Press, 1979); Stuart Creighton Miller, *The Unwelcome Immigrant: The American Image of the Chinese 1785-1882* (Berkeley and Los Angeles: University of California Press 1969), 10; Emory S. Bogardus, *Immigration and Race Attitudes* (Boston: D.C. Heath 1928), 46; Rubin F. Weston, *Racism in U.S. Imperialism: The Influence of Racial Assumptions on American Foreign Policy, 1893-1946* (Columbia, South Carolina: University of South Carolina Press, 1972), 23; Gary B. Nash and Richard Weiss, *The Great Fear: Race in the Mind of America* (NY: Holt, Rinehart and Winston, 1970); Thomas F. Gossett, *Race: The History of an Idea in America* (NY: Oxford University Press, 1997); Steven W. Mosher, *China Misperceived: American Illusions and Chinese Reality* (NY: New Republic, 1990); Archibald T. Steele, *The American People and China* (NY: McGraw-Hill, 1966); George Charles Roche III, *Public Opinion and the China policy of the United States, 1941-1951* (Ph.D. dissertation, University of Colorado, 1965); Ronald Takaki, *Strangers from a Different Shore: A History of Asian Americans* (Boston: Little, Brown, 1989); Warren I. Cohen, "American Perception of China," in Michael Oksenberg and Robert B. Oxnam eds., *Dragon and Eagle: United States-China Relations: Past and Future,* (NY: Basic, 1973).

[30] Michael Hunt, *Ideology and U.S. Foreign Policy* (New Haven and London: Yale University Press 1987).

[31] Isaacs, 71.

[32] Sandra M. Hawley, "The Importance of Being Charlie Chan," in Jonathan Goldstein, Jerry Israel and Hilary Conroy eds., *America Views China: American Images of China Then and Now* (NJ: Lehigh University Press, 1991).

[33] Miller, 9-10; Steele, 21; Isaacs, 164-176.

[34] On the history of the American garrison in China since 1901 see: Dennis L. Noble, *The Eagle and the Dragon: The United States Military in China, 1901-1937* (NY and Westport, Conn.: Greenwood Press, 1990).

[35] David M. Shoup, *The Americans in China 1927-1928: The China Expedition which Turned out to be the China Exhibition* (Hamden, Connecticut: Archon Books, 1987).

[36] Edward M. Coffman, "The American 15th Infantry Regiment in China, 1912-1938: A Vignette in Social History," *The Journal of Military History*, 58 (January 1994): 57-74.

[37] "Conditions of Service in China," *Infantry Journal* 29 (August 1926): 167-174.

[38] Forrest C. Pogue, *George C. Marshall: Education of a General,* (NY: Viking Press, 1963).

[39] Coffman, 64.

[40] Oliver J. Caldwell, *A Secret War: Americans in China 1944-1945* (London: Feffer and Simons, 1972), 205.

[41] Entry 16, box 1128, Intelligence Reports 1941-45, RG 226, OSS, National Archives.

[42] Graham Peck, *Two Kinds of Time* (Boston: Houghton Mifflin, 1950), 421; White and Jacoby, 160.

[43] White and Jacoby, 161; Tuchman, 421.

[44] "Anti-Chinese Feelings of American Armed Forces in China," 17 September 1943, State Department Decimal Files, 893.20/791, RG 59, National Archives also U.S. Department of State, *Foreign Relations of the United States, 1944, China* (Washington, DC: Government Printing Office, 1967), 164.

[45] Miles, 433-434.

[46] Bertrand Russell, *The Problem of China* (NY: Century, 1922), 198.

[47] Smith, 98-106; Ch'en, 59-91.

[48] Quoted in Dower, 167.

[49] Report on Chinese Activities in San Francisco, Federal Bureau of Investigation, 18 December 1942, microfilm LM65, roll 21, State Department Decimal Files 893.20211/10, RG 59, National Archives.

[50] Report on the Morale of the Chinese People and their Reaction to the War, box 723, OSS, Intelligence Reports 1941-45, RG 226, National Archives.

[51] Dower, 168-169.

[52] Tu Wei-ming, "Chinese Perceptions of America," in Michael Oksenberg and Robert B. Oxnam eds., *Dragon and Eagle: United States-China Relations: Past and Future* (NY: Basic, 1973).

[53] Report from the Embassy in Chungking to the Secretary of State, 2 March 1944, box 804, OSS, Intelligence Reports 1941-45, RG 226, National Archives.

[54] Ibid.

[55] Report on the Morale of the Chinese People and their Reaction to the War, box 723, OSS, Intelligence Reports 1941-45, RG 226, National Archives.

[56] *Foreign Relations of the United States*, 1945 vol. vii (Washington, DC: Government Press Office, 1969), 10.

[57] U.S. Department of State, *Foreign Relations of the United States, 1944, China* (Washington, DC: Government Printing Office, 1967), 48, 67-68. Also "Report About the Conduct of American Troops in Chengtu," 17 April, 1944, box 3734, file 811.22/338, Department of State, Decimal File 1940-1944, RG 59, National Archives.

[58] Peck, 482-483.

[59] Ch'en, 79-80.

[60] Romanus, *Time Runs Out in CBI*, 348.

[61] Ibid, ibid.

[62] Oliver J. Caldwell, *A Secret War: Americans in China 1944-1945* (London: Feffer and Simons, 1972), 207.

[63] Report about the conduct of American troops in Chengtu, 17 April 1944, box 3734, file 811.22/338 Department of State, Decimal File 1940-1944, RG 59, National Archives; Department of State, *Foreign Relations of the United States, 1944, China* (Washington, DC: Government Printing Office, 1967), 28-29.

[64] Larry I. Bland and Sharon R. Ritenour, eds. *The Papers of George Catlett Marshall* vol. I; *"The Solidiery Spirit,"* December *1880-June 1939* (Baltimore: Johns Hopkins University Press, 1981), 273.

[65] Pogue, 240.

[66] Ch'en, 243.

[67] Caldwell, 209.

[68] Peck, 636.

[69] Thomas W. Collier, "The Chinese Language Officer Program of the U.S. Army, 1919-43," Unpublished thesis for the department of History, Duke University, 1966.

[70] On Stilwell's language experience see Tuchman, 76-83.

[71] Romanus, *The Stilwell Mission,* 27

[72] Coffman, 67-68.

[73] Tuchman, 361; Romanus, *Time Run Out in CBI,* 375.

[74] Lyle S. Powell, *A Surgeon in Wartime China* (Kansas: University of Kansas Press, 1946), 53.

[75] Milton E. Miles, *A Different Kind of War: The Little Known Story of the Combined Guerrilla Forces in China by the U.S. Navy and the Chinese during World War II* (NY: Doubleday, 1967), 481-482.

[76] Romanus, *Stilwell Command Problems,* 34; Miles, 109.

[77] Letter from Brig. General H.L. Boatner, box 126, Records of the Army Staff, Records of the Office of the Chief of Military History, Publications and Unpublished Manuscripts, 1943-77, RG 319, National Archives.

[78] Ibid.

[79] Miles, 109.

[80] Eldridge, 142; Tuchman,, 419.

[81] Arthur H. Smith, *Chinese Characteristics* (NY: Fleming H. Revell, 1894); Carl Crow, *The Chinese Are Like That* (NY: Harper & Brothers, 1938).

[82] Crow, 84.

[83] Claire L. Chennault, *Way of a Fighter* (NY: G.P. Putnam, 1949), 76

[84] David Morris, *China Changed My Mind* (Boston: Houghton Mifflin, 1949), 104.

[85] Morton H. Fried, *Fabric of Chinese Society* (NY: Frederick A. Praeger, 1953); Olga Lang, *Chinese Family and Society* (New Jersey: Oxford University Press, 1946); Francis L. K. Hsu ed., *Kinship and Culture* (Chicago: Aldine Pub. Co., 1971).

[86] See the chapter on the family and the individual in China in Davies, 46-56.

[87] Theodore H. White, "Life Looks at China," *Life*, 1 May 1944, 99-110.

[88] Powell, 24.

[89] Ibid., 23.

[90] U.S. Department of State, *Foreign Relations of the United States, 1944, China,* (Washington, DC: Government Printing Office, 1967), 211; Eldridge, 145-146.

[91] David Morris, *China Changed My Mind* (Boston: Houghton Mifflin, 1949), 98.

[92] U.S. Department of State, *Foreign Relations, 1944, China*, 164. See also *Chicago Daily News* journalist Leland Stowe's report on the "Burma Road racket" which was published in 1942. Stowe was the first correspondent to report in detail about the corrupt practices of Chinese officials who profited from steeling Lend-Lease articles supplied by the U.S. His findings angered many Americans and tarnished the overwhelming sympathy toward the Chinese. Stowe was heavily criticized for his role in revealing the reality nobody at the time wanted to acknowledge. Leland Stowe, *They Shall Not Sleep* (NY: Alfred A. Knopf, 1944), 62-85.

[93] Sterling Seagrave, *The Soong Dynasty* (NY: Harper & Row, 1985), 391; Peck, 478.

[94] For commercial contacts and smuggling of goods between Chinese and Japanese forces see Eldridge, 60.

[95] Entry 16, box 1110, Intel reports 1941-45, RG 226, National Archives.

[96] Ent. 16, file 104798, Intel reports 1941-45, RG 226, National Archives.

[97] Chennault, 78.

[98] Romanus, *Stilwell's Mission*, 217; Eldridge, 146-147; Romanus, *Time Runs Out in CBI*, 168.

[99] Max Weber, *The Religion of China* (NY and London: Free Press, 1964), 237, 244.

[100] Fukuyama, 83-95.

[101] Dorn, 73.

[102] Ibid, 72.

[103] Tuchman, 364.

[104] Romanus, *Time Runs Out in CBI*, 165.

[105] Smith, 17.

[106] Davies, 53.

[107] Max Weber, *The Religion of China* (NY and London: Free Press, 1964), 234.

[108] Tuchman, 164-165.

[109] Romanus, *Stilwell's Mission*, 35.

[110] Romanus, *Stilwell's Command Problems*, 348, 351-352; Romanus, *Time Runs Out in CBI*, 235.

[111] Romanus, *Time Runs Out in CBI*, 232.

[112] Davies, 299.

[113] Albert C. Wedemeyer, *Wedemeyer Reports!* (NY: Henry Holt, 1958), 298-300.

[114] Ibid., 300.

[115] Romanus, *Time Runs Out in CBI*, 154.

[116] Box 1087, OSS Intelligence Reports 1941-45, RG 226, National Archives.

[117] White and Jacoby, 141.

[118] Memorandum on military intelligence in China by Ambassador Gauss, 23 November 1943, File 893.20/798, State Department, Decimal Files 1940-1944, RG 59, National Archives; White and Jacoby, 141; Eldridge, 55, 205.

[119] White and Jacoby, 141.

[120] Memorandum on military intelligence in China by Ambassador Gauss, 23 November 1943, file 893.20/798, State Department, Decimal Files 1940-1944, RG 59, National Archives.

[121] U.S. Department of State, *Foreign Relations of the United States, Diplomatic Papers, China, 1942* (Washington, DC: Government Press Office, 1956), 13-14.

[122] Memorandum on military intelligence in China by Ambassador Gauss, 23 November 1943, file 893.20/798, State Department, Decimal Files 1940-1944, RG 59, National Archives.

123 White and Jacoby, 140.

124 Romanus, *Stilwell's Command Problems*, 348.

125 Entry 16, box 1128, Intel reports 1941-45, RG 226, National Archives.

126 White, 140.

127 Tuchman, 421.

128 Eldridge, 102-103.

129 Report on the Health of the Chinese Troops at Lanchaw, box 804, OSS Intelligence Reports 1941-45, RG 226, National Archives.

130 Report from the Embassy in Chunking to the Secretary of State, 14 January 1943, box 804, OSS Intelligence Reports 1941-45, RG 226, National Archives. On the Terrible conditions in Chinese hospitals see Powell, 94-95, 99-100.

131 Powell, 98-99.

132 Ibid., 219.

133 Magruder, "The Chinese as a Fighting Man."

134 White and Jacoby, 144.

135 Ibid, Ibid.

136 Col. Paul L. Jones as told to Hugh Crumpler, "May, 1942: Fifty Years Ago This Month, The Withdrawal from Burma and the Stillwell Walkout," *Ex-CBI Roundup (May 1992): 6.*

137 File 893.20/12-1844, State Department, Decimal Files 1940-1944, RG 59, National Archives.

138 Romanus, *Time Runs Out in CBI*, 369-371.

139 White and Jacoby, 133. Theodore White described the case of one unit that lost 30% of its troops due to the deplorable conditions through a 500-mile march. See *Life*, 1 May 1944.

140 Report from the Embassy in Chunking to the Secretary of State, 14 January 1943, box 804, OSS Intelligence Reports 1941-45, RG 226, National Archives.

141 Romanus, *Time Runs Out in CBI*, 67.

142 Davies, 221.

143 Liang, 21.

144 Hanson W. Baldwin, *Great Mistakes of the War* (NY: Harper, 1950), 60.

145 Romanus, *Stilwell's Mission,* 372-373; Miles, 332; Wedemeyer, 305.

146 Romanus, *Stilwell's Mission*, 157.

[147] Harold Isaacs, "One Man's Fight Against Corruption," *Newsweek,* 13 November 1944, 45-46.

[148] Davies, 325.

[149] Romanus, *Time Runs Out in CBI,* 15.

[150] David Morris, *China Changed My Mind* (Boston: Houghton Mifflin, 1949), 112.

[151] Eldridge, 140.

[152] This advisory group was no bigger than 70 men headed by General Hans von Seeckt who was also mentioned in Chapter 3 as an advisor to the Ottoman Army during WWI. See Walsh K. Billie, "The German Military Mission in China 1928-38," *Journal of Modern History* vol. 46 no. 3, (1974): 500-513; Carlson, 15-17.

[153] Wilma Fairbank, *America's Cultural Experiment in China 1942-1949* (Washington, DC: Department of State, 1976); U.S. Department of State, *Foreign Relations of the United States, 1942, China* (Washington, DC: Government Printing Office, 1956), 699.

[154] The American Historical Association, *Our Chinese Ally* (Washington, DC: The War Department, 1944).

[155] Weber, 146.

[156] Francis L.K. Hsu, "Eros, Affect and Pao," in F.L.K. Hsu ed., *Kinship and Culture* (Chicago: Aldine, 1971), 462.

[157] Chiang-kun Yang, *Religion in the Chinese Society* (Berkeley and Los Angeles: University of California Press, 1961); Weber.

[158] David H. Hackworth and Julie Sherman, *About Face* (NY: Simon and Schuster, 1989), 247.

[159] Max Hastings, *The Korean War* (NY and London: Touchstone, 1987), 287-312, 239-242.

[160] Roy Appleman and Walter Hermes, *United States Army in the Korean War: South to the Naktong, North to the Yalu* (Washington DC: Center for Military History), 385-389.

[161] Advisor's Handbook, U.S. Military Advisory Group in the Republic of Korea, box 2189, Record of the Army Staff, National Archives.

[162] Frances Fitzgerald, *Fire in the Lake: The Vietnamese and the Americans in Vietnam* (Boston: Little, Brown, 1972); Westmoreland, *A Soldier Reports* (NY: Dell, 1980).

CHAPTER 5: COALITION OF PROHIBITION: U.S. AND SAUDI ARABIA IN THE GULF WAR

[1] David Holden and Richard Johns, *The House of Saud* (London: Holt, Rinehart and Winston, 1981), 406.

[2] Alan Munro, *An Arabian Affair: Politics and Diplomacy Behind the Gulf War* (London: Brassey's, 1996), 191.

[3] Said K. Aburish, *The Rise, Corruption and Coming Fall of the House of Saud* (NY: St. Martin's Press, 1994).

[4] On U.S.-Saudi military cooperation see: Nadav Safran, *Saudi Arabia: The Ceaseless Quest for Security* (Cambridge, Mass.: Belknap Press of Harvard University Press, 1985); Michael A. Palmer, *Guardians of the Gulf: A History of America's Expanding Role in the Persian Gulf 1833-1992* (NY: Free Press, 1992); Anthony H. Cordesman, *Saudi Arabia: Guarding the Desert Kingdom* (Boulder, Colo.: Westview Press, 1997); F. Gregory Gause III, *Oil Monarchies: Domestic and Security Challenges in the Arab Gulf States* (NY: Council on Foreign Relations Press, 1994).

[5] On the American negotiations with Saudi Arabia to allow a troop deployment in the country see Lawrence Freedman and Efraim Karsh, *The Gulf Conflict 1990-1991: Diplomacy and War in the New World Order* (Princeton: Princeton University Press, 1993), 92-93.

[6] Khaled bin Sultan, *Desert Warrior: A Personal View of the Gulf War by the Joint Forces Commander* (NY: Harper Perennial, 1995), 197.

[7] Hans J. Morgenthau, *American Foreign Policy: A Critical Examination* (London: Methuen, 1952), 175.

[8] Bob Woodward, *The Commanders* (NY: Simon and Schuster, 1991), 240.

[9] *The Washington Post*, 11 September 1990.

[10] "Ulama Council Supports Actions of King Fahd," FBIS-DR-90-157, 14 August 1990.

[11] Mordechai Abir, *Saudi Arabia: Government, Society and the Gulf Crisis* (London and NY: Routledge, 1993), 178.

[12] On religious opposition to the Bin Baz's *fatwa* see Joshua Teitelbaum, *Holier than Thou: Saudi Arabia's Islamic Opposition* (Washington, DC: The Washington Institute for Near Easy Policy, 2000), 28-32.

[13] Norman H. Schwarzkopf, *It Doesn't Take a Hero* (NY: Linda Grey Bantam, 1992), 335.

[14] *The Washington Post*, 11 August 1990.

[15] Munro, *Arabian Affair,* 99.

[16] Abir, 175.

[17] Schwarzkopf, 305.

[18] Khaled, 37.

[19] The French contingent remained under Khaled's command during Desert Shield, but joined the American forces before Desert Storm.

[20] United States Department of Defense, *Conduct of the Persian Gulf War: Final Report to Congress* (Washington, DC: Department of Defense, 1992), 557-558.

[21] Richard M. Swain, *"Lucky War:" Third Army in Desert Storm* (Fort Leavenworth, Kansas: U.S. Army Command Staff College Press, 1997), 56.

[22] Khaled, 194.

[23] Ibid., 204.

[24] Ibid., 192.

[25] Michael R. Gordon and Bernard E. Trainor, *The Generals' War* (NY: Little Brown and Co., 1995), 73.

[26] Khaled, 324-325.

[27] Ibid., 324.

[28] Munro, 157.

[29] Ibid., 137.

[30] Ibid., 287.

[31] Abir, 174; George Bush and Brent Scowcroft, *A World Transformed* (NY: Knopf, 1998), 321.

[32] Rick Francona, *Ally to Adversary: An Eyewitness of Iraq's Fall from Grace* (Annapolis, MD: Naval Institute Press, 1999), 97-98; Khaled, 325-331.

[33] Peter W. Wilson and Douglas F. Graham, *Saudi Arabia: The Coming Storm* (NY: M.E. Sharpe, 1994), 162; *The Washington Post*, 15 November 1990.

[34] Ibid.

[35] Aburish, 92.

[36] Schwarzkopf, 339-340.

[37] Eliot A. Cohen and Thomas A. Keaney, *The Gulf War Air Power Survey, vol. II, Part I: Operations* (Washington, DC: GPO, 1993);

Gordon and Trainor, 265; Kenneth M. Pollack, "The Influence of Arab Culture on Arab Military Effectiveness," (Ph..D dissertation, Massachusettes Institute of Technology, 1996), 526-529.

[38] Schwarzkopf, 340.

[39] Wilson and Graham, 156-158; Pollack, 522.

[40] Ibid., 155-156; *The Washington Post*, 20 April 1991, A14.

[41] Pollack, 534.

[42] Schwarzkopf, 340.

[43] Similar observations were made by Kenneth Pollack, 519-535.

[44] Aburish, 190.

[45] Author's interviews with Saudi nationals and U.S. military officials, May 2000.

[46] Schwarzkopf, 348; Nora Bensahel, 55

[47] Interview Schwarzkopf, PBS documentary: http://www.pbs.org/wgbh/pages/frontline/gulf/oral/schwarzkopf/4.html

[48] Gordon and Trainor, 170-171.

[49] Ibid., 172.

[50] Francona, 57-59.

[51] Ibid, Ibid.

[52] Munro, 173.

[53] Francona, 61.

[54] *The Washington Post*, 23 August 1990.

[55] Ibid.

[56] Michael W. Suleiman, *The Arabs in the Mind of America* (Brattleboro, Vermont: Amana Books, 1988); Richard J. Payne, *The Clash with Distant Cultures: Values, Interests and Force in American Foreign Policy* (Albany: State University of New York, 1995), 96-98; Meg Greenfield, "Our Ugly Arab Complex," *Newsweek,* 5 December 1977, 110.

[57] Hooshang Amirahmadi, Elaine C. Condon and Abraham Resnik, "Middle East Studies and Education in the United States: Retrospect and Prospects," in Hooshang Amirahmadi ed., *The United States and the Middle East: A Search for New Perspectives* (Albany, NY: State University of New York Press, 1993); Suleiman, 87.

[58] *The Washington Post*, 23 August 1990.

[59] Some of the popular books were Robert Lacey, *The Kingdom* (NY: Harcourt Brace Jovanovich, 1982); Sandra Mackey, *The Saudis: Inside the Desert Kingdom* (Boston: Houghton Mifflin, 1987); David

Holden, Richard Johns, and James Buchan, *The House of Saud: The Rise and Rule of the Most Powerful Dynasty in the Arab World* (NY: Holt, Rinehart, and Winston, 1981).

[60] Author's interviews U.S. Army and Marine servicemen, March 2000.

[61] Abir, *Saudi Arabia,* 93.

[62] Swain, 155.

[63] Author's interviews with U.S. Foreign Area Officers, December 2001.

[64] Khaled bin Sultan, "The Gulf War and its Aftermath: A Personal Perspective," *RUSI Journal*, (December 1993): 2.

[65] Gus Pagonis, *Moving Mountains: Lessons in Leadership and Logistics from the Gulf War* (Boston: Harvard Business School, 1992), 106.

[66] Ibid., 107.

[67] Ibid, Ibid.

[68] Schwarzkopf, 334.

[69] Pagonis, 109; also author's interview with U.S. Army personnel, October 2001.

[70] Robert Fisk,"1,400 Pilgrims killed in Mecca Tunnel," *The Independent*, 4 July 1990; *The New York Times,* 4 July 1990. Accidents of this kind are almost part and parcel of the *Hajj*. In 1994, 270 pilgrims died in a stampede while pilgrims were performing the "stoning the devil" ritual. During the 1997 pilgrimage, fires driven by high winds tore through an overcrowded tent city outside Mecca, killing more than 340 pilgrims and injuring 1,500. In the following year, about 180 pilgrims died in a stampede and in 2001, 35. All of these accidents could have been avoided had the Saudi regime been more inclined to learn the lessons from past incidents.

[71] Soraya Nelson, "Every Soldier is an Ambassador for the U.S.," *Army Times*, 27 August 1990: 26.

[72] On the nature of Saudi justice system see: "The Brutality of the Saudi Arabian Justice System," *Associated Press*, 28 March 2000 Cairo, Egypt.

[73] Francona, 62.

[74] Richard Mead, 39.

[75] Aburish, 224.

[76] Francona, 58; Schwarzkopf, 336.

[77] Schwarzkopf, 336; Munro, 99.

[78] Desert Shield General Order 1, http://www.3ad.com/history/gulf. war/general.order.1.htm.

[79] Schwarzkopf, 338.

[80] Rick Maze, "U.S. Troops Keep Worship under Wraps," *Army Times*, 24 December 1990: 8.

[81] Francona, 58.

[82] Munro, 190.

[83] Schwarzkopf, 396.

[84] Ibid., Ibid.

[85] *The New York Times*, 25 December 1990.

[86] Author's interview with a Marines officer, 5 March 2000.

[87] Khaled, 213; Schwarzkopf, 332.

[88] Francona, 58-59.

[89] Munro, 98.

[90] Interview LTC John R. Vines, Commander 4th Battalion, 325th Infantry (82nd Airborne Division), Oral History Interview, DSIT AE 017, U.S. Army Center of Military History, Washington, DC.

[91] Munro, 189; Khaled, 213.

[92] Schwarzkopf, 378.

[93] Francona, 58; Khaled, 214.

[94] Khaled, 214.

[95] On the status of women in Saudi Arabia see: Eleanor Abdella Doumato, "Women and Stability in Saudi Arabia," *Middle East Report,* vol. 21 no. 4 (July 1991); Saddika Arebi, *Women and Words in Saudi Arabia* (NY: Columbia University Press, 1994); Mackey, *The Saudis.*

[96] Molly Moore, *A Woman at War: Storming Kuwait with the U.S. Marines* (NY: Charles Scribner's, Sons 1993) 31.

[97] "Only Male Marines Deploy to Saudi Arabia," *Army Times*, 27 August 1990: 14.

[98] Khaled, 211; Francona, 63.

[99] Pagonis, 116; Schwarzkopf, 332.

[100] Interview General Schwarzkopf, "Waging War," PBS Documentary.

[101] Maj. Deborah Gilmore, quoted in Steven J. Alvarez, Army Reserve Women Weather "The Storm," *American Forces Press Service,* http://

www.defenselink.mil/news/Mar2001/n03202001_200103203. html

[102] Munro, 86.

[103] Khaled, 211.

[104] *The Washington Post*, 23 August 1990; Moore, 33.

[105] Francona, 62.

[106] Khaled, 211.

[107] Teitelbaum, 30-31; *The Washington Post*, 7 November 1990, A17; Abir, *Saudi Arabia,* 179.

[108] Khaled, 212.

[109] Schwarzkopf, 336-337.

[110] Khaled, 212; Schwarzkopf, 388.

[111] Khaled, 279-281; Munro, 187.

[112] Edward J. Marolda and Robert J. Schneller, *Shield and Storm: The United States Navy and the Persian Gulf War* (Annapolis: Naval Institute Press, 2001), 161; Pagonis, 130.

[113] Swain,19.

[114] Ibid, 33.

[115] Ibid, Ibid.

[116] Schwarzkopf, 277.

[117] I thank Peter Bechtold from the Foreign Service Institute for this input.

[118] Khaled, 208.

[119] TV interview with Lt. General Calvin Waller Deputy Commander CENTCOM, "The Gulf War," *Frontline*, PBS, http://www.pbs.org/ wgbh/pages/frontline/gulf/oral/waller/1.html

[120] Munro, 320-321.

[121] Rick Atkinson, *Crusade: The Untold Story of the Persian Gulf War* (NY: Houghton, Mifflin, 1993), 72.

[122] Gordon and Trainor, 72.

[123] Moore, 155.

[124] Gordon and Trainor, 72.

[125] Soraya Nelson, 26.

[126] Schwarzkopf, 338.

[127] TV interview with Peter de la Billiere, "The Gulf War," *Frontline*, http://www.pbs.org/wgbh/pages/frontline/gulf/oral/billiere/2.html

[128] Winston S. Churchill, *The Second World War: Triumph and Tragedy* (Cambridge, Mass: Houghton Mifflin, 1953), 397-398.

[129] Gordon and Trainor, 73.

[130] Pagonis, 129.

[131] Author's interview with U.S. military personnel, December 2001.

[132] R. Hrair Dekmejian, "The Rise of Political Islamism in Saudi Arabia," *Middle East Journal* vol 48 no. 4 (Autumn 1994): 627-643.

[133] Interview LTC John R. Vines, Commander 4th Battalion, 325th Infantry (82nd Airborne Division), Oral History Interview, DSIT AE 017, U.S. Army Center of Military History, Washington, DC.

[134] Arkin, *Stars and Stripes*.

[135] *The Washington Post*, 4 December 2001.

[136] *The Washington Post*, 7 January 2002.

[137] *USA Today*, 18 April 2001.

[138] Munro, 130.

[139] Schwarzkopf, 332.

[140] *The Washington Post*, 20 April, 1991, A14.

[141] Schwarzkopf, 498.

CHAPTER 6: SABRAS AMONG THE CEDARS: ISRAEL AND THE SOUTH LEBANON ARMY, 1985-2000

[1] On Israel's ties with the Christians in Lebanon see Beate Hamizrachi, *The Emergence of the South Lebanon Security Belt* (NY and Westport, Connecticut: Praeger, 1988), 63-67; Ze'ev Schiff and Ehud Ya'ari, *Israel's Lebanon War* (NY: Simon and Schuster, 1984), 25; Rephael Eitan, *A Soldier's Story* (Tel Aviv: Ma'ariv, 1985), [Hebrew], 151-153; Ronen Bergman, "The Gamble," *Ha'aretz*, Weekend Supplement, 3 January 1997, 14-18.

[2] Yossi Melman, "In and Out of a Nightmare: How the Security Zone Was Created and How Israel's Involvement in it Increased Between 1975 and 2000," *Ha'aretz*, 25 May 2000.

[3] Schiff and Ya'ari, 16.

[4] Author's interview with an Israeli Intelligence officer, 21 February 2001.

[5] Thomas L. Friedman, *From Beirut to Jerusalem* (NY: Farrar Straus Giroux, 1989), 138.

[6] Eitan, 189; Friedman, 136-137.

[7] Friedman, 137.

[8] *Ha'aretz*, 10 May 1985.

[9] Author's interview with Lebanon Liaison Unit (LLU) officer, 29 May 2001.

[10] Ibid.

[11] Arieh O'Sullivan and David Rudge, "Fighting Against Time," *Jerusalem Post,* 31 July 1998.

[12] Author's interview with IDF Colonel Rafik Said, former Head of Civil Affairs Administration in south Lebanon, 5 June 2001.

[13] Yaakov Perry, *Strike First* (Tel Aviv: Keshet, 1999), [Hebrew], 115-116.

[14] Andrew Rathmell, "The War in South Lebanon," *Jane's Intelligence Review* 1 April 1994; Ronen Bergman, "Fighting Blind," *Ha'aretz Magazine,* 14 May 1999.

[15] Clive Jones, "Israeli Counter-Insurgency Strategy and the War in South Lebanon 1985-97," *Small Wars and Insurgencies* vol. 8 no.3 (Winter 1997): 82-108.

[16] Ariela Ringel Hoffman, "Protect Me from My Friend," *Yediot Ahronot*, Weekend Supplement, 5 March 1999, 4.

[17] Author's interview with Col. (ret.) Moshe Zur, former Head of Intelligence, Northern Command, 25 May 2001.

[18] *Ma'ariv*, 1 October 1999.

[19] Gal Luft, "Securing Israel's North," in Patrick Clawson and Michael Eisenstadt eds., *The Last Arab-Israeli Battlefield?* (Washington, DC: The Washington Institute for Near East Policy, 2000), 92-93.

[20] Author's interviews with IDF officers.

[21] *Ha'aretz*, 25 May 1993.

[22] Yossi Beilin, *A Guide to an Israeli Withdrawal from Lebanon* (Tel Aviv: Hakibbutz Hameuchad, 1998), [Hebrew], 15-18; Jones, "Israeli Counter-Insurgency Strategy," 102-103.

[23] Over the years, more than 10,000 south Lebanese were sentenced to various punishments by the Lebanese government for collaborating with Israel. See "SLA Still in Denial on IDF Leaving Southern Lebanon," *Ha'aretz*, 28 February 2000.

[24] *The Christian Science Monitor*, 28 December 2001.

[25] Yoav Limor, "It's Hard to Trust the SLA," *Ma'ariv*, Weekend Supplement, 26 March 1999.

[26] *Ha'aretz*, 18 February 2000.

[27] *Ha'aretz*, 26 November 1999.

[28] Ariela Ringel Hoffman, "Protect Me from My Friend," *Yediot Ahronot*, Weekend Supplement, 5 March 1999, 4.

[29] Ronen Bergman, "Fighting Blind."

[30] Yoav Limor, "It's Hard to Trust the SLA."

[31] Gal Luft, "Israel's Security Zone in Lebanon - A 'Tragedy'? " *Middle East Quarterly* vol.7 no.3 (September 2000): 13-20.

[32] Ronen Bergman, "Thanks for Your Cooperation," *Ha'aretz Magazine*, 29 October 1999.

[33] Yochanan Peres, " Ethnic Relations in Israel," *American Journal of Sociology* vol. 76 no. 6 (1971):1021-47.

[34] David K. Shipler, *Arab and Jew: Wounded Spirits in a Promised Land*, (NY: Times Books, 1986), 222-223.

[35] Peres, 1041.

[36] Ibid, 1039.

[37] Shipler, 183, 232; *Ha'aretz*, 24 January 1999.

[38] On the attitude and prejudices of Israeli Jews toward Israeli Arabs see: Ian Lustick, *Arabs in the Jewish State: Israel's Control of a National Minority* (Austin and London: University of Texas Press, 1980); Jacob M. Landau, *The Arab Minority in Israel, 1967-1991* (Oxford: Clarendon Press, 1993); Ori Stendel, *The Arabs in Israel* (Brighton, UK: Sussex, 1996); Fouzi El-Asmar, *To be An Arab in Israel* (London: Frances Pinter, 1975); Shipler, *Arab and Jew,* 181-313.

[39] Israel's Central Bureau of Statistics, http://www.cbs.gov.il

[40] Sepharadic Jews were also more supportive of the war in Lebanon than Ashkenazis see Asher Arian, *Israeli Public Opinion and the War in Lebanon,* JCSS Momorandum no. 15, (Tel Aviv: Tel Aviv University, 1985), 1-2. See also Shipler, 241-245.

[41] Peres, 1025.

[42] Friedman,128, 133.

[43] Ibid., 131.

[44] Ibid., 135.

[45] Augustus Richard Norton, *Amal and the Shi'a: Struggle for the Soul of Lebanon* (Austin: University of Texas Press, 1987),107.

[46] Norton, 113; Friedman, 179-180.

[47] Norton, 107.

[48] Author's interview with former LLU officer, 2 June 2001.

[49] Hamizrachi, 63-67.

[50] Interview Rafik Said.

[51] Ibid.

[52] *Ha'aretz*, 2 June 2000.

[53] Landau, 85.

[54] *Ha'aretz*, 24 January 1999.

[55] Author's interview with Colonel (Ret.) Yitzhak Hershkovitz, former artillery liaison officer to the LLU, 24 January 2002.

[56] Interview Rafik Said.

[57] Israel Central Bureau of Statistics, Statistical Abstract of Israel.

[58] See Gabriel Ben-Dor, *The Druze in Israel: A Political Study* (Jerusalem: Magnes Press, 1979); "The Druze in the IDF: Equal Rights," *Ba'Machane,* 27 November 1991, 52-59.

[59] On the integration of Druze soldiers in the IDF, see: Alon Peled, *A Question of Loyalty: Military Manpower Policy in Multiethnic States* (Ithaca and London: Cornell University Press, 1998).

[60] Author's interview with former LLU officer, 2 June 2001.

[61] Author's interview with former LLU officer, Lt. Colonel Yasser Hatib, 5 June 2001.

[62] Author's interviews with former LLU officers.

[63] Schiff and Ya'ari, *Israel's Lebanon War,* 242.

[64] Author's interviews with former LLU officers.

[65] Hamizrachi, 52.

[66] Ibid, ibid.

[67] See Jonathan C. Randel, *Going All the Way* (NY: Viking Press, 1983), 12; Robert Fisk, *Pity the Nation* (NY: Simon & Schuster, 1990). .

[68] Oz Almog, *The Sabra: The Creation of a New Jew* (Berkeley and LA: University of California Press, 2000), 197.

[69] Amnon Kaveh, "Mo'diin - Sechora overet la'socher," *Matara* 22 (Tel Aviv: El Ha'matara, 1991): 4-7.

[70] The debate over the Israeli responsibility in the massacre is still inconclusive. Most Israelis admit indirect responsibility but claim that the IDF could not foresee such atrocious behavior nor did it have any concrete information pointing to such a possibility. Some

of the Israeli military interviewees admitted that the IDF knew that the Phalanges would act against the Palestinians but could not anticipate the ferocity and cruelty of their action. Others, such as journalists Thomas Friedman and Robert Fisk believed the Israelis knew exactly what they were doing when they let the Phalangists into the camps. See: Friedman, 164; Robert Fisk, 383.

[71] Friedman, 22-23.

[72] David C. Jordan, *The Republic of Lebanon* (Boulder: Westview Press, 1983), 33.

[73] Interview, Colonel (ret.) Aviel Garafi, former head of intelligence, LLU, 28 May 2001.

[74] Interview Colonel (ret.) Alias Salame, former head of intelligence, SLA, 28 May 2001.

[75] Interview Yasser Hatib.

[76] Sania Hamady, *Temperament and Character of the Arabs* (NY: Twayne Publishers, 1960), 34-39.

[77] Raphael Patai, *The Arab Mind* (NY: Charles Scribner's Sons, 1983), 90-94.

[78] *Ha'aretz*, 28 February 2000.

[79] Author's interview with former LLU officer.

[80] Author's interviews with IDF officers.

[81] William Harris, *Faces of Lebanon: Sects, Wars and Global Extensions* (Princeton: Markes, Wiener, 1997), 317.

[82] Author's interview with former LLU officer.

[83] Eitan, 156.

[84] Interview Garafi.

[85] Interview Rafik Said.

[86] Interview Garafi.

[87] Interview Hatib.

[88] Author's interview with former LLU officer.

[89] Interview, Hershkowitz.

[90] Author's interview with former LLU officer.

[91] Interview Hershkowitz.

[92] Tal Bashan, "Interview with General Lahad," *Ma'ariv*, Weekend Supplement, 1 October 1999.

[93] Human Rights Watch, "Persona non Grata: The Expulsion of Civilians from Israeli-Occupied Lebanon," http://www.hrw.org/reports/1999/lebanon/

[94] Interview Uri Lubrani, former coordinator of government affairs in Lebanon, Virginia, 17 October 2001.

CHAPTER 7: DOES CULTURE STILL MATTER?

[1] A statement by President Bill Clinton, Press Release, The Oval Office, 16 December 1998.

[2] *The Washington Post*, 30 October 2001.

[3] *The Washington Post*, 15 November 2001.

[4] Ibid.

[5] *Associated Press*, 23 September 2001.

[6] *The New York Times,* 12 October 2001 and *The Boston Globe,* 13 October 2001.

[7] *The Times* (London), 21 September 2001.

[8] Steve Bowman, "Historical and Cultural Influences on Coalition Operations," in **Thomas J. Marshall, ed.,** *Problems and Solutions in Future Coalition Operations* (Carlisle, PA: Strategic Studies Institute, U.S. Army War College, 1997), 9-10.

[9] *The New York Times*, 12 September, 2002.

[10] David Shalit, "PhD in Joint Patrols," *Ma'ariv*, Weekend Supplement, 17 November 2000.

[11] Leslie McLoughlin, *Ibn Saud Founder of a Kingdom* (Basingstoke, Hampshire: Macmillan, 1993), 166-167.

[12] Hackworth, 117-118.

[13] Richard A. Williams, "Bright Star: Almost Business as Usual," The Washington Institute for Near East Policy, Policywatch No. 574, 15 October 2001.

[14] *The Times* (London), 21 September 2001.

[15] *The Daily Telegraph* (London), 4 April, 2000.

EPILOGUE

[1] Pollack, 764.

INDEX

China   x-xx, 9, 18, 48, 50,
66-68, 70, 74-5, 81, 91,
94, 96, 101, 146, 214,
218, 220, 222, 226,
232-3, 236, 240, 244-5
African-American troops
in   116
China-Burma-India *see* CBI
Chinese Air Force   116
Chinese Army   104-5, 107-8,
124, 130, 133, 135-6,
140, 142
Chinese familism   126
Chinese Language Officer
Program   119, 142, 236
Chinese military
conscription   135-7
Chinese obsession with face
108, 127-30, 141, 145
Chinese time perception
122
Chinese troops   105-6, 109,
126, 128, 136, 139
chonchim   196, 209, 216-7
Chungking   103, 108-9, 116,
126-7, 133
Churchill, Colonel A.J.   92
Churchill, Prime Minister
Winston S.   xvii, 7, 95,
127, 185
Clark, General Wesley   xxii
Clausewitz, Carl von   5-6
Clinton, President Bill
220
Coalition Information
Center   229
Committee of Union and
Progress (CUP)   25

Communication   10-11,
42-3, 61, 80, 86-89, 108,
119, 121-2, 169, 171,
184, 208-9, 221-2, 227,
236, 238-240, 243
high context   16
low context   16
non-verbal   14, 235, 238
verbal   11, 88, 208, 235
Communications and
Integration Cell   155
Confucianism   123, 144
corruption   24, 39, 57, 123,
125-6, 140-1, 145, 218,
226, 237
Crimean War   x, 23, 38, 69
cross-cultural cooperation
xii, xiv, xx, xxii, 98, 225,
241
Crow, Carl   111
crusade   56, 115, 230
crusade effect   247-8
cultural acclimatization   xxii,
42, 168, 187, 238
culture, definition of   1-2
high contact   14
low contact   14
monochronic   15
polychronic   15
culture shock   xviii, 57, 141,
240

D

Davies, John P.   101, 127, 140
Defense Language Institute
Foreign Language
Center   169

Made in the USA
Lexington, KY
26 July 2011